São Tomé and Príncipe

WORLD BIBLIOGRAPHICAL SERIES

General Editors:
Robert G. Neville (Executive Editor)
John J. Horton

Robert A. Myers   Ian Wallace
Hans H. Wellisch   Ralph Lee Woodward, Jr.

John J. Horton is Deputy Librarian of the University of Bradford and currently Chairman of its Academic Board of Studies in Social Sciences. He has maintained a longstanding interest in the discipline of area studies and its associated bibliographical problems, with special reference to European Studies. In particular he has published in the field of Icelandic and of Yugoslav studies, including the two relevant volumes in the World Bibliographical Series.

Robert A. Myers is Associate Professor of Anthropology in the Division of Social Sciences and Director of Study Abroad Programs at Alfred University, Alfred, New York. He has studied post-colonial island nations of the Caribbean and has spent two years in Nigeria on a Fulbright Lectureship. His interests include international public health, historical anthropology and developing societies. In addition to *Amerindians of the Lesser Antilles: a bibliography* (1981), *A Resource Guide to Dominica, 1493-1986* (1987) and numerous articles, he has compiled the World Bibliographical Series volumes on *Dominica* (1987), *Nigeria* (1989) and *Ghana* (1991).

Ian Wallace is Professor of German at the University of Bath. A graduate of Oxford in French and German, he also studied in Tübingen, Heidelberg and Lausanne before taking teaching posts at universities in the USA, Scotland and England. He specializes in contemporary German affairs, especially literature and culture, on which he has published numerous articles and books. In 1979 he founded the journal *GDR Monitor*, which he continues to edit under its new title *German Monitor*.

Hans H. Wellisch is Professor emeritus at the College of Library and Information Services, University of Maryland. He was President of the American Society of Indexers and was a member of the International Federation for Documentation. He is the author of numerous articles and several books on indexing and abstracting, and has published *The Conversion of Scripts, Indexing and Abstracting: an International Bibliography* and *Indexing from A to Z*. He also contributes frequently to *Journal of the American Society for Information Science, The Indexer* and other professional journals.

Ralph Lee Woodward, Jr. is Professor of History at Tulane University, New Orleans. He is the author of *Central America, a Nation Divided*, 2nd ed. (1985), as well as several monographs and more than seventy scholarly articles on modern Latin America. He has also compiled volumes in the World Bibliographical Series on *Belize* (1980), *El Salvador* (1988), *Guatemala (Rev. Ed.)* (1992) and *Nicaragua (Rev. Ed.)* (1994). Dr. Woodward edited the Central American section of the *Research Guide to Central America and the Caribbean* (1985) and is currently associate editor of Scribner's *Encyclopedia of Latin American History*.

VOLUME 172

São Tomé and Príncipe

Caroline S. Shaw

Compiler

CLIO PRESS

OXFORD, ENGLAND · SANTA BARBARA, CALIFORNIA
DENVER, COLORADO

British Library Cataloguing in Publication Data

São Tomé and Príncipe – (World
bibliographical series; vol. 172)
I. Shaw, Caroline S.   II. Series
016.96715

ISBN 1-85109-181-5

Clio Press Ltd.,
Old Clarendon Ironworks,
35A Great Clarendon Street,
Oxford OX2 6AT, England.

ABC-CLIO,
130 Cremona Drive,
Santa Barbara,
CA 93116, USA.

Designed by Bernard Crossland.
Typeset by Columns Design and Production Services Ltd, Reading, England.
Printed and bound in Great Britain by
Bookcraft (Bath) Ltd., Midsomer Norton

THE WORLD BIBLIOGRAPHICAL SERIES

This series, which is principally designed for the English speaker, will eventually cover every country (and many of the world's principal regions), each in a separate volume comprising annotated entries on works dealing with its history, geography, economy and politics; and with its people, their culture, customs, religion and social organization. Attention will also be paid to current living conditions – housing, education, newspapers, clothing, etc. – that are all too often ignored in standard bibliographies; and to those particular aspects relevant to individual countries. Each volume seeks to achieve, by use of careful selectivity and critical assessment of the literature, an expression of the country and an appreciation of its nature and national aspirations, to guide the reader towards an understanding of its importance. The keynote of the series is to provide, in a uniform format, an interpretation of each country that will express its culture, its place in the world, and the qualities and background that make it unique. The views expressed in individual volumes, however, are not necessarily those of the publisher.

VOLUMES IN THE SERIES

Contents

Contents

Contents

xi

Introduction

The Democratic Republic of São Tomé and Príncipe consists of the two islands of São Tomé and Príncipe and a number of smaller islets, and is situated in the Gulf of Guinea. São Tomé lies approximately 180 miles from the coast of Gabon with its southernmost tip crossed by the equator, while Príncipe is about 160 miles from the coast of Equatorial Guinea. The republic is the second smallest state in Africa: São Tomé has a land surface of 330 square miles, and Príncipe only 42 square miles. It is a former colony of Portugal, from whom it gained its independence in 1975. The population in 1992 was around 120,000.

The islands are volcanic in origin, and as a result of these beginnings are characterized by extensive mountain systems, unusual rock formations and rich soils. The centre of the island of São Tomé is dominated by mountains which rise to a height of 6,639 feet above sea level and whose dramatic peaks are often shrouded in cloud. No less dramatic are the deep valleys cut through the mountains by fast-flowing rivers and waterfalls. São Tomé and Príncipe is part of the 'Cameroon line', a range of mountains across Central Africa all of which were formed by volcanic activity. The principal markers are the Cameroon highlands in Cameroon, the four Gulf of Guinea islands of Fernando Pó, Príncipe, São Tomé and Annobon, and the South Atlantic island of St. Helena. All the volcanoes on São Tomé and Príncipe are thought to be long extinct but craters can still be seen.

São Tomé and Príncipe's climate is tropical, with two rainy seasons around the months of March and September, and it is greatly influenced by the confluence of the wind systems of the Atlantic and the Sahara. Topography has created a number of island microclimates with altitude, in particular, strongly influencing temperature. This climate, combined with the fertility of the soil, makes the islands capable of supporting a great variety of natural vegetation.

The islands have an immense natural beauty and a wealth of plant and animal life, much of it endemic. The sandy beaches are fringed by palm

Introduction

trees and the mountains are covered in dense tropical forest. Virgin forest at higher, inaccessible altitudes is thought to still contain plants unknown to botany amongst its lianas, ferns, orchids and the trees whose canopy is so high as to make identification impossible. This part of the forest has been protected from commercial exploitation by its inaccessibility. The islands' inhabitants have developed an extensive knowledge of the medicinal qualities of some of the species of flora which may yet prove to be one of the country's most valuable natural resources.

Bird life is also impressive, with the islands being home to a number of rare species: the forest is the second most important in Africa for endangered species of birds. It is not necessary, however, to be an ornithologist to witness the common sight of large birds of prey, such as the black kite, even around the main harbour of São Tomé city. The noisy African grey parrots returning to their evening roosts in the town of Santo António, capital of Príncipe, are equally distinctive.

In the absence of conclusive evidence to the contrary, it is generally held that the islands were uninhabited until their discovery by the Portuguese in the 15th century. The date of discovery is not certain, although it is usually credited to Pêro de Escobar and João de Santarém in December 1470 and January 1471. Escobar and Santarém were sea-captains in the employ of Fernão Gomes, who had leased the right to the West African Guinea trade from the Portuguese crown, and had undertaken to explore 100 leagues of the coast each year. The settlement of the islands did not take place, however, until 1485, some fifteen years after the assumed date of discovery. Some historians take this as an indication that the islands were not in fact discovered until perhaps as late as 1478.

In the southern part of São Tomé exists the community known as the Angolars. They may have inhabited the island prior to the arrival of the Portuguese but the popular belief is that they are the descendants of survivors of a slave ship from Angola which was wrecked off the southern shore of São Tomé in 1540. They inhabited the mountainous and heavily forested southern part of the island, away from the plantations and city which were developing in the northeast. Until the late 19th century the Angolars were still a separate and autonomous population.

The settlement of the islands followed a pattern similar to that which the Portuguese had adopted in the other Atlantic islands discovered in the 15th century – Madeira, the Azores and the Cape Verde islands. Territory and authority were granted by the Portuguese crown to 'captains' who were obliged to settle and cultivate these lands. The captaincy to São Tomé, held first by João de Paiva in 1485, also gave the right to trade along an area of coast around the Portuguese fort of São Jorge da Mina in present day Ghana.

xiv

The settlers all looked to sugar cane to make their fortunes. São Tomé was well-suited to produce this crop: the soil was fertile; the climate ideal; and the land in the northeast of the island was level and easily cleared. Moreover, the rivers running off the mountains provided the power the water mills needed to crush and process the canes. The island was also near to a vast source of labour on the continent of Africa.

Under the captaincy of Álvaro de Caminho, granted in 1493, São Tomé began to develop rapidly whilst Príncipe was settled seven years later, in 1500. Caminho brought with him large numbers of settlers from Europe, including Portuguese criminals and 2,000 Jewish children. These were the children of the Jews who had sought refuge in Portugal after having been expelled from Castille in 1492. The unfortunate children, all under the age of ten, were removed from their parents, baptized and sent to São Tomé to be brought up as Christians.

Caminho also brought slaves from the African mainland. These people probably originated from the Bight of Benin, Biafra, and parts of the powerful kingdom of Kongo in the Congo basin. As well as supplying labour for the sugar plantations, Africans also provided domestic comforts for the settlers: in order to increase the islands' population Caminho gave female slaves to the male Europeans. From these mixed-race alliances powerful *mestiço* families were to emerge to form the islands' élite. By the end of the 15th century some estimates put the population as high as 10,000, despite the ravages of tropical diseases upon a European community without natural immunities.

During the 16th century wealthy São Tomense families were very influential in the affairs of the other nations of the Gulf of Guinea. Their most important rôle was in the highly profitable slave trade when the islands were used as 'warehouses' for slaves destined for Brazil and the Americas. The writ of the Portuguese crown was not easy to enforce so far from Lisbon and the São Tomense routinely flouted the crown's trade monopolies. They became heavily involved in the trade and internal politics of the kingdom of Kongo and they were also the first to form a settlement at Luanda, now the capital city of modern Angola and then the site of a valuable source of cowry shells used as currency. The islands also exercised religious power through the see of São Tomé, which covered the whole of West Africa from Côte d'Ivoire to the Cape of Good Hope: the São Tomense clergy used their influence to further their own interests in the slave trade.

By the middle of the 16th century São Tomé was the world's biggest producer of sugar and an important destination for European mercantile shipping. This prosperity, however, was not to last. The sugar cane became afflicted by disease and by a depletion of the soil's fertility. The quality of the processed sugar had never been very high, the humidity of

Introduction

the climate making drying difficult, and when Brazil entered the world market the islands could not compete. By 1615 fifty-nine of the former seventy-two plantations had been abandoned.

Political as well as agricultural and economic factors contributed to the islands' declining importance. There was incessant feuding within the São Tomense élite and as public office became the one reliable source of income these posts were the subject of intense competition. Relations between the clergy and secular authorities frequently broke down, and excommunications were risibly common. The only real power came to lie in the landowners' private armies of slaves.

Threats to the settlement's stability also came from the interior of the island. There were numerous slave uprisings, the first recorded being as early as 1517, and many slaves escaped into the forest, often joining forces with the Angolars to raid plantations. In 1547 the town of São Tomé was attacked, and again in 1574 when it was set on fire. The Angolar 'King' Amador led a massive uprising in 1595 which almost succeeded in conquering the entire island. Although the leaders of the rebellion were captured and executed, complete pacification of the interior was not achieved until Mateus Pires came to an accord with the Angolars in 1693. This atmosphere of insecurity, together with economic decline, contributed to the decision of many of the sugar planters to migrate to Brazil.

The irreversible decline of the sugar economy meant that São Tomé and Príncipe retained only a minor rôle on the international stage. The islands had never been sufficiently supplied with military resources, and their vulnerability to foreign sea-borne attacks was proved repeatedly in the 17th and 18th centuries. Dutch and French ships plundered and burned the islands' settlements on a number of occasions. The most significant of these attacks was the Dutch invasion and occupation of the city of São Tomé between 1641 and 1648. The Dutch were at this time attempting to usurp the Portuguese in Brazil and in order to take control of the supply of slaves to Brazil they also occupied Luanda and São Tomé. The planters soon came to a *modus vivendi* with the Dutch, and were happy to use their ships as the only means of trading through the blockade on Portuguese shipping. The Dutch were eventually routed in Brazil, and gradually lost their hold on the Gulf of Guinea. Under the leadership of governor Lourenço Pires de Tavora the Dutch on São Tomé were confined to their fortress and eventually abandoned the islands completely in 1648.

After the end of the sugar boom the most lucrative economic activity available to the São Tomense élite was the slave trade to Brazil, which persisted into the 19th century. In 1815 Britain and Portugal agreed to abolish the trade in zones north of the equator which, of course, could

xvi

only benefit traders operating from Angola which lies in indisputably southern latitudes. The São Tomense traders could also exploit the island's equatorial position to claim that slave ships found around its coast had simply been blown slightly off course. Portugal finally abolished the slave trade altogether in 1836, and the institution of slavery in 1875.

In the 19th century São Tomé and Príncipe entered a second phase of prosperity, again based on luxury crops for the European market. This time it was coffee and cocoa that were to transform the economy, landscape and society of the two islands. Coffee was first introduced, on Príncipe, in 1800 and flourished on the higher slopes. The real boom lay in the cacau tree, which was first introduced, again on Príncipe, in 1822. By 1910 the islands were producing fifteen per cent of the world's cocoa and making a crucial contribution to Portugal's trade balance. Vast areas of forest were cleared, the primary forest only surviving at the highest altitudes. Enormous plantations were carved out: in 1963 it was found that just twenty-three plantations owned eighty-five per cent of the land. A typical plantation would occupy a swathe of land from the heights of the mountainous interior down to the coast. Access to the sea facilitated the export of the crop: transport within the plantation was often provided by private railways, vestiges of which can still be seen. The plantation buildings formed remote quasi-towns in the midst of the forest. Owners built imposing mansions and, in later years, equally grand hospitals. Workers' living quarters, however, were little more than barracks.

The first plantation owners were drawn from the indigenous *mestiço* élite. They already owned land and slaves and in many cases had been involved in the slave trade. Titles to land had rarely been formalized, and in the unseemly scramble to occupy and clear the forest many small-scale indigenous farmers (known as *forros*) were dispossessed. Social dignity prevented this class of São Tomense from taking up plantation employment, work which carried the social status of slavery. They came to form a marginalized, disaffected class, drifting to the fringes of the city of São Tomé.

The Angolars were also badly affected by the growth of the plantations. As the southern part of São Tomé was brought into cultivation, they were driven out of the forest and on to a narrow coastal strip around the fishing village of São João dos Angolares. In 1875 troops entered the village and Portuguese colonial rule was finally imposed. The Angolars, like the *forros*, refused to become plantation labour and lived instead by their skills as foresters and fishermen.

Finding a work force for the plantations soon emerged as a major problem. Slaves emancipated in 1875 showed an unsurprising reluctance to work for their former masters, and tended to merge with the class of dispossessed *forros*. Since no indigenous labour force existed that would accept the discipline and indignities offered by plantation work, the planters looked instead to other Portuguese colonies in Africa – Angola, Cape Verde and Mozambique. They were never prepared to offer wages that were in any way attractive and so had to rely on a variety of methods of coercion in order to bring workers to the islands.

The most brutal, and eventually scandalous, form of coercion took place in Angola. Deep in the interior of the country slave caravans would be formed and slaves rounded up and force-marched across hundreds of miles of barren and inhospitable land. Often shackled, many died on this horrific journey. On arrival at the coast, with a hypocrisy fully endorsed by the Portuguese colonial authorities, the slaves would be taken before an official to be 'redeemed' from slavery under the terms of the legislation which had been enacted to abolish the slave trade and slavery. It would quickly be decided that these unfortunate former slaves, so far from their native lands, should be given an opportunity to earn their living by becoming contracted to work on the cocoa plantations of São Tomé and Príncipe. Although there was full compliance with all the requirements of the law, the contracted workers neither knew, nor gave their consent, to the procedures that were determining their fate. In theory the contracts should only have lasted for a finite number of years, typically five. In practice, however, the contracts for Angolans were for life, and recontracting took place on the islands with as little regard for the understanding or consent of the individuals involved as had been shown in obtaining the original contracts.

An important source of labour in the 20th century was the drought-stricken Cape Verde islands. The colonial authorities in Cape Verde ensured that the desperate victims of drought were given no viable alternatives to contracting themselves to work on the plantations of São Tomé and Príncipe. The drought of 1903 saw the first arrivals in any number, and the flow continued until the 1970s. The terrible droughts of the 1940s produced particularly large numbers of these 'forced' emigrants. Unlike the Angolan workers, the Cape Verdeans generally knew their rights, arrived with family members, and if they did not succumb to disease often managed to return to their homes after completing their contracts. Some remained, and the 1981 census showed that five per cent of the population were of Cape Verdean origin. Nevertheless, plantation life and its attendant humiliations were deeply resented.

The need for continuous recruitment of new labour from abroad lay in the appallingly high mortality rate for plantation workers. In the first decade of the 20th century the annual mortality rates on the plantations of São Tomé and Príncipe were estimated at an astonishing 100 per 1,000 workers and 200 per 1,000 workers respectively. The islands had always been notorious for malaria and other fevers and the Cape Verdeans in particular had a low resistance to these tropical diseases. Large numbers of people, often in a debilitated state after surviving the journey across Angola on foot, crowded together in insanitary conditions in the middle of tropical forest naturally facilitated the spread of many fatal diseases. Príncipe was scourged by sleeping sickness, probably introduced in the 1820s with the import of infected cattle from Gabon. The eradication of the tsetse fly responsible for the transmission of the disease was the subject of a famous public health campaign between the years of 1911 and 1914. Suicide was not uncommon: Angolans, apparently, wished to return to their homes as spirits, given that a corporeal return was denied them. Informally, medical officers ascribed many of the deaths of Angolans simply to 'sadness'.

During the 19th century and for much of the present century, life on the plantations as well as being dangerously unhealthy was bleak in many other ways, with most plantations functioning like remote fiefdoms. They had poor communication links with the rest of the island and a trip to São Tomé city could take several days on foot through the forest. Life was regulated with dreary monotony, the plantation bell ringing the hours of a 62-hour working week. Education, religious services and entertainment were largely lacking and the plantation provided the only shop. Living quarters would be wooden barracks, periodically burnt to the ground for hygiene reasons, although some plantations later replaced them with stone-built terraces. These would still lack private kitchens, let alone plumbing, and whole families might have to live in a single room only separated from their neighbours by a partition that failed to reach the ceiling. The plantation managers and foremen had immense powers over the workers, with corporal punishment and other affronts to human dignity not uncommon. Those workers who managed to reach the *Curador* (curator), the official appointed to oversee their welfare on the islands, have deposited some distressing testimony. Even when overt cruelty was not practised, plantation life closely resembled slavery up until the 1920s when repatriation was implemented for workers who had completed their contracts.

By the beginning of the 20th century news of the horrors of the neo-slave trade in Angola began to reach the outside world through the reports of European missionaries. Investigations by journalists and humanitarian groups such as the Aborigines Protection Society and the Anti-Slavery Society provoked a scandal of international proportions.

Introduction

British public opinion was particularly outraged and the British Foreign Office became involved at a diplomatic level with the Portuguese Colonial Ministry. Pressure was put upon the British cocoa manufacturers to boycott cocoa from São Tomé and Príncipe until repatriation and improvements in recruitment methods were put into place. The islands' cocoa was eventually boycotted in 1909, but not until an alternative supply from Ghana had been secured.

The cocoa boom, like that of sugar before it, was to prove unsustainable, with a variety of causes contributing to the decline in production and profitability. In the latter decades of the 19th century indigenous landowners entered into a period of financial difficulties. These were eagerly exacerbated and exploited by the Banco Nacional Ultramarino, the monopoly colonial bank. The bank and a number of other large consortiums based in Lisbon managed to acquire the most important plantations which meant that profits were returned to Lisbon, rather than being re-invested in São Tomé and Príncipe. The islands' infrastructure and public amenities were indeed notoriously poor. A lack of re-investment in the plantations themselves meant that the cacau trees were allowed to age without sufficient replanting taking place. Crops were affected by devastating infestations of insect pests and a decline in soil fertility. At the same time competition arose from more efficient new producers in other parts of the world. The decline in production was matched by a reduction in the number of foreign plantation workers on the islands, from 38,000 in 1921 to 17,000 in 1954: over the same period production fell from 30,000 tonnes per year to under 10,000 tonnes. One beneficiary of this decline was the forest, with secondary forest establishing itself on abandoned land.

One of the first acts of the post-independence government, which came to power in 1975, was to nationalize the plantations although this went no way towards solving the industry's problems. Apart from a brief period of profitability based on unusually high world cocoa prices, the decline continued. Production fell from 11,586 tonnes in 1973 to 3,378 tonnes in 1984. European managers and technicians had fled the islands before independence and there were few experienced São Tomense amongst those who replaced them. Plantation work was no less unpopular than it had been in colonial times, but a top-heavy and unproductive adminstrative layer soon developed.

The new government did not fail to recognize the necessity of diversifying away from a monoculture which left the islands' economy entirely at the mercy of the international commodity markets. Ironically, the only way to generate the resources necessary for diversification seemed to be by producing more cocoa. In an attempt to increase production the plantations were opened to private enterprise in 1986 and a number of joint ventures with foreign companies were set up. Nevertheless, the plantations themselves are probably obsolete institutions: the experience of countries like Ghana has shown that cocoa can be produced more efficiently by small-scale farmers. Gradually this is being acknowledged in São Tomé and Príncipe and plantation workers have in some cases been allocated their own plots of land to cultivate. The increase in small-scale farming has also helped reduce the islands' reliance on imports of foodstuffs.

It was the unpopularity of plantation work that led to the 1953 Batepá Massacre, the defining event of the islands' recent political history. The governor, Carlos Gorgulho, had ordered the formation of a number of work brigades to be drawn from the economically marginal *forros*. Believing that this would lead to enforced work on the plantations, the *forros* protested only to be met by an armed response from troops and forces organized by the plantation owners. Estimates of the number of deaths range from 50 to 1,032.

Until 1953 there had been little political activity on the islands, and no opposition movement to Portuguese rule. The massacre, however, shocked the São Tomense and politicized many. Opposition groups began to form amongst students in Lisbon, and these later moved to bases in friendly independent African states. The most enduring of these small groups was the Comité de Libertação de São Tomé e Príncipe, formed in 1960 under the leadership of Miguel Trovoada. At various times it was based in Guinea, Gabon and Equatorial Guinea. Renamed the Movimento de Libertação de São Tomé e Príncipe (MLSTP) in 1972, it formed strong and important links with the other organizations fighting for the liberation of Portuguese Africa. Its contacts with the islands and islanders were not, however, so well developed.

São Tomé and Príncipe's independence was not the result of any action taken by the MLSTP or by the islands' population. The repressive right-wing régime in Portugal had, since 1961, been fighting increasingly unpopular and irresolvable wars against the guerillas of the independence movements of Angola, Guinea-Bissau and Mozambique. In April 1974 a left-wing coup led by disaffected junior army officers in Lisbon overthrew the government. The main concern of the new powers in Lisbon was to bring an end to the African wars and Portugal's presence in that continent. The MLSTP successfully negotiated the granting of independence to São Tomé and Príncipe and an interim government was set up, including members of the MLSTP and representatives of the Portuguese government. Independence was achieved in July 1975.

The one-party system devised by the MLSTP enshrined the party as the sole source for the republic's political leadership. In practice it was impossible to distinguish the party from the state and, although the MLSTP remained in power from 1975 until 1991, there were a number of symptoms of political dysfunctionality. The president, Manuel Pinto da Costa, accumulated more and more of the important offices of state: between 1982 and 1984 he was President, Prime Minister, Commander-in-Chief of the Armed Forces, Minister of Defence and National Security, and President of the MLSTP; in 1985 he also became Minister of Planning, which he exhanged in 1986 for Minister of Agriculture and Fisheries. Members of his family were also prominent in the government. Before independence the party had had a history of splits, factions and internal feuds: this did not change with the accession to power. Competition for the economic security of public office probably intensified the internal jockeying for position, whilst stifling genuine opposition.

The government also acquired a paranoia for its own security, with the result that senior party members were imprisoned or fled into exile. These included the former Prime Minister, Miguel Trovoada, who spent two years in prison without trial before being allowed to leave the country in 1981. Two possible attempted invasions by mercenaries of foreign-based opposition groups, in 1978 and 1988, fuelled the atmosphere of suspicion. After the first of these attempts Pinto da Costa appealed to the Angolan government to send troops to protect the islands. The garrison which arrived was deeply unpopular and served mainly to maintain the President's hold on power. The troops were not withdrawn until 1991.

The relationship with Angola, built up between the MLSTP and the Movimento Popular de Libertação de Angola in the years before independence, was of immense importance to the islands. As well as providing troops, the Angolan government supplied oil on extremely favourable terms until 1991. The termination of this arrangement has left the islands facing regular fuel shortages: the ceramics factory, for example, has resorted to burning wood as the only reliable energy source.

Foreign aid has come to play an essential role in São Tomé and Príncipe. Although the country was non-aligned during the Cold War, the Eastern bloc provided a certain amount of development assistance. The former East Germany was an important source of industrial aid, their most notable contribution being the construction of a brewery in Neves. This was, however, at the cost of the pre-arranged sale of cocoa at below market prices. Some of the aid and development loans were squandered through mis-management or 'white elephant' projects. The European Community, Portugal, and France have all been significant donors, with the latter keen to increase its influence in the region.

Despite – and in some respects because of – foreign aid, the economy remains fragile. The International Monetary Fund closely monitors economic policy and in 1987 it enforced a stringent programme of structural adjustment. By 1992 the islands had a debt of $189 million, equivalent to a debt of $1,500 per capita, and there was also a trade deficit of $8,349 million. Despite a modest growth in the economy of 0.8 per cent over the years 1987-92, this could in no way match an annual growth of 2.5 per cent in the population.

The rapidly growing population is indubitably putting a strain on the islands' resources: forty-six per cent of the São Tomense are under the age of fifteen. Primary education is free and compulsory, but the service can only cope by operating a three-shift system and offering a curtailed curriculum. This is storing up problems for future development prospects and already donor countries which offer places on higher education courses are finding that the São Tomense students are inadequately prepared. Health services, which are also very dependent on foreign aid, are similarly stretched. Life expectancy at 65 years is relatively good, but mortality rates have increased from 7.7 per 1,000 at the beginning of the 1980s to 11.5 per 1,000 at the decade's end. There has been evidence of malnutrition among children and malaria remains endemic. There are few more depressing sights than the unmarked rows of tiny, freshly dug, graves in the lushly overgrown cemetery in São Tomé city.

As an acknowledgement of the stagnation within São Tomé and Príncipe's politics and economy, and perhaps in response to the momentous changes in Eastern Europe, by 1990 the MLSTP had decided to open up the political arena. A new constitution was drawn up and approved by a referendum in 1990, and multi-party elections to the legislative assembly were held in January 1991. Exiles returned and new political parties were formed. The main opposition to the MLSTP-Partido Social Democrático (MLSTP-PSD), the renamed MLSTP, was the Partido de Convergência Democrática (PCD) led by Miguel Trovoada, which duly won the elections. Foreseeing his own defeat, Pinto da Costa decided not to stand in the presidential elections and Trovoada was elected in March 1991.

The new PCD government brought no radical change in direction, the MLSTP having already adopted many free market policies in the mid-1980s. Internal political conflicts have not ended either: in April 1992 the President dismissed his Prime Minister, Daniel Daio, in a dispute over the respective powers of the two offices. The MLSTP-PSD were victorious in local elections in December 1992, probably as a protest against continuing economic hardships. There have also been signs of discontent within the army.

For five centuries the islands have been caught up in the powerful flow of peoples and commodities between Africa, the Americas and Europe. Somehow in the midst of this maelstrom a strong indigenous culture took root and survived. The clearest manifestation of this human tenacity lies in the creation of three new languages. These are creole languages which have a grammatical substructure from Bantu and Congolese languages, and a vocabulary largely derived from archaic and modern Portuguese. The creole spoken on Príncipe is usually known as *lungwa iyé* ('island language'), that of São Tomé as *forro* or *lungwa san tomé*. *Lungwa angola* is spoken by a diminishing number of the Angolars. Many similarities exist between these languages and the creole language spoken on the island of Annobon. Portuguese is an official language and in practice it is also the written language, the language of law and of education. Nevertheless it is the creole languages which are the mother tongues of the population: they are the spoken languages and the medium for popular culture.

The islands' popular culture embraces a number of genres. Riddles, proverbs and oaths abound in everyday discourse, and like many African societies there is a rich opus of oral literature. Some of the folk tales have affinities with Portuguese stories; others feature a rather shifty turtle 'trickster' hero; yet others pass comment on slavery and plantation life. Popular music is lively and highly danceable, and the islands boast a variety of specialized dance forms. A number of adaptations of Roman Catholic rites, involving music, dance and processions, also form part of local culture. At various times in the islands' history the authorities perceived this indigenous culture to be a threat and attempted to enforce restrictions and prohibitions, but without lasting effect.

Most extraordinary of all the manifestations of popular culture are the islands' spectacular theatrical performances, the most remarkable of which is the *tchiloli*. At its core is the 16th-century play by Baltasar Dias, *Marquez de Mantua* (Marquis of Mantua), which dramatizes one of the episodes from the mediaeval romances of the Emperor Charlemagne. Around this verse text, which is spoken in its original 16th-century Portuguese idiom, a prose play of modern origin has been constructed. In this modern text themes of power, law and the state have been drawn out from Dias' play and developed in such a way as to become highly satirical of the Portuguese colonial state. To add to the spectacle all the characters move across the performance area by dancing to a musical accompaniment from flutes and percussion instruments. The actors, who are all men, wear elaborate costumes and are virtually always masked. They are an astonishing sight as they emerge from the forest into the clearing which is to be used for the performance. Belonging to disciplined troupes, the actors keep their roles, often inherited from family members, for life. Vestiges of African religious practices have been noted in some aspects of the actors' ritualized behaviour. On Príncipe, on Saint Lawrence's day, the whole town of Santo António is given over to the performance of another story from the Charlemagne cycle, the *Auto da Floripes* (Drama of Floripes).

The islands have also produced a number of writers and poets, contributors to the richness of the literature which has emerged from the Portuguese-speaking countries of Africa in the last hundred years. Many of the first generation of published poets were the illegitimate children of São Tomense women and Portuguese fathers. Through their fathers they had access to a Portuguese education, but their personal experience was of a mixed-race heritage. Poets such as Caetano da Costa Alegre (1864-90) were amongst the first of the Portuguese African writers to address the questions of race and racism.

The greatest of the São Tomense poets, and one who can stand comparison on a far larger stage, was Francisco José Tenreiro (1921-63). As well as being a distinguished geographer and author of several indispensable texts about São Tomé and Príncipe, Tenreiro was one of the first Portuguese African poets to take up the message of *negritude*. His poetry celebrates the beauty and tragedy of his country and the wider experience of the African diaspora. This diaspora was, of course, the force which created the modern society of São Tomé and Príncipe.

It is a complex society which has emerged from a largely unedifying history to inherit a somewhat precarious future. The plantations have not only scarred the forest, but the people as well and there are now two worlds existing in parallel on the islands. The first is the unregulated sprawl of wooden houses which can be found on the fringe of the elegant colonial architecture of São Tomé city, straggling beside roads, and along the coasts. These informal settlements are within easy reach of haphazardly planted fruit trees, or beaches for landing fish caught from dugout canoes. The other world is that of the remote, enclosed plantations and their rows of sub-standard workers' barracks. Most of the islands' inhabitants have no reason to feel any loyalty towards these plantations, certainly not the dispossessed *forros*, nor the descendants of emancipated slaves, nor the children of imported contract workers. It is hard to resist the impression, however naïve, that the only way to throw off this terrible history is to break up the plantations and allow the São Tomense to cultivate their land for their own account.

The bibliography

In compiling a bibliography of such a remote and small nation there have been inevitable difficulties. As I was memorably informed in the stationers shop in São Tomé city, 'This is São Tomé. We neither publish

Introduction

books, nor do we sell them'. Proprietors told of the constant struggle to publish their newspapers: one week a paper shortage, the next a power cut. The simple fact is that very little is published in the islands, and relatively little is written about them. The great exception to this is the published outpourings of accusation and defence that resulted from the labour scandals of the early-20th century. Nevertheless, through research in the Arquivo Histórico de São Tomé e Príncipe, the Biblioteca Nacional de Lisboa, the British Library, the School of Oriental and African Studies (London) and the Internet I hope I have been able to discover sufficient material to achieve two objectives. My first aim for this bibliography is that it should provide the user with an impression of these beautiful islands and a guide to the most obvious and accessible resources; the second is that it might offer a starting point for more specialized research.

Acknowledgements

I would like to take this opportunity to express my gratitude to a number of individuals: to Patrick Chabal for his encouragement; to Keith Davis for friendship in Lisbon; to Christopher Doutney and other colleagues at the British Library of Political and Economic Science; to Alda Espírito Santo of the União Nacional dos Escritores e Artistas de São Tomé e Príncipe; to Senhora Rodrigues of the Arquivo Histórico de São Tomé e Príncipe; to my companions in São Tomé and Príncipe, Cathy Shaw, Mick Clementson and Peter Livesey; and to Christine Smallwood.

The Country and Its People

1   **Angola, Moçambique, S.Tomé.** (Angola, Mozambique, São Tomé.)
    J. Carlos Rates.   Lisbon: Tipografia Didot, 1929. 226p.
The chapter on São Tomé and Príncipe (p. 209-26) provides a general description of both islands, covering public administration and communications, agriculture, labour and social services. There are some interesting black-and-white photographs of plantation life.

2   **Aspectos e problemas da expansão portuguesa.** (Aspects and problems
    of Portuguese expansion.)
    Orlando Ribeiro.   Lisbon: Junta de Investigações do Ultramar, 1962.
    213p. (Estudos de Ciências Políticas e Sociais, no. 59).
A general discussion of the history and society of São Tomé and Príncipe (p. 161-72) is largely drawn from Francisco Tenreiro's richly-praised *Ilha de São Tomé* (*estudo geográfico*) (q.v.). Nevertheless, Ribeiro's insights are always worth having: for example, this description of the 'double personality of the island: on one side that which could have been its harmonious and spontaneous development, on the other the economic stimulation of a capitalism which sacrificed everything to its greed for profit' (p. 172).

3   **Cabo Verde, Guiné, São Tomé e Príncipe: curso de extensão
    universitária, ano lectivo de 1965-1966.** (Cape Verde, Guinea, São
    Tomé and Príncipe: university extension course, academic year
    1965-1966.)
    Foreword by Adriano Moreira.   Lisbon: Universidade Técnica de
    Lisboa, Instituto Superior de Ciências Sociais e Política Ultramarina,
    1966. 1036p. 21 maps. bibliog.
Relevant essays are: Raquel Soeiro de Brito, 'Guiné, Cabo Verde e São Tomé e Príncipe: alguns aspectos da terra e dos homens' (Guinea, Cape Verde and São Tomé

and Príncipe: aspects of land and people) (p.13-46); António de Almeida, 'Das etnonímias da Guiné Portuguesa, do arquipélago de Cabo Verde e das ilhas de São Tomé e Príncipe' (Ethnic names from Portuguese Guinea, Cape Verde and São Tomé and Príncipe) (p.109-48); Jorge Morais-Barbosa, 'Cabo Verde, Guiné e São Tomé e Príncipe: situação linguística' (Cape Verde, Guinea and São Tomé and Príncipe: the linguistic situation) (p.149-64); José Júlio Gonçalves, 'A informação na Guiné, em Cabo Verde e em São Tomé e Príncipe' (Information in Guinea, in Cape Verde and in São Tomé and Príncipe) (p.165-376) (q.v.); Maria Palmira de Moraes Pinto Duarte, 'O serviço social em Cabo Verde, na Guiné e em São Tomé e Príncipe' (Social services in Cape Verde, Guinea and São Tomé and Príncipe) (p.377-440) (q.v.); Alberto Feliciano Marques Pereira, 'Temas actuais que servem à formação da juventude portuguesa, referidos às províncias de Cabo Verde, Guiné e São Tomé e às restantes em geral' (Current themes in the development of Portuguese youth in Cape Verde, Guinea and São Tomé and in general) (p.441-58); A. Ribeiro, 'Estruturas eclesiásticas de Cabo Verde, Guiné e São Tomé e Príncipe' (Ecclesiastical structures in Cape Verde, Guinea and São Tomé and Príncipe) (p.459-74); Joaquim Angélico de Jesus Guerra, 'Occupação missionária de Cabo Verde, Guiné e São Tomé e Príncipe' (Missionary work in Cape Verde, Guinea and São Tomé and Príncipe) (p.475-546); João Baptista Nunes Pereira Neto, 'Movimentos subversivos da Guiné, Cabo Verde e São Tomé e Príncipe' (Subversive movements from Guinea, Cape Verde and São Tomé and Príncipe) (p.547-600); José Maria Gasper, 'Questões do trabalho' (Labour issues) (p.601-16); Armando M. Marques Guedes, 'Organização político-administrativa: os conselhos legislativos e os conselhos do governo' (Political and administrative organization: legislative councils and government councils) (p.617-48) (q.v.); Luís Maria da Câmara Pina, 'Ideia geral do valor estratégico do conjunto Guiné-Cabo Verde e da ilha de São Tomé' (The strategic value of Guinea-Cape Verde and São Tomé) (p.697-720); Vasco Fortuna, 'Estruturas económicas de Cabo Verde, Guiné e São Tomé e Príncipe' (Economic structure of Cape Verde, Guinea and São Tomé and Príncipe) (p.721-72); José Júlio Cravo Silva, 'Aspectos do rendimento nacional de Cabo Verde, Guiné e São Tomé e Príncipe' (National income for Cape Verde, Guinea and São Tomé and Príncipe) (p.773-852); José Pereira Neto, 'Comércio externo de Cabo Verde, Guiné e São Tomé e Príncipe' (Foreign trade of Cape Verde, Guinea and São Tomé and Príncipe) (p.853-920); Óscar Barata, 'O povoamento de Cabo Verde, Guiné e São Tomé' (The population of Cape Verde, Guinea and São Tomé) (p.921-58); Carlos Rebello Marques de Almeida, 'O presente e o futuro da agricultura de São Tomé e do Príncipe' (Present and future of agriculture in São Tomé and Príncipe) (p.1007-36) (q.v).

4 **Historia ethnographica da ilha de S.Thomé.** (Ethnographic history of the island of São Tomé.)
António Lôbo de Almada Negreiros.   Lisbon: Antiga Casa Bertrand-José Bastos, 1895. 369p.

A lively book containing the author's impressions, opinions and prejudices about the way of life of the various ethnic groups on the island. A continuing theme is the need for a better kind of colonialism, one which will invest, develop and educate rather than casually tolerate degeneration. The first part of the book constitutes a history of the islands with an emphasis on the topics of race and ethnic origin. The second part begins with a chapter detailing the complex hierarchy of race and class and the moral character of each of its subdivisions. The family life of the indigenous São Tomense is covered next. Men often abandon their families and marriage is not a strong institution: the men who are considered the most honest are those who actually support their 'harem' of women. A chapter on customs covers a broad range of topics, including courtship, festivals, music and song, elections, and the chaotic and easily-abused system of land ownership. São Tomense religious practice is seen to be a surface of Catholicism on a bedrock of 'fetichism'. To the São Tomense *feiticeiros* (sorcerors) are as important as priests in interpreting the divine and festivals, funeral rites and prayers are described in some detail in this text. Medicine too can be in the hands of the *feiticeiros* and a chapter is devoted to traditional medicine, including a substantial list of medicinal plants and their uses. There are also chapters on both the plantation workers and the Angolars, with a description of life on the plantations. Although Negreiros believes that the contract system is good for Africans he does remark on the epidemics of suicide and the 'indefinable sadness' of the Angolan workers. The history of the Angolars is recounted with some admiration and their achievements as sailors, fishermen, foresters and in craftwork are praised. The Angolars are still largely self-governing despite the occupation of their town by government forces in 1878 and the loss of much of their land to the plantations. A final chapter discusses São Tomense creole. Proverbs, poetry (including that of Francisco Stockler) and vocabulary are cited, and a rudimentary grammar is sketched.

5 **Império ultramarino português (monografia do império). II Guiné (continuação). S.Tomé e Príncipe.** (The Portuguese overseas empire [monograph on the empire]. II Guinea [continuation]. São Tomé and Príncipe.)
Henrique Galvão, Carlos Selvagem. Lisbon: Empresa Nacional de Publicidade, 1951. 421p. 6 maps. bibliog.

This is a colonial handbook, covering São Tomé and Príncipe's discovery and settlement, geography and natural history, population and society. Political and administrative organization, transport and communications, agriculture and other economic activities, as well as finance are also examined (p. 181-416).

6 **Leve esboço da vida material dos nativos das ilhas de São Tomé e do Príncipe.** (Brief outline of the material life of the natives of the islands of São Tomé and Príncipe.)
Januário da Graça do Espírito Santo. In: *Conferência Internacional dos Africanistas Ocidentais 6ª Sessão. Volume V.* [Lisbon]: Commission for Technical Co-operation in Africa South of the Sahara, Scientific Council for Africa South of the Sahara, 1956, p. 149-58.

Describes the food, housing, clothing and subsistence agriculture of the indigenous population of São Tomé and Príncipe. A summary in English is provided.

7 **A província de São Tomé - a terra e o homen.** (The province of São Tomé - land and people.)
Mário Moreira da Silva. *Revista do Gabinete de Estudos Ultramarinos*, no. 13 (May-August 1956), p. 30-45.

Da Silva presents a general survey, full of the imperial spirit, and memorable for its demonstration of the noble and civilizing influence of the homesick Portuguese settlers, and its view that São Tomé and Príncipe is a fine example of tropical Portuguese culture.

8   **S.Tomé e Príncipe.** (São Tomé and Príncipe.)
    União Nacional de S.Tomé e Príncipe.   [São Tomé]: Imprensa Nacional
    da Colónia de S.Tomé e Príncipe, 1948. 177p.

This is a collection of reports, mostly prepared by officials and administrators, and published under the auspices of the União Nacional (National Union). This body was the official political association of the pre-democratic Portuguese state. Portugal's achievements in renovating and developing São Tomé and Príncipe are, unsurprisingly, praised in this book. Reports cover a wide range of topics: civil administration and the Curadoria Geral dos Serviçais e Indígenas (General Curator of Contract Workers and Natives); health services (Joaquim Ferreira da Silva); economic statistics (Augusto Bagôrra); the Catholic Church (José Gonçalves Pereira); public finance (Hilario Lemos de Carvalho); customs and excise (Jorge Barbosa); the judiciary (A. L. da Cruz); public works (L. F. F. Colaço); postal services and telecommunications (J. Upendra Naique Countó); the military (Augusto Bagôrra); ship-ping; the work of the Câmara Municipal de S.Tomé (São Tomé city council) (João Ribeiro); meat (José António Ribeiro); general improvements (J. B. Ferreira Semedo); historical churches and buildings (Rocha); Portugal's record on labour history and the abolition of slavery (Ivo de Cerqueira); agriculture and forestry (Salustino da Graça); and Príncipe's history and economy (Fernandes Ramos).

9   **São Tomé and Príncipe: from plantation colony to microstate.**
    Tony Hodges, Malyn Newitt.   Boulder, Colorado: Westview Press,
    1988. 173p. 5 maps. bibliog. (Profiles. Nations of Contemporary Africa).

Although so much has changed since it was first published, there can be little doubt that this is the most important English-language work about São Tomé and Príncipe. It is an impressive synthesis of information and analysis, without any sacrifice of clarity. Chapters cover geography, history up until 1974, society, internal politics since independence, foreign relations and the problems of an island monoculture economy. A final chapter, 'Conclusion: finding a viable vocation', is still relevant. Despite the advent of multi-party democracy in 1991 the islands' problems remain: a growing population far exceeds any employment opportunities which the cocoa plantations could offer. This book is very well served by its photographs, tables and bibliography.

10   **São Tomé e Príncipe: breve memória descritiva e histórica e sintese
     estatistica.** (São Tomé and Príncipe: brief descriptive and historical
     record and statistical synthesis.)
     [São Tomé]: [s.n.], 1969. 161p. 2 maps.

Simultaneously in Portuguese, French and English, this reference work was produced for the VI Congress of the International Association of Asthmology which was held in São Tomé and Príncipe in 1969. It begins with a general description of the islands and in particular offers information on health and medical services. This is followed by a section on the islands' role in the international relief effort for Biafra during the Nigerian civil war. São Tomé was used as the base for airlifting relief to Biafra and sick Biafran children were cared for on the islands. Caritas International was the main charity involved in this work. The book also includes a section on folklore and a full range of statistical data.

Geography

General

11 **Conservação dos ecossistemas florestais na República Democrática de São Tomé e Príncipe.** (Conservation of forest ecosystems in the Democratic Republic of São Tomé and Príncipe.) P. J. Jones, J. P. Burlison, A. Tye. Gland, Switzerland; Cambridge, England: União Internacional para a Conservação da Natureza e dos Recursos Naturais, 1991. 78p. 6 maps. bibliog.

The forests of São Tomé and Príncipe are of immense ecological importance. The biodiversity of the bird and plant life is well-recognized: it is the second most important African forest for endangered bird species. The authors undertook this report as part of a European Development Fund regional programme for the conservation and rational utilization of Central African forest ecosystems. A forest inventory was carried out in 1989 when it was found that around one third of the islands' area is primary forest (*obó*), still intact because it is located in inaccessible mountain areas. Another third consists of secondary forest (*capoeira*) where the shade trees of abandoned plantations have been taking over. Although this is a good habitat for birds, the dominant *Elaeis guineensis* palm has begun encroaching on the primary forest-land. Plantations constitute the remaining land, with shade trees growing there. Recommendations are made for environmental protection and wildlife conservation: quick-growing trees should be planted for use as fuel for households and the cocoa-drying sheds; shade trees should be encouraged to grow on the plantations to mimic the forest habitat; pesticide use should be limited; the export of parrots and turtles should be banned; and the primary forest should be made into nature reservations. The authors also warn that a major threat would occur if the plantations were to be rehabilitated. The legal and administrative situation concerning the forest and other conservation issues is not at present regularized or enforced and proposals are made to remedy this. A useful bibliography includes Food and Agriculture Organization reports and in addition there is appended material on bird life taken from *Threatened birds of Africa and related islands. The ICBP/IUCN red data book: part 1* by N. J.

5

Collar and S. N. Stuart (Cambridge, England: International Council for Bird Preservation/International Union for the Conservation of Nature, 1985. 3rd ed. 761p.). See also Salvador Sousa Pontes, 'The forest and its importance in São Tomé and Príncipe' in *Conservation of West and Central African rainforests* (Washington, DC: World Bank, 1992, p. 40-43).

12 **A floresta e a ocupação humana na ilha de São Tomé.** (The forest and human settlement in the island of São Tomé.)
Francisco José Tenreiro. *Garcia de Orta*, vol. 9, no. 4 (1961), p. 549-56.

In many respects this interesting article serves as a history of agriculture on São Tomé. Tenreiro begins by noting the striking similarity in the patterns of Portuguese settlement on the Atlantic islands of Madeira, the Azores, Cape Verde and São Tomé and Príncipe where the cultivation of sugar cane battled against the differences in geography. Until the introduction of coffee and cocoa only the littoral zones of São Tomé were cultivated, since sugar needs level ground and deep soil. By the 20th century, however, little of the natural vegetation remained below an altitude of 1000 metres - a testimony to the effectiveness of 19th-century clearing undertaken for the coffee and cocoa plantations. This article describes the plantation system from a broad geographical perspective: the author sees it as pre-capitalist in origin, the first stage in opening up the land to human settlement. He also makes the interesting observation that in São Tomé the strength of the forest is inversely proportional to the strength of the economy.

13 **A ilha de São Tomé (estudo geográfico).** (The island of São Tomé [geographic study].)
Francisco José Tenreiro. Lisbon: Junta de Investigações do Ultramar, 1961. 279p. 12 maps. bibliog. (Memórias da Junta de Investigações do Ultramar, no. 24).

This could be the definitive textbook on São Tomé: it is an indispensable source. The first two chapters describe physical geography: the mountainous relief of the island and its formation by volcanic activity and erosion by water courses; the climate, soil and vegetation and man's impact on them. The third chapter, which treats colonization and acculturation, is a history of the island from settlement and the sugar boom, through the two hundred years when 'São Tomé seemed like an empty warehouse, in which there lingered only the persistent smell of abandoned merchandise' (p. 74), to the 19th-century 'rediscovery' of the island. The plantation system's profound impact on the island's geography is covered in both its physical aspect, with the removal of the forest, and its human effect on the dispossessed indigenous population. This chapter also contains an interesting section on São Tomé as a crossroads for plants from the continents of Africa, America, Asia and Europe. The next chapter looks at the contemporary population, covering demography, the location and layout of settlements and the organization of the plantations. Domestic architecture, small-scale agriculture and fishing are also described in admirable detail. The penultimate chapter looks at contemporary economy and society, making a clear distinction between the world of the plantation and that of the marginalized indigenous São Tomense. This chapter covers popular culture, ways of life and relations between the various races, social groups and nationalities. In contradiction to the myth of the racial harmony of the Portuguese colonizing mission, Tenreiro finds that island society is neither plural nor integrated. He quotes M. Ferreira Ribeiro from 1877, 'where everything should breathe happiness, only sadness and isolation can be found' (p. 217). The final chapter looks at the island's economy in the context of the international markets and finds the signs of an impending crisis. As a geographer the author sees the fundamental problem to be an antiquated spatial organization. There is a pressing need to diversify away from cocoa, and to make use of the productive capacity of the indigenous population. His conclusion compares São Tomé to the islands of Cape Verde, and this comparison highlights the social instability caused by plantation agriculture. The book contains seventy-three black-and-white photographs of a wide variety of subjects. Finally, mention must be made of the impressive 369-item bibliography. It is arranged into thirteen subject areas, and many entries have annotations. Similar themes are covered in Tenreiro's article 'São Tomé: um exemplo de organização do espaço' (São Tomé: an example of spatial organization) (*Estudos de Ciências Políticas e Sociais*, no. 51 [1961], p. 67-83).

Mudança na paisagem das ilhas de S.Tomé e Príncipe.
See item no. 245.

Soils

14   **Carta dos solos de São Tomé e Príncipe.** (Map of the soils of São Tomé and Príncipe.)
J. Carvalho Cardoso, J. Sacadura Garcia.   Lisbon: Junta de Investigações do Ultramar, 1962. 306p. 2 maps. bibliog.
Detailed soil surveys of both islands were undertaken between 1956 and 1958 and a general review of geomorphology, geology, climate and vegetation is followed by a description of the working methods used in the field and the laboratory. The main body of the book is a classification and description of the soil types found. These are identified as lithosols, regosols, alluvial soils, black tropical soils, dark brown tropical soils, red tropical fersiallitic soils, yellow tropical fersiallitic soils and hydromorphic soils. This section also includes tables of chemical analyses. The Missão de Estudos Agronómicos do Ultramar (Mission for Overseas Agronomic Studies) prepared two maps with a scale of 1:50,000, one for each island, which are shaded to show the location of different soil types. Contours, roads and settlements are also indicated and a summary in English is provided. A preliminary study was also carried out by Cardoso: *Caracterização das principais unidades pedológicos do 'Esboço da carta dos solos de São Tomé e Príncipe'* (Description of the principal pedological types from the 'Outline of the map of the soils of São Tomé and Príncipe') (Lisbon: Junta de Investigações do Ultramar, 1958. 85p. bibliog. [Estudos, Ensaios e Documentos, no. 53]). A progress report in English can be found in Cardoso and Garcias 'The soils of S.Tomé e Príncipe islands' (*Garcia de Orta*, vol. 8, no.3 [1960], p. 737-48).

15 **Estudo da fertilidade de alguns solos de S.Tomé. I - ensaio em vasos pelo método subtractivo.** (Study of the fertility of some soils from São Tomé. I - pot study using the subtractive method).
J. Contreiras, J. Vieira da Silva, J. Esteves Baptista, M. A. Rosado Dias, M. A. Ribeiro Nunes. *Garcia de Orta*, vol. 8, no. 2 (1960), p. 443-501. bibliog.

This is one of a series of reports on experiments into the fertility of the soils of São Tomé. Also published in *Garcia de Orta* are J. M. d'Arriaga e Cunha and J. de Sousa Lopes 'Estudo da fertilidade de alguns solos de São Tomé. II - determinação do fósforo lábil, por diluição isotópica, e da taxa de utilização do fosfato monocálcico em solos de São Tomé e Príncipe' (Study of the fertility of some soils from São Tomé. II - determination of labile phosphorous by isotype dilution and the rate of monocalcium phosphate utilization in soils from São Tomé and Príncipe) (vol. 8, no. 2 [1960], p. 503-10) and F. M. C. Henriques and A. P. S. Cardoso 'Estudos sobre a fertilidade dos solos da ilha de S.Tomé. V - dinâmica do potássio em três solos em relação com a absorção por uma cultura esgotante de azevém (*Lolium multiflorum* L.)' (Studies on the fertility of soils from the island of São Tomé. V - dynamics of potassium absorption by rye grass [*Lolium multiflorum* L.]) (vol. 17, no. 2 [1969], p. 167-79. bibliog.). All have summaries in English.

16 **Fertilité et fertilisation des sols à vocation cacaoyère de São Tomé.** (Fertility and fertilization of soils used for cacao in São Tomé).
P. Jadin. *Café Cacao Thé,* vol. 32, no. 2 (April-June 1988), p. 111-26. 2 maps. bibliog.

Soil samples from various cocoa plantations were subjected to chemical analysis and the soils' fertility and potential for mineral fertilization assessed. The soils were found to be rich, with surplus phosphorus and magnesium. Given improvements in agricultural techniques on the plantations, use could be made of potash fertilizer. Potentially useful future studies concerning the role of shade legumes and boron deficiency are outlined. There is a summary in English.

17 **Mineralogia dos solos de São Tomé e Príncipe.** (Mineralogy of the soils of São Tomé and Príncipe.)
J. Bailim Pissarra, J. Carvalho Cardoso. Lisbon: Junta de Investigações do Ultramar, 1965. 144p. bibliog. (Estudos, Ensaios e Documentos, no. 118).

This study of the mineral composition of the islands' soils has a summary in English. See also Pissara 'Mineralogical composition of paraferrallitic soils of São Tomé e Príncipe islands' (*Garcia de Orta*, vol. 13, no. 1 [1965], p. 117-22) and Pissara and Maria Ana Fontes 'Clay minerals and genesis of some soils of São Tomé e Príncipe islands' in the same journal issue (p. 123-24). Further mineralogical investigations are reported in Pissara and A. Tavares Rochas 'Contribuição para o estudo mineralógico e da microfauna dos regossolos psamíticos calcários de São Tomé' (Contribution to the study of minerals and microfauna in the calcareous psammitic regosols of São Tomé) (*Garcia de Orta*, vol. 11, no. 1 [1963], p. 171-78. map. bibliog.).

18 **Note on the plans of work of the Missions for Agronomical Studies of Cabo Verde, Guiné and S. Tomé e Príncipe.**
J. Carvalho Cardoso. *Garcia de Orta*, vol. 8, no. 1 (1960), p. 202-12. bibliog.

Submitted to the Third Inter-African Soil Conference at Dalaba, this document describes the soil research projects undertaken in the three countries. In São Tomé and Príncipe these concentrate on soil fertility and water economy. Included is a brief description of the Missions' organizational and administrative structure. More information on the situation in the islands can be found in 'Breve notícia sobre a actividade da Brigada de S. Tomé e Príncipe' (Short note on the activity of the Mission for São Tomé and Príncipe) (*Garcia de Orta*, vol. 8, no. 2 [1960], p. 511-13).

19 **Previsão da 'vida' dos solos de S. Tomé em relação ao agente causador da murchidão vascular da bananeira, *Fusarium oxysporium* Schl. f. *cubense* Sny. & Hans.** (Forecast of the behaviour of the soils of São Tomé in relation to the agent causing banana wilt disease, *Fusarium oxysporium* Schl. f. *cubense* Sny. & Hans).
A. do Rosário Noronha. *Garcia de Orta*, vol. 15, no. 3 (1967), p. 333-48. bibliog.

Numerous soil samples were studied to determine which types favour or hinder this serious banana disease (sometimes known as Panama disease). The results are detailed here and there is a summary in English.

20 **Santomenses (agricultores) cuidado com a erosão.** (São Tomense [farmers] beware of erosion.)
Manuel Pires dos Santos. São Tomé: The Author, 1990. 16p. bibliog.

The causes and consequences of soil erosion are explained in this pamphlet which also outlines some simple techniques to help prevent erosion. São Tomé's mountainous topography, coupled with the shallowness of much of its soil, makes it vulnerable to erosion once vegetation is removed.

21 **Os solos de S.Tomé e Príncipe perante a nova classificação de solos americana.** (The soils of São Tomé and Príncipe according to the new American soil classification.)
J. Carvalho Cardoso. *Garcia de Orta*, vol. 10, no. 4 (1962), p. 733-52. bibliog.

The author attempts to classify the soils of São Tomé and Príncipe, which were surveyed in 1958, according to the United States Department of Agriculture Soil Survey Staff's *Soil classification: a comprehensive system. 7th approximation*, 1960. The text is summarized in English.

Maps and mapping

22 **Archipelagic straight baselines: São Tomé and Príncipe.**
R. W. Smith.   Washington, DC: US Department of State, Bureau of
Intelligence and Research, 1983. 8p. map. (Limits in the Seas, no. 98).
The maritime boundaries which São Tomé and Príncipe established in 1978 are
mapped here, as they were amended in 1982. The system of enclosing archipelagic
sovereign waters which was used is judged to conform with the law of the sea.

23 **Descobrimento e cartografia das ilhas de S.Tomé e Príncipe.** (The
discovery and cartography of the islands of São Tomé and Príncipe.)
Armando Cortesão.   Lisbon: Junta de Investigações do Ultramar,
1971. 18p. 6 maps. (Agrupamento de Estudos de Cartografia Antiga.
Secção de Coimbra, no. 62).
It is generally held that João de Santarém and Pêro de Escobar discovered the island
of São Tomé on 21 December 1470 and that of Príncipe on 17 January 1471. Cortesão
points out that the Portuguese often seemed to find islands by accident, and then not
chart them but leave mysterious references in early 15th-century documents. There is
an interesting discussion of the 15th-century use of the word *descobrimento*, when it
often implied the establishment of regular relations with an already 'discovered' land.
Cortesão's main theme in this study is the islands' cartographic history. There are six
reproductions of maps of the islands. They are the work of Pedro Reinel (1483);
Valentim Fernandes (1507); Luís Teixeira (1606); anonymous (1664); João Teixeira
Albernaz (1665); and Gago Coutinho (1921).

24 **Engenhos de água na ilha de São Tomé no século XVI.** (Water mills
on the island of São Tomé in the 16th century.)
Francisco Tenreiro.   Coimbra, Portugal: Associação Portuguesa para o
Progresso das Ciências, 1957. 9p. map.
This study is based on a map and description of the island published in Cornelius
Claess' *Caert-thresoor, inhoudende de tafelendes gantsche werelts landen* (Treasury
of maps, containing tableaux of all the countries of the world) (Middleburgh,
Netherlands: [s.n.], 1597). The north-east of the island of São Tomé contained
numerous sugar plantations and one of the important features marked on this map is
the location of the water mills which were used for sugar processing. Tenreiro has
used this early map to annotate a more accurate map, published here, which gives a
full cartographical description of the island at the end of the 16th century. It shows
rivers and forests, the sugar industry, and other economic activity such as the
cultivation of coconuts and bananas. The 1597 description mentions the presence of
fugitive and rebellious Africans in the south and Tenreiro marks this area as inhabited
by the Angolars.

25 **A evolução da geodesia e a ocupação geodésica do ultramar português em África.** (The development of geodesic mapping in Portugal's African colonies.)
José Farinha da Conceição. Lisbon: Junta de Investigações do Ultramar, 1970. 81p. 7 maps. bibliog. (Estudos, Ensaios e Documentos, no. 127).

Includes notes on the mapping work undertaken in São Tomé and Príncipe and the degree of precision achieved. Geodesic maps of the two islands are reproduced.

26 **Exposição de cartographia nacional (1903-1904).** (Exhibition of national cartography [1903-1904].)
Edited by Ernesto de Vasconcellos. Lisbon: Sociedade de Geographia de Lisboa, 1904. 279p.

The section on São Tomé and Príncipe (p. 151-53) lists ten maps, with brief annotations.

27 **Plano hidrográfico da Baía de Âna Chaves.** (Hydrographic plan of Ana Chaves Bay.)
Missão Hidrográfica de Angola. Lisbon: Ministério do Ultramar, Junta das Missões Geográficas e de Investigações do Ultramar, 1955.

This is a 1:10,000 coloured plan of the bay, showing water depths, buildings and roads on the coast. It also contains information for ships on where to drop anchor and provides tide tables. A 1:1,000 map produced by the Missão Hidrográfica, *Plano hidrografico da ponta de S.Sebastião na Baía de Ana Chaves* (Hydrographic plan of St. Sebastian's point in Ana Chaves Bay), in 1916 shows the area around the fort in great detail. It also marks the harbour, warehouses, water depths and tidal information.

28 **Reconhecimento da ilha de S.Tomé 1916 a 1918.** (Reconnaisance of the island of São Tomé, 1916 to 1918.)
Missão Geodésica de S.Tomé e Príncipe. Lisbon: [s.n.], 1920.

This is an extremely detailed 1:50,000 coloured map of the island with an inset 1:5,000 map of the islet of Sete Pedras. The maps show contours, rivers, roads and settlements.

29 **Relação dos nomes geográficos de São Tomé e Príncipe.** (Register of the geographical names of São Tomé and Príncipe.)
Lisbon: Junta de Investigações do Ultramar, Centro de Geografia do Ultramar, 1968. 82p.

Around 38,000 place names are listed.

30   **S.Tomé e Príncipe.** (São Tomé and Príncipe.)
      [São Tomé]: Centro de Informação e Turismo de S.Tomé e Príncipe,
      1971. [2p.] 5 maps.
Produced with the assistance of the Repartição Provincial dos Serviços Geográficos e
Cadastrais (Provincial Office of Geographic and Cadastral Services), this single sheet
contains all the maps the visitor could hope to find. Two coloured 1:75,000 maps, one
for each island, mark contours, roads, watercourses, waterfalls, settlements,
plantations and beaches. There are also street plans for São Tomé city (1:10,000) and
Santo António, the capital of Príncipe (1:5,000) and the fifth map encompasses the
Gulf of Guinea and its continental coast. The sheet includes colour reproductions of
three of Pascoal Viégas' beautiful naïve paintings, showing performances of the
tchiloli, the *Danço Congo* (Congo Dance) and the *Ussua Nova* dance. Copies of the
map made available after independence have had references to the islands' colonial
status carefully blacked out or pasted over.

**Catálogo sumário da exposição bibliográfica e cartográfica de S.Tomé e
Príncipe.**
See item no. 413.

Geology

31 **Bibliografia geológica do ultramar português.** (Geological
bibliography of the Portuguese overseas territories.)
Francisco Gonçalves, Jaime Caseiro. Lisbon: Junta de Investigações
do Ultramar, 1959. 272p.

Entries are usually accompanied by a brief abstract, and are arranged by author and
indexed by geographical area, author and subject. Forty-eight entries in this volume
refer to São Tomé and Príncipe.

32 **Contribuição para o estudo geológico e geomorfológico da ilha de
S.Tomé e dos ilhéus das Rolas e das Cabras.** (Contribution towards
the geological and geomorphological study of the island of São Tomé
and the islets of Rolas and Cabras.)
J. M. Cotelo Neiva. In: *Conferência Internacional dos Africanistas
Ocidentais 6ª Sessão. Volume II.* [Lisbon]: Commission for Technical
Co-operation in Africa South of the Sahara; Scientific Council for
Africa South of the Sahara, 1956, p. 147-53. map. bibliog.

The principal geological and geomorphological features of the islands, both volcanic
and sedimentary, are described by Neiva. In the same volume he contributes four
more papers on the geology of São Tomé, Príncipe and the other smaller islands of
the archipelago.

Geology

33 **A ilha do Príncipe e a "linha dos Camarões" (estudo petrológico).**
(The island of Príncipe and the 'Cameroon line' [petrological study].)
Luís Aires Barros. Lisbon: Junta de Investigações do Ultramar, 1960.
127p. map. bibliog. (Memórias da Junta de Investigações do Ultramar,
2nd series, no. 17).

The first part of this study is a geological description of the island of Príncipe. The
second part analyses the petrochemistry of all the islands and volcanoes belonging to
the 'Cameroon line': Cameroon, Fernando Pó, Príncipe, São Tomé, Annobon, St.
Helena and Ascension. Barros concludes that, with the exception of Ascension, these
sites are linked by petrological similarities and the notable alignment of the volcano
peaks. A. N. Halliday, A. P. Dickin, A. E. Fallick and J. G. Fitton in 'Mantle
dynamics: a Nd, Sr, Pb and O isotopic study of the Cameroon line volcanic chain'
(*Journal of Petrology*, vol. 29, no. 1 [1988], p. 181-211, map, bibliog.) also find
significant relationships between space, time and geochemistry along the 'line'. See
also H. M. Dunlop and J. G. Fittons 'The Cameroon line, West Africa, and its bearing
on the origin of oceanic and continental alkali basalt' (*Earth and Planetary Science
Letters*, vol. 72 [1985], p. 23-38, map, bibliog.) and 'A K-Ar and Sr-isotopic study of
the volcanic island of Principe, West Africa - evidence for mantle heterogeneity
beneath the Gulf of Guinea' (*Contributions to Mineralogy and Petrology,* no. 71
[1979], p. 125-31).

34 **Lateritos das ilhas de S.Tomé e do Príncipe. Algumas hipóteses
acerca da sua génese.** (Laterites from the islands of São Tomé and
Príncipe. Some theories on their origins.)
M. Monteiro Marques, A. F. A. Sanches Furtado. *Garcia de Orta:
Série de Geologia*, vol. 3, no. 1-2 (1979), p. 1-16. map. bibliog.

The authors conduct a mineralogical analysis of these clays which have been
produced by the weathering of rocks in a tropical climate. In addition, they draw
some conclusions about the formation of the islands' coastlines.

35 **Novos elementos para geoquímica das lavas de São Tomé.** (New
contributions to the geochemistry of the lavas of São Tomé.)
Luís Aires-Barros, M. J. Matias, J. M. Marques. *Garcia de Orta:
Série de Geologia*, vol. 13, no. 1-2 (1990), p. 1-7. bibliog.

Drawing on a variety of petrological studies the authors consider the island's
magmatic evolution: it is 'an alkaline series derived from basic magma by fractional
crystallization'. Other studies of the chemical composition of the igneous rocks of
São Tomé are C. Torre de Assunção 'Alguns aspectos da petrografia da ilha de
S.Tomé' (Some aspects of the petrography of the island of São Tomé) (*Garcia de
Orta*, vol. 5, no. 3 [1957], p. 497-515. bibliog.); and J. M. Cotelo Neiva 'Quelques
laves vacuolaires de l'île de St.-Thomé et de l'îlot de Rolas' (Some vacuolar lavas
from the island of São Tomé and the islet of Rolas) (*Garcia de Orta*, vol. 2, no. 1
[1954], p. 53-59 and 'Chimisme des roches eruptives des îles de S.Thomé et Prince'
(The chemistry of the volcanic rocks of the islands of São Tomé and Príncipe)
(*Congrès Géologique International*, no. 21 [1954], p. 321-33, bibliog.).

36 **Petrochemistry of the volcanic rocks of the island of Principe, Gulf of Guinea.**
J. G. Fitton, D. J. Hughes. *Contributions to Mineralogy and Petrology*, vol. 64 (1977), p. 257-72. map. bibliog.

Príncipe has attracted considerable interest amongst geologists. It is formed almost entirely of two generations of volcanic rock and is deeply dissected, although there are no signs of any recent volcanic activity. This paper gives mineralogical and chemical data on the igneous rocks of the island and discusses their evolution. New information on the geological structure is also presented in this work which is part of a larger project on the petrochemical evolution of the volcanoes of the Cameroon line. Other studies of the lavas of Príncipe are Luís Aires-Barros, M. J. Matias and J. M. Marques 'Considerações petrogenéticas sobre as piroxenas das lavas da ilha do Príncipe' (Considerations of rock evolution applied to the pyroxene lavas from the island of Príncipe) (*Geociências: Revista da Universidade de Aveiro*, vol. 6, no. 1-2 [1991], p. 17-24, bibliog.); Luís Aires-Barros, M. J. Matias and L. Chambel 'Sobre a natureza do magma paterno e da fonte mantélica das lavas da ilha do Príncipe' (On the nature of the paternal magma and the mantle source of the lavas from the island of Príncipe) (*Garcia de Orta, Série Geologia*, vol. 9, nos. 1-2 [1986], p. 15-26, bibliog.); Aires-Barros' 'A geoquímica dos "elementos imóveis" das rochas vulcânicas como caracterizadora do seu enquadramento geotectónico. O caso das lavas das ilhas de Príncipe e da Madeira' (The geochemistry of the 'stationary elements' of volcanic rocks as a characterization of their geotectonic framework. The case of the lavas from the islands of Príncipe and Madeira) (*Garcia de Orta, Série de Geologia*, vol. 6, nos. 1-2 [1983], p. 127-136, bibliog.); Aires-Barros 'A geoquímica dos elementos higromagmatófilos das lavas da ilha do Príncipe e seu enquadramento na geotectónica da linha dos Camarões' (The geochemistry of hygromagmatic elements of the lavas of the island of Príncipe and their place in the geotectonics of the Cameroon line) (*Boletim da Sociedade Geológica de Portugal*, no. 23 [1982], p. 7-13); J. M. Cotelo Neiva 'Phonolites de l'île du Prince' (Phonolites from the island of Príncipe) (*Garcia de Orta*, vol. 3, no. 4 [1955], p. 505-15).

Flora

General

37 **Afromontane elements in the flora of S.Tomé: variation and taxonomy of some 'nomads' and 'transgressors'.**
F. White. *Garcia de Orta: Série de Botânica*, vol. 6, nos. 1-2 (1983-84), p. 187-202. 2 maps. bibliog.
White offers a study of fourteen species of tree which are found on both São Tomé and the African mainland. Their taxonomy is problematic in that 'as Darwin observed, wide ranging, much diffused and common species vary most' (p. 188). The annotations for each species are particularly concerned with their distribution and variation.

38 **Catalogue of the vascular plants of S.Tomé (with Principe and Annobon).**
Arthur Wallis Exell. London: British Museum (Natural History), 1944. 428p. 3 maps.
Exell visited the Gulf of Guinea islands in 1932 and 1933 to carry out botanical research. The main body of this important work is the 'General systematic list' (p. 56-382) of all the species which have been recorded, with brief descriptions and locations. These are indexed by Latin name, and there is also a glossary of vernacular and English names. The first of two introductory chapters looks at the islands' climate, topography and geology as they pertain to botany. The history of cultivation is also of importance and it is noted that the islands allow 'the unusual opportunity of studying territory unmodified by man until 1470' (p. 6). The plantations have greatly affected the islands' vegetation and today there is no unbroken stretch of natural vegetation from mountain to coast. Nonetheless, the Angolars' settlement was particularly fruitful for botanical research 'as their methods of cultivation did not involve the complete destruction of the forest which accompanied the formation of European-owned plantations' (p. 6). Príncipe is less botanically-favoured than São

Tomé because it is smaller, has a lower altitude and was comprehensively cleared during the campaign against sleeping sickness. The mountains of São Tomé provided the most interesting endemic species: the rain forest contained lianas, ferns, lichens, mosses, orchids and trees so tall that they were difficult to identify. The only unique habitat is the Lagoa Amelia swamp which is located in the crater of an extinct volcano. In this chapter Exell also lists the other botanical and scientific expeditions to the islands, and although there is no bibliography there are many references throughout the text to useful sources. By the 1860s 'knowledge of the vegetation of S.Tomé and Príncipe was now fairly advanced compared with that of the adjacent areas of the continent - indeed many characteristic tropical African species were first described from the islands' (p. 11). The second chapter considers the origins of the flora and the geographical distribution of non-introduced plants is shown in tabular form. Statistics show affinities between the four Gulf of Guinea islands. Exell concludes that the flora is predominantly West African. In *Supplement to the catalogue of the vascular plants of S.Tomé (with Principe and Annobon)* (London: British Museum [Natural History], 1956, 58p.) he updates and corrects the original work, especially in the light of six more collections having become available. The introduction includes some comments on endemism and the differences between the species found on São Tomé and on Príncipe.

39 **Cianófitas de S.Tomé e Príncipe.** (Cyanophyceae of São Tomé and Príncipe.)
    Joaquim Sampaio.   Lisbon: Junta de Investigações do Ultramar, 1958. 80p. bibliog. (Estudos, Ensaios e Documentos, no. 47).

This is a study of algae found on the two islands and has a summary in English.

40 **Contribuição para o estudo das Begoniáceas de S.Tomé e Príncipe.** (Contribution to the study of the Begoniaceae of São Tomé and Príncipe.)
    José Henrique Pereira de Barros Ferreira.   *Garcia de Orta*, vol. 13, no. 4 (1965), p. 525-44. bibliog.

The nine species of the genus *Begonia* L. which represent the Begoniaceae family in São Tomé and Príncipe are described here. See also J. M. Reitsma 'Begonia section *Baccabegonia Reitsma*, sect. nov.' (in the Agricultural University of Wageningen's *Papers,* vol. 84, no. 3 [1984], p. 95-111). Reitsma looks at two endemic species: *Begonia baccata* and *Begonia crateris*. Ferreira's other studies of the islands' flora include: 'Contribuição para o estudo das Malváceas de S.Tomé e Príncipe' (Contribution to the study of the Malvaceas of São Tomé and Príncipe) (*Garcia de Orta*, vol. 11, no. 1 [1963], p. 27-55); 'Contribuição para o estudo das Melastomataceae de S.Tomé e Príncipe' (Contribution to the study of the Melastomataceae of São Tomé and Príncipe) (*Garcia de Orta,* vol. 16, no. 1 [1968], p. 69-86, bibliog.); and 'Um Tristemma novo para a ciência, o *Tristemma thomensis* sp. nov.' (A new Tristemma for science, the *Tristemma thomensis* sp. nov.) (*Garcia de Orta*, vol. 16, no. 1 [1968], p. 63-68). Most of the articles have summaries in English.

41 **A diagrammatic method of analysing the inter-relationship of the fauna or flora of several localities.**
C. B. Williams. *Proceedings of the Linnean Society of London,*
vol. 158, no. 2 (1947), p. 99-103.

Williams uses data from the *Catalogue of the vascular plants of S.Tomé (with Principe and Annobon)* (q.v.) to diagrammatically examine the relationships between the flora of the four Gulf of Guinea islands. The diagrams show on which island which species can be found, and indicate the degree of commonality. In the same journal issue Williams continues his calculations in 'The logarithmic series and the comparison of island floras' (p. 104-08). The results obtained are commented upon by Arthur Wallis Exell in 'Discussion of the percentage relationship calculated by Dr. Williams' (p. 108-10).

42 **Estudo farmacognósico de cascas de *Cinnamonum cassia* (Nees) Nees ex Blume de S.Tomé.** (Pharmacological study of the bark of *Cinnamonum cassia* [Nees] Nees ex Blume.)
A. Correia Alves, L. Nogueira Prista. *Garcia de Orta,* vol. 7, no.2 (1959), p. 325-30. bibliog.

Cinnamon is grown commercially on some plantations and the bark and an essential oil which is prepared from the bark are chemically analysed in this study.

43 **Flora de S.Tomé e Príncipe: ácidos gordos e proteínas de algumas sementes.** (Flora from São Tomé and Príncipe: fatty acids and proteins from some seeds.)
J. Mendes Ferrão.   Lisbon: Junta de Investigações Científicas do Ultramar, 1979. 185p. bibliog. (Estudos, Ensaios e Documentos, no. 132).

The islands' flora is studied from the perspective of its nutritional potential. There is a summary in English.

44 **Flora de S.Tomé e Príncipe: Caesalpinaceae.** (Flora from São Tomé and Príncipe: Caesalpinaceae.)
Maria Cândida Liberato.   Lisbon: Junta de Investigações do Ultramar, Jardim e Museu Agrícola do Ultramar, 1976. 29p.

Liberato describes the members of this family which can be found on São Tomé and Príncipe, with notes on when and where they have been recorded. The same author has also produced several similar studies on other plant families found in the islands, all published in Lisbon by the Junta de Investigações do Ultramar, Jardim e Museu Agrícola do Ultramar: *Flora de S.Tomé e Príncipe: Connaraceae* (Flora from São Tomé and Príncipe: Connaraceae) (1980, 14p.); *Flora de S.Tomé e Príncipe: Dichapetalaceae* (Flora from São Tomé and Príncipe: Dichapetalaceae) (1982, 7p.); *Flora de S.Tomé e Príncipe: Rosaceae* (Flora from São Tomé and Príncipe: Rosaceae) (1980, 13p.).

45 **Madeiras de S.Tomé: características anatómicas e físicas.** (Wood from São Tomé: anatomical and physical characteristics.) Maria Clara P. G. de Freitas. Lisbon: Instituto de Investigação Científica Tropical, 1987. 119p. bibliog.

The woody tissues of eighteen species of tree from São Tomé were examined, with a particular view to their potential use in small-scale industries.

46 **Nomes crioulos e vernáculos de algumas plantas de S.Tomé e Príncipe.** (Creole and vernacular names of some plants from São Tomé and Príncipe.) Joaquim do Espírito Santo. *Boletim Cultural da Guiné Portuguesa,* vol. 24, no. 93 (1969), p. 193-211.

There has been considerable confusion regarding the vernacular names of the islands' flora: the same name has been applied to different plants and different names for the same plant. Names have even been applied which are in fact unknown in the area. This article lists around 300 vernacular names together with their botanical names and *vice versa.* See also H. Lains e Silva 'Nomes vulgares de algumas plantas de São Tomé e Príncipe (com notas sobre a origem dos nomes e a utilidade das plantas)' (Common names for some plants from São Tomé and Príncipe [with notes on etymology and uses for the plants]) (*Garcia de Orta,* vol. 7, no. 2 [1959], p. 293-323. bibliog.). Some of Lains e Silva's annotations are quite substantial and include historical references for the more important plants.

47 **Nótulas para o conhecimento da flora de S.Tomé e Príncipe.** (Notes towards the understanding of the flora of São Tomé and Príncipe.) L. Gonçalves Sobrinho. *Garcia de Orta,* vol. 7, no. 1 (1959), p. 89-95.

The 524 samples of plants collected by H. Lains e Silva are listed with brief annotations. A large number were introduced species, new to the islands.

48 **Plantas úteis da África portuguesa.** (Useful plants of Portuguese Africa.) F. de Mello de Ficalho, edited and with a foreword by Ruy Telles Palhinha. Lisbon: Agência Geral das Colónias, 1947. 2nd ed. 301p.

Palhinha's preface gives an account of the Conde de Ficalho's scientific achievements together with the history of this massive work, which was first published in 1884. Ficalho's own introduction (p. 5-72) treats cultivated and spontaneous plants separately, and includes a history of botany and exploration in Portuguese Africa. He alludes specifically to São Tomé and Príncipe (p. 63-64). The main body of the work is a listing by family of the 'useful' plants. It has substantial annotations on the uses to which they are put, their distribution, from whence they originate and their names in a variety of languages. The plants are indexed by Portuguese and vernacular name, including those of the creole languages of São Tomé and Príncipe, and by botanical name. This is a book of botanic, ethnographic and historic interest.

49   **Revisão das algas de S.Tomé e Príncipe do herbário do Instituto
      Botânica de Coimbra.** (Review of the seaweeds from São Tomé and
      Príncipe held in the herbarium of the Botanical Institute of Coimbra.)
      J. E. de Mesquita Rodrigues.   *Garcia de Orta,* vol. 8, no. 3 (1960),
      p. 583-95. bibliog.

The collection of Phaephyceae in Coimbra is described and photographs and a
summary in English are included.

Medicinal plants

50   **Algumas plantas medicinais e venenosas de São Tomé e Príncipe.**
      (Some medicinal and poisonous plants from São Tomé and Príncipe.)
      Joaquim do Espírito Santo.   *Boletim Cultural da Guiné Portuguesa,*
      vol. 24, no. 96 (1969), p. 917-40.

Fifty-four medicinal and poisonous plants are listed in this volume, along with
botanical descriptions and their vernacular names. The author includes information on
the various uses of the medicinal plants and their preparation and the introduction
notes that over 122 medicinal plants have been identified from the islands. One of the
aims of this study is to clarify the vernacular nomenclature.

51   **Contribuição para o estudo das dioscoreáceas das nossas províncias
      ultramarinas.** (Contribution to the study of the Dioscoreaceae of our
      overseas provinces.)
      A. Correia Alves, L. Nogueira Prista, A. Figueira de Sousa.   *Garcia de
      Orta,* vol. 8, no. 4 (1960), p. 821-35. bibliog.

The alkaloids found in the São Tomense yam *Dioscorea dumetorum* Pax are studied
here. This particular yam is an important foodstuff and is also used in the local
medicine for the treatment of burns, some skin diseases and as a vesicatory. There is a
summary in English.

52   **Pesquisa de alantoína em algumas plantas de S.Tomé usadas no
      tratamento de feridas.** (Search for allantoine in some São Tomense
      plants used in the treatment of wounds.)
      L. Nogueira Prista, A. Correia Alves, Maria Fatima C. de Araújo.
      Garcia de Orta, vol. 8, no. 2 (1960), p. 327-31. bibliog.

Four plants used in the traditional medicine of São Tomé for treating wounds were
subjected to an analysis for the presence of allantoine, a substance known to be
effective in healing. The plants were *Pycanthus angolensis, Sterculia tragacantha,
Craterispermum ethiopicum* and *Santiriopsis trimera.* The bark of the first of these
was found to contain 0.2% allantoine, and is also used for the treatment of inflamed
mouths. The chemical analysis is described in Prista, Alves and M. C. Healy P. da

Costas 'Investigação fitoquímica de cascas de *Pycanthus angolensis* (Welw.) Exell' (Phytochemical research into the bark of *Pycanthus angolensis* [Welw.] Exell), (*Garcia de Orta*, vol. 8, no. 2 [1960], p. 315-26).

53 **Plantas úteis da flora de S.Tomé e Príncipe - medicinais, industriais e ornamentais.** (Useful plants from the flora of São Tomé and Príncipe - medicinal, industrial and decorative.)
Luis Lopes Roseira, preface by Carlos Alberto de Araújo.   [s.l.]: Serviços Gráficos da Liga dos Combatentes, 1984. 100p. map. bibliog.
A brief introduction to the islands' geography and plant life is followed by a thorough inventory of the useful flora that can be found there. The plants are listed by family, with both Latin and local names, botanical descriptions and notes on their use and method of preparation in the islands' traditional medicine. A number of black-and-white photographs are included in this useful guide to one of the islands' most-noted natural resources.

54 *Rauwolfia vomitoria* **Afz. de S.Tomé - contribuição para o seu estudo botânico e químico.** (*Rauwolfia vomitoria* Afz. from São Tomé - contribution towards its botanical and chemical study.)
A. Correia Alves, L. Nogueira Prista.   *Garcia de Orta*, vol. 6, no. 4 (1958), p. 689-96.
An analysis of the roots of this plant shows that they are high in alkaloids and so may have pharmaceutical potential. It is known locally as *cata pequena* and is taken as an infusion to treat stomach pains and abcesses. The authors supply a summary in English.

55 **Relação das plantas medicinais estudadas no Agrupamento Científico de Farmacognosia.** (Report on the medicinal plants studied at the Scientific Group for Pharmacognosy.)
Garcia de Orta, vol. 8, no. 4 (1960), p. 847-54.
The results of experiments on samples of fourteen medicinal plants, eight of which come from São Tomé, are briefly summarized in this report.

56 **Sobre o *Lonchocarpus sericeus* H. B. e K. colhido em S. Tomé.**
(On the *Lonchocarpus sericeus* H. B. e K. collected in São Tomé.)
A. Correia Alves, L. Nogueira Prista.   *Garcia de Orta*, vol. 8, no. 4 (1960), p. 837-46. bibliog.
The bark of this plant is used in São Tomé as a laxative. However, the chemical analysis detailed in this article which was intended to determine the cause of its pharmacological properties failed to discover any quinones, saponins, alkaloids or rotenone, although ascorbic acid was found. The results are summarized in English.

Medicina tradicional.
See item no. 184.

Fauna

General

57 **Alguns araneídeos das ilhas de São Tomé e do Príncipe.** (Some araneids from the islands of São Tomé and Príncipe.)
Amélia Bacelar.   In: *Conferência Internacional dos Africanistas Ocidentais 6ª Sessão. Volume IV.* [Lisbon]: Commission for Technical Co-operation in Africa South of the Sahara; Scientific Council for Africa South of the Sahara, 1956, p. 37-46. bibliog.
Bacelar lists and describes the spiders from the two islands.

58 **Alguns dos anfíbios e répteis da província de S.Tomé e Príncipe.** (Some of the amphibians and reptiles of the province of São Tomé and Príncipe.)
Sara Manaças.   In: *Livro do homenagem ao Prof. Fernando Frade.*
Lisbon: Junta de Investigações do Ultramar, 1973, p. 219-30. bibliog.
Manaças lists and briefly describes, including vernacular names, the amphibians and reptiles from São Tomé and Príncipe which are held at the Centro de Zoologia, Junta de Investigações do Ultramar (Centre for Zoology, Council for Overseas Research). The introduction outlines the history of the study of the islands' amphibians and reptiles, chronicling the various scientific expeditions, collectors and zoologists. Together with the bibliography, this is a very useful guide to the subject and also has a summary in English.

59   An asymmetric dental formula in a mammal. The São Tomé island
      fruit bat *Myonycteris brachycephala* (Mammalia: Megachiroptera).
      Javier Juste, Carlos Ibáñez.   *Canadian Journal of Zoology*, vol. 71,
      no. 1 (January 1993), p. 221-24. bibliog.
Possibly due to the evolutionary effects of the island's isolation, the dentition of the
São Tomé fruit bat is very unusual in its asymetric lack of a lower internal incisor.

60   Aves e mamíferos das ilhas de São Tomé e Príncipe - notas de
      sistemática e de protecção à fauna. (Birds and mammals of the
      islands of São Tomé and Príncipe - notes on classification and animal
      protection.)
      Fernando Frade.   In: *Conferência Internacional dos Africanistas
      Ocidentais 6ª Sessão. Volume IV.*   [Lisbon]: Commission for
      Technical Co-operation in Africa South of the Sahara; Scientific
      Council for Africa South of the Sahara, 1956, p. 137-49. bibliog.
Some bird species not previously recorded on the islands are listed in this article, with
suggestions for their protection. There are also notes on rodent pests, civet cats, bats,
monkeys (*Cercopithecus mona*) and the insectivore *Sorex crocidura* thomensis. There
is a summary in English.

61   Freshwater snails of São Tomé, with special reference to *Bulinus
      forskalii* (Ehrenberg), host of *Schistosoma intercalatum.*
      D. S. Brown.   *Hydrobiologia*, vol. 209, no. 2 (1991), p. 141-53.
      bibliog.
This is a full and illustrated description of the distinctive São Tomé variants of this
snail host. The tropical flatworm, *Schistosoma intercalatum* is implicated in the
transmission of bilharzia. The snails have an unusual shell morphology, and Brown
suggests that they should be labelled as *Bulinus forskalii* São Tomé.

62   A new *Tadarida* of the subgenus *Chaerephon* (Chiroptera:
      Molossidae) from Sao Tome island, Gulf of Guinea (West Africa).
      Javier Juste, Carlos Ibanez.   *Journal of Mammalogy*, vol. 74, no. 4
      (November 1993), p. 901-07. bibliog.
The identification of this new species of free-tailed bat, found on São Tomé, brings to
four the number of families of bat known on the island.

63   Ofídeos venenosos da Guiné, S.Tomé, Angola e Moçambique.
      (Venomous snakes from Guinea-Bissau, São Tomé, Angola and
      Mozambique.)
      Sara Manaças, Margarida Pinheiro.   *Garcia de Orta: Série de
      Zoologia,* vol. 10, nos. 1-2 (1981-82), p. 13-46. bibliog.
There are two venomous snakes on São Tomé: the semi-aquatic *Naja melanoleuca*,
known locally as 'cobra-preta' (black cobra); and *Dendroaspis viridis*, known as the
'serpente das bananeiras' (banana-tree snake), which can reach a length of 2.5 metres.

The species are described, with an introductory essay on snake venom and methods for treating victims of snake bites. A summary in English is also provided.

64   **Os ratos na ilha de S. Thomé.** (Rats on the island of São Tomé.)
      António Lôbo de Almada Negreiros. *Revista Portugueza Colonial e Marítima*, vol. 5, no. 25 (1899), p. 30-40.

Negreiros explains the damage caused to the cocoa crop by rats and suggests the introduction of the mongoose to control their numbers.

Birds

65   **Aves de S.Tomé e Príncipe (colecção do Centro de Zoologia).** (Birds from São Tomé and Príncipe [the Centre for Zoology's collection].)
      Fernando Frade, J. Vieira dos Santos. *Garcia de Orta: Série de Zoologia*, vol. 6, nos. 1-2 (1977), p. 3-18. bibliog.

This checklist, summarized in English, covers the 501 specimens collected in 1970 by the Centro de Zoologia, Junta de Investigações Científicas do Ultramar (Centre for Zoology, Council for Overseas Scientific Research).

66   **Avian systematics and evolution in the Gulf of Guinea - the J. G. Correia Collection.**
      Dean Amadon. *Bulletin of the American Museum of Natural History*, vol. 100 (1953), p. 393-452. map. bibliog.

José G. Correia, a former cooper on a whaling ship, visited the islands of the Gulf of Guinea in 1928-29 as part of an ornithological mission. Although he managed to make a representative collection from São Tomé and Príncipe for the American Museum of Natural History he was unable to visit Annobon and was hampered on Fernando Pó by sleeping sickness. Amadon begins by describing the geology, flora and fauna of the islands and suggests that São Tomé and Príncipe and Annobon were never connected to the mainland; 'and the avifauna has the unbalanced and impoverished yet highly endemic aspect usual in islands that have always been well isolated' (p. 401). This valuable work lists the resident non-marine birds of the islands drawn from Correia's collection, which was never previously fully reported, as well as from other sources. Extensive descriptive notes accompany each species, covering the location of Correia's specimens and with particular attention paid to any indication of variation from their mainland equivalents. Issues of taxonomy are raised. The article concludes with a fascinating essay on evolutionary factors (p. 442-48) in these isolated islands. Amadon calculates that, combining species and subspecies, the rate of endemism in São Tomé and Príncipe is 57 per cent and 47 per cent respectively: the few species that managed to reach the islands became highly differentiated from their mainland relatives. Plumage is more subdued amongst the islands' birds since there are fewer species from which they need to distinguish themselves. Feathers are softer since flight is less important and the general size and length of bill are often greater. Birds have also adopted a more generalized mode of life which is reflected in their morphology. The article includes black-and-white photographs of specimens.

67 **The birds of São Tomé and Príncipe in the Gulf of Guinea.**
D. W. Snow. *The Ibis*, vol. 92, no. 4 (1950), p. 579-95.

Snow visited both islands between 4 September and 3 October 1949, although 'formalities demanded by the police and civil authorities used up a good deal of the already inadequate time at our disposal' (p. 581). He confesses himself intrigued by the differences between the bird life of São Tomé and that of Príncipe, and sees potential for a future study of ecological and evolutionary issues. As he points out, 'Of the forty resident land-birds that have been recorded for São Tomé and the twenty-eight for Príncipe, only thirteen species are common to the two islands. Of these, four are either very rare or extinct on Príncipe, and four are sub-specifically different, leaving only five identical forms existing on both islands' (p. 582). Endemic species seem to have been comparatively stable, with the non-endemic species more likely to be subject to fluctations by introduction and extinction. The article continues as an annotated list of the species observed, which covers the location of specimens, their calls, behaviour, feeding habits, nests and numbers.

68 **A field guide to the birds of West Africa.**
Gérard J. Morel, William Serle. London: Collins, 1977. 351p. map.

An invaluable guide to the identification of birds in the field. Of the 1,097 species which have been recorded in the area roughly bounded by the Sahara, the Congo and the watershed of the White Nile, and including São Tomé and Príncipe, 726 are dealt with in the body of the text. Descriptions cover visual identification, song, distribution, habitat, nesting and a note on allied species where appropriate. The other 371 bird families are briefly annotated in a full checklist of species. There are 515 birds illustrated, 335 of which are in colour, by Wolfgang Hartwig. The book is indexed by English and scientific name, and there is also a list of Latin, English, Spanish, French and German names.

69 **La moucherolle endémique de l'île de São Tomé, *Terpsiphone atrochalybeia* (Thomson 1842).** (The endemic paradise flycatcher *Terpsiphone atrochalybeia* [Thomson 1842].)
R. de Naurois. *Alauda*, vol. 52, no. 1 (1984), p. 31-44. map. bibliog.

The numbers of this flycatcher have been declining in recent years due to the use of pesticide. Naurois has contributed much to the knowledge about the birds of São Tomé and Príncipe and has published similarly detailed descriptions of several other species: see, for example, '*Chaetura (Rhaphidura) thomensis* Hartert 1900 endémique des îles de São Tomé e Príncipe (Golfe de Guinée)' ('The São Tomé spinetailed swift *Chaetura [Rhaphidura] thomensis* Hartert 1900, endemic to São Tomé and Príncipe, Gulf of Guinea, West Africa) (*Alauda*, vol. 53, no. 3 [1985], p. 209-22); and 'Une nouvelle sous-espèce de tisserin: *Ploceus velatus peixotoi* (île de S. Tomé, Golfe de Guinée)' (A new sub-species of weaver: *Ploceus velatus peixotoi* [São Tomé, Gulf of Guinea]) with Fernando Frade (*Garcia de Orta*, vol. 12, no. 4 [1964], p. 621-26. bibliog.).

70   **New records of non-resident birds, and notes on some resident ones in Sao Tome and Principe islands.**
Fernando Frade.   *The Ostrich*, supplement no. 3 (1959), p. 317-20. bibliog.

Based on research carried out in 1954, this article lists new records of non-resident birds (rather absurdly several of the specimens were located at the airport). It also contains some notes on resident birds, updating the existing information on the subject.

71   **The status and conservation of the endemic bird species of São Tomé and Príncipe, West Africa.**
P. Atkinson, N. Peet, J. Alexander.   *Bird Conservation International*, vol. 1, no. 3 (1991), p. 255-82.

Surveys of bird life were carried out between June and September 1990. The importance of the forest habitat for birds in these areas is stressed, and this includes not only primary forest but also secondary forest and the shade trees found on plantations. The surveys record the first sightings since the 1920s of two very rare species, *Bostrychia bocagei* and *Lanius newtoni*. *Amaurocichla bocagii* was also spotted but it was found that *Oriolus crassirostris* is now rare.

Conservação dos ecossistemas florestais na República Democrática de São Tomé e Príncipe.
See item no. 11.

Aves e mamíferos das ilhas de São Tomé e Príncipe - notas de sistemática e de protecção à fauna.
See item no. 60.

Insects

72   **A broca do café em S.Tomé (*Stephanoderes hampei* Ferr.).** (The coffee borer on São Tomé [*Stephanoderes hampei* Ferr.].)
Armando Jacques Favre Castel-Branco.   *Garcia de Orta*, vol. 17, no. 1 (1969), p. 97-106. bibliog.

Describes these pests of the coffee bush and the damage which they cause. There is a summary in English.

73 **Entomofauna da Guiné Portuguesa e das ilhas de São Tomé e do
    Príncipe.** (Insects from Portuguese Guinea and the islands of São Tomé
    and Príncipe.)
    In: *Conferência Internacional dos Africanistas Ocidentais 6ª Sessão.*
    Volume IV. [Lisbon]: Commission for Technical Co-operation in
    Africa South of the Sahara; Scientific Council for Africa South of the
    Sahara, 1956, p. 11-22; 47-60; 79-90; 235-40; 257-64. bibliog.

This volume covers the subject matter in five parts: Armando Jacques Favre Castel-
Branco 'I. Hemípteros (coccídeos e psilídeos) e himenópteros' (I. Hemiptera
[coccidium and *Psyllidae*] and Hymenoptera) (p. 79-90); M. Luisa Gomes Alves 'II.
Coleópteros' (II. Coleoptera) (p. 11-22); Guilherme C. Tordo 'III. Coleópteros e
hemípteros' (III. Coleoptera and Hemiptera) (p. 257-64); João Tendeiro 'IV.
Malófagos' (IV: Mallophaga) (p. 235-64); Amélia Bacelar 'V. *Lepidoptera*
(*Rhopalocera*)' (V. *Lepidoptera* [*Rhopalocera*]) (p. 47-60).

74 **Entomofauna de S.Tomé: insectos do cacaueiro.** (Insects from São
    Tomé: insects of the cacao.)
    Armando Jacques Favre Castel-Branco. Lisbon: Junta de
    Investigações do Ultramar, 1963. 94p. bibliog. (Estudos, Ensaios e
    Documentos, no. 107).

The descriptions of these pests include the type of damage done by the insects
together with suggestions for their control. The introduction gives some background
to the present situation: between 1910 and 1920 shade plants were removed from the
cocoa plantations and this led to their devastation by such pests as *Selenotrips
rubrocinctus*. The replanting after this disaster was carried out in great haste and
without any planning. There is a current trend to abuse insecticides, but experiments
are taking place in biological control. There is a substantial summary in English and
some attractive colour illustrations.

75 **Entomofauna de S. Tomé e Príncipe (contribuição para o seu
    conhecimento). Coleópteros-cerambicídeos - I.** (Insects from São
    Tomé and Príncipe [contributions to their study]. Coleoptera-
    Cerambycidae - I.)
    Guilherme C. Tordo. In: *Estudos de zoologia.* (Studies in zoology).
    Lisbon: Junta de Investigações Científicas do Ultramar, 1974,
    p. 237-48, bibliog. (Memórias da Junta de Investigações Científicas do
    Ultramar, no. 58).

Lists and describes some species of Cerambycidae, many of which were not
previously recorded on the islands. The study includes a description of a new species
of genera, Ancylonotus, and has a summary in English. Tordo has conducted valuable
research into the islands' insects. See also 'Entomofauna da ilha de S.Tomé
(contribuição para o seu conhecimento). Uma nova espécie do género *Cethera* (*Hem.
Reduviidae*)' (Insects from the island of São Tomé [contributions to their study]. A
new species of the genus *Cethera* [*Hem. Reduviidae*].) (*Garcia de Orta*, vol. 17, no. 1
[1969], p. 71-74).

76 **Entomological note I - a fruit-fly attacking coffee cherries in São Tomé.**
Carl T. Schmidt. *Garcia de Orta*, vol. 15, no. 3 (1967), p. 329-32.
This note reports on a large infestation of *Dacus bivittatus* Bigot larvae found on coffee berries on São Tomé.

77 **Uma espécie nova de coccinela entomófaga da ilha do Príncipe (Ins. col.).** (A new species of insectivorous ladybird from the island of Príncipe [Ins. col.].)
Maria Luisa Gomes Alves, Armando Jacques Favre Castel-Branco.
Garcia de Orta, vol. 10, no. 4 (1962), p. 643-46.
Contains a description of the newly discovered *Scymnomorphus principensis* sp.n.

78 **O gorgulho da bananeira em S.Tomé.** (The banana borer in São Tomé.)
Carl T. Schmidt. *Garcia de Orta*, vol. 13, no. 3 (1965), p. 343-50. bibliog.
Cosmopolites sordidus is a serious pest of the banana tree in São Tomé. Schmidt describes the insect, the damage it causes and methods of control that are available. The problem is exacerbated by the casual way in which bananas are grown on the island. They are extremely widespread, and are often planted for shade rather than commercial cultivation. Hence little attention is paid when they become infested with borers, and the insects are then able to spread.

79 **Himenópteros da África portuguesa I. Esfecóides de Cabo Verde, Guiné e S.Tomé.** (Hymenoptera of Portuguese Africa I. Sphecoids from Cape Verde, Guinea and São Tomé.)
Manuel de Assunção Diniz. *Garcia de Orta*, vol. 12, no. 2 (1964), p. 233-40.
The species from São Tomé studied in this article are *Ampulex sibirica* Fab. and *Sceliphron spirifex* L. A summary in English is provided.

80 **Luta biológica.** (The biological fight.)
Armando Jacques Favre Castel-Branco. *Garcia de Orta*, vol. 10, no. 4, (1962), p. 635-42.
The advantages of biological control over the use of insecticides are outlined in this article. Reference is made to the control of *Aspidiotus destructor* on Príncipe by the use of *Cryptognatha nodiceps*, and to research into the biological control of *Icerya purchasi* Mask on São Tomé. See also Castel-Branco 'Luta biológica contra *Aspidiotus destructor*, Sign., na ilha do Príncipe' (The biological fight against *Aspidiotus destructor*, Sign., on the island of Príncipe) (*Garcia de Orta: Série de Zoologia*, vol. 1, no. 1 [1972], p. 17-36). Both articles have summaries in English.

81 Uma nova cochonilha da ilha do Príncipe (*Asterolecanium pustulans* Ckll., var. nov. *princeps*). (A new scale insect from the island of Príncipe [*Asterolecanium pustulans* Ckll., var. nov. *princeps*].)
Armando Jacques Favre Castel-Branco. *Garcia de Orta*, vol. 12, no. 4 (1964), p. 627-32. bibliog.

Scale insects are a pest of cocoa and coffee plants. This is a description of a new subspecies which was found on Príncipe. See also Castel-Branco 'Uma cochonilha nova para a fauna de S.Tomé: *Asterolecanium pustulans* Cockerell' (A new scale insect for the fauna of São Tomé: *Asterolecanium pustulans* Cockerell) (*Garcia de Orta*, vol 11, no. 2 [1963], p. 253-56. bibliog.) and Idinha Mónica Fernandes 'Estudo de algumas cochonilhas de S.Tomé' (Study of some scale insects from São Tomé) (*Garcia de Orta: Série de Zoologia*, vol. 3, no. 1 [1974], p. 1-4. bibliog.).

82 Nova contribuição para o conhecimento da ixodofauna (*Acarina, Ixodoidea*) da República Democrática de S.Tomé e Príncipe. (A new contribution towards the understanding of ticks [*Acarina, Ixodoidea*] from the Democratic Republic of São Tomé and Príncipe.)
J. Travassos Dias. *Garcia de Orta: Série de Zoologia*, vol. 15, no. 1 (1988), p. 35-40. bibliog.

In addition to this study of ticks another can be found in João Tendeiro 'Ixodídeos encontrados na província de S.Tomé e Príncipe' (Ticks found in the province of São Tomé and Príncipe) (in: *Conferência Internacional dos Africanistas Ocidentais 6ª Sessão. Volume IV*. [Lisbon]: Commission for Technical Co-operation in Africa South of the Sahara; Scientific Council for Africa South of the Sahara, 1956, p.245-50).

83 *Pachymerus lacerdae* Chevr. - espécie nova (Ins. col. *Bruchidae*) para a fauna da ilha de S.Tomé. (*Pachymerus lacerdae* Chevr. - a new species (Ins. col. *Bruchidae*) for the fauna of the island of São Tomé.)
Armando Jacques Favre Castel-Branco. *Garcia de Orta*, vol. 13, no. 2 (1965), p. 179-84.

This pest of the palm tree was found for the first time on São Tomé and Príncipe. A summary in English is provided.

84 Panorama geral da entomologia de S. Tomé e Príncipe. (A general view of the entomology of São Tomé and Príncipe.)
Edited by Armando Jacques Favre Castel-Branco. Lisbon: Província de S. Tomé e Príncipe, 1970. 259p.

A conference of entomologists took place on the islands during two weeks in August 1967 and this volume contains transcripts in French and Portuguese of the various discussions, workshops and papers. The conference focused on the insect pests of cocoa, coffee, palms, bananas and pineapples, and the methods for combatting them. The participants were A. S. Balachowsky, P. Bovey, R. Cabral, Passos de Carvalho, Castel-Branco, Maria Augusta Brazão Ferreira, P. Grison, B. Hurpin, R. Quinta and Magalhães Silva.

85   O reaparecimento da *Glossina palpalis palpalis* na ilha do Príncipe.
(The reappearance of *Glossina palpalis palpalis* on the island of
Príncipe.)
João Fraga de Azevedo, João Tendeiro, L. T. de Almeida Franco, M. da
Costa Mourão, J. M. de Castro Salazar.   Lisbon: Junta de
Investigações do Ultramar, 1961. 224p. 10 maps. (Estudos, Ensaios e
Documentos, no. 89).

A bilingual text, in English as well as Portuguese, this describes the return of the
tsetse fly in 1956 after its eradication from the island in 1914. Within twelve days of
its identification a control team arrived on Príncipe. Humans and domestic animals
were tested, but no trypanosomiasis was found, nor were any of the flies found to be
agents of sleeping sickness. The measures taken to eradicate the fly for this second
time are described. Wild pigs and stray dogs were destroyed, domestic animals were
bathed in insecticide, tsetse habitats were cleared and sprayed with insecticide, and
flies were trapped. Numerous photographs accompany the text. The same authors
produced an earlier report 'Notícia sobre a tsé-tsé da ilha do Príncipe' (Note on the
tsetse on the island of Príncipe) (*Garcia de Orta*, vol. 4, no. 4 [1956], p. 507-22). A
further report can be found in Azevedo, Mourão, Salazar *A erradicação da Glossina*
palpalis palpalis da ilha do Príncipe (1956-1958) (The eradication of the *Glossina*
palpalis palpalis from the island of Príncipe [1956-1958]) (Lisbon: Junta de
Investigações do Ultramar, 1961, 181p. map. [Estudos, Ensaios e Documentos, no.
91]).

86   Sobre os vectores da malária em São Tomé e Príncipe. (On the
vectors of malaria in São Tomé and Príncipe.)
H. Ribeiro, Helena da Cunha Ramos, C. Alves Pires.   *Garcia de Orta:*
Série de Zoologia, vol. 15, no. 2 (1988), p. 135-52. 2 maps. bibliog.

This is a study of the taxonomy, distribution, biology and medical importance of
Anopheles gambiae Giles and *Anopheles coustani* A. Both are potential vectors for
the transmission of malaria, a disease which is endemic in both islands. The former is
probably of greater importance: experiments with live human 'bait' showed it to be
very aggressive. Summary in English.

The biological problems of cacao in S.Tomé e Príncipe.
See item no. 253.

Marine life

87   Baleias em S.Tomé. (Whales in São Tomé.)
Machado de Sousa.   *Boletim de Informação, Propaganda e*
Estatística, vol. 1, no.8 (September-October 1951), p. 11-17.

Brief descriptions of the whale species which sometimes frequent the seas around the
islands accompany this report on the opening of a whaling station near Neves in the
north of São Tomé.

88 **Contribuição para o conhecimento dos foraminíferos do arquipélago de S.Tomé e Príncipe.** (Contribution to the understanding of the foraminifers from the archipelago of São Tomé and Príncipe.)
Manuel de Assunção Diniz. *Garcia de Orta*, vol. 7, no. 3 (1958), p. 471-82. 2 maps. bibliog.

Lists and describes the species which can be found in the waters around São Tomé and Príncipe. Fossil foraminifers are studied by G. Henriques da Silva in 'Contribuição para o conhecimento da microfauna do Miocénio marinho da ilha do Príncipe' (Contribution to the understanding of microfauna of the maritime Miocene from the island of Príncipe) (*Garcia de Orta*, vol. 6, no. 3 [1958], p. 507-10. bibliog.) and Armando Reis Moura in 'Contribuição para o conhecimento dos foraminíferos das praias levantadas de S.Tomé e Príncipe' (Contribution to the understanding of the foraminifers of the raised beaches of São Tomé and Príncipe) (*Garcia de Orta*, vol. 9, no. 4 [1961], p. 751-58. bibliog.). Moura found the fossil foraminifers to be almost identical to contemporary members of the family.

89 **Copépodes marinhos das águas de S.Tomé e do Príncipe.** (Marine copepods from the waters of São Tomé and Príncipe.)
Emerita Marques. In: *Livro do homenagem ao Prof. Fernando Frade.* Lisbon: Junta de Investigações do Ultramar, 1973, p. 231-60. bibliog.

Marques provides a description of forty species of these minute crustacea found in samples taken from the coastal waters around São Tomé and Príncipe in September and October 1967. He has also published 'Copépodes parasitas de peixes marinhos de S.Tomé' (Copepod parasites of sea fish from São Tomé) (*Garcia de Orta*, vol. 13, no. 2 [1965], p. 185-92, bibliog.) and 'Copépodes marinhos da ilha de São Tomé' (Marine copepods from the island of São Tomé) (In: *Conferência Internacional dos Africanistas Ocidentais 6ª Sessão. Volume IV.* [Lisbon]: Commission for Technical Co-operation in Africa South of the Sahara; Scientific Council for Africa South of the Sahara, 1956, p. 193-204, bibliog.). Summaries in English are included.

90 **Investigações sobre os peixes de superfície e a pesca nas ilhas de São Tomé e Príncipe.** (Research into shallow-water fish and fishing in the islands of São Tomé and Príncipe.)
Fernando Frade, F. Correia da Costa. In: *Conferência Internacional dos Africanistas Ocidentais 6ª Sessão. Volume IV.* [Lisbon]: Commission for Technical Co-operation in Africa South of the Sahara; Scientific Council for Africa South of the Sahara, 1956, p. 151-68. bibliog.

Species of fish are listed and described, together with notes on the fishing industry and its methods. There are also photographs and a summary in English.

91 **The marginellids of São Tomé, West Africa.**
Serge Gofas, Francisco Fernandes. *Journal of Conchology*, vol. 33, part 1 (May 1988), p. 1-30. map. bibliog.

Marine molluscs of the Marginellidae family found in the waters around São Tomé are described in this paper. Twelve varieties are known, eleven of which differ from mainland species. Seven of these are newly documented in this article: *Marginella spinacia, Volvarina insulana, Granulina parilis, 'Cysticus' gutta, Gibberula modica, Gibberula punctillum* and *Gibberula cucullata.* The authors emphasize the taxonomical importance of examining living specimens in order that the soft parts as well as the shell are taken into consideration. The article is well illustrated. See also Francisco Fernandes, Emilio Rolán 'The Marginellidae (Mollusca: Gastropoda) of Principe island (Republica de S.Tomé e Príncipe)' (*Journal of Conchology,* vol. 34, part 2 [January 1992], p. 85-90. map). The species found on the island of Príncipe during a visit in 1990 are described, including a new species '*Cystiscus' josephinae* n.sp.

Tourism, Transport and Communications

92   **Central Africa - a travel survival kit.**
Alex Newton.   Hawthorn, Australia: Lonely Planet, 1994. 2nd ed.
599p. maps. (Lonely Planet Travel Survival Kits).
The second edition of this popular travel guide is much revised and improved in its coverage of São Tomé and Príncipe (p. 434-51) and contains three maps. The islands receive a thorough and enthusiastic write-up as far as the more independent and adventurous holidaymaker is concerned. The islands' government has recently become more open to tourism and will no doubt welcome the kind of endorsement with which the section on São Tomé and Príncipe begins, 'A veritable paradise on earth awaits the visitor to these remote islands' (p. 434). The compressed history and summary of political and economic conditions is reliable and admirably up-to-date. Detailed information is introduced on air and maritime links to the islands, visa requirements, foreign currency exchange, hotels, restaurants, night-clubs, internal transport, beaches and places of interest for the visitor. Catering for the deep-sea fishing end of the tourist market is the recently opened luxury resort of Bom Bom on Príncipe. See David Clement-Davies' 'Bom Bom for the sweet life' (*The Sunday Telegraph* [22 May 1994], p. 22. map.).

93   **Lista telefónica nacional 92-93.** (National telephone directory 92-93.)
Companhia Santomense de Telecomunicações.   Lisbon: Directel -
Listas Telefónicas Internacionais, 1992. 120p.
In such a small country the telephone book doubles up as a convenient directory of businesses and services. This slim volume is divided into official bodies, personal subscribers and businesses.

94   **Reseaux ferres de l'ouest africain.** (Railway networks in West Africa.)
E. T. Honig.   Krefeld, Germany: Rohr, 1988. maps.
The first volume of this collection of maps and photographs covers Ghana, Togo, Benin, Nigeria, Cameroon, Gabon and São Tomé and Príncipe and Honig explains how the islands' plantations often built private railway track in order to carry cocoa to the coast.

95 S.Tomé e Príncipe.

Lisbon: Agência-Geral do Ultramar, [1959?]. 32p.

This is an English-language brochure containing photographs and information for the visitor of the islands, concerning customs, visas and transport.

96 Studies to determine the contribution that civil aviation can make to the development of the national economies of African states - São Tomé and Príncipe.

F. Pratt. [Montreal]: International Civil Aviation Organization, 1976. 39p.

Reports on a study mission to the islands in April 1976 which was carried out under the auspices of the International Civil Aviation Organization and the United Nations Development Programme.

97 Viagem a S.Tomé e Príncipe: encontro com o equador. (Journey to São Tomé and Príncipe: encounter with the equator.)

Vasco Callixto. Lisbon: The Author, 1992. 111p. map.

Callixto spent two weeks in 1991 travelling around the islands. This account of his visit contains a lot of useful information about hotels, restaurants, beaches, transport and places of interest. He shows a particular interest in the monuments of the colonial era and regrets that so many have been removed. The Museu Nacional de São Tomé e Príncipe (National Museum of São Tomé and Príncipe) in the Fortaleza de S. Sebastião (St. Sebastian Fort) is described in some detail. Callixto also visited Príncipe, the village of São João dos Angolares, and made a stomach-churning boat trip to the equator. Difficulties with transport are something of a leitmotif in the book and travel on the ruinous roads was not helped by the unreliability of Callixto's car. It had been dropped in the sea whilst being unloaded from the ship which brought it to São Tomé and had never fully recovered. It had to be towed back from São João dos Angolares, and on another occasion it took an hour simply to open the bonnet. The book also contains a summary of a lecture given by Callixto 'Quando os primeiros aviões aterraram em S.Tomé' (When the first aeroplanes landed on São Tomé). The first landing was in 1928 when one thousand men worked for two weeks to prepare a landing strip. This is followed by a brief history of aviation in São Tomé and Príncipe. A final chapter covers the history of telecommunications on the islands, from the very first private telephones used to communicate between the main plantation complex and its outlying stations, to the satellite technology of the 1980s. An African Development Bank loan paid for the installation of a digital system, and in 1989 the government set up a joint venture with the Companhia Portuguesa de Rádio Marconi.

A informação na Guiné, em Cabo Verde e em São Tomé e Príncipe (achegas para o seu estudo).
See item no. 391.

Travellers' Accounts

16th century

98 **O manuscrito 'Valentim Fernandes'.** (The 'Valentim Fernandes' manuscript.)
Edited by Joaquim Bensaúde, António Baião. Lisbon: Academia Portuguesa da História, 1940. 240p. maps.

This attractive transcription of the Munich codex retains its original spelling and includes some facsimile pages, one of which is a map of the island of São Tomé. The account dates from 1506 (p. 121-29) and Fernandes' informant on São Tomé is Gonçalo Piriz, a sailor. He first describes the population, stating that many of the Jewish children who were brought to the island in 1493, have died. Miscegenation is already well-established: he notes that 'more white women have children by black men and black women by white men' (p. 122). Deported criminals, who would have been executed in Portugal, have been allowed slaves and many are prospering. Fernandes' account lists items which are important for survival in a new settlement, such as food crops and domestic animals, the large tasty rats, birds, rivers, fish, and the fat black venomous snakes who 'stare at men and don't flee' (p. 124). This is an immensely valuable document on the early history of the islands.

99 **Navigation de Lisbonne à l'île São Tomé par un pilote portugais anonyme (vers 1545).** (Voyage from Lisbon to the island of São Tomé by an anonymous Portuguese pilot [around 1545].)
Translated by Serge Sauvageot, with notes by T. Monod, R. Mauny. *Garcia de Orta*, vol. 9, no. 1 (1961), p. 123-38. bibliog. map.

This is a wonderfully vivid eye-witness account of the island in its first century of occupation. This translation is accompanied by a facsimile of the original, published in J. B. Ramusio's collection *Delle navigationi et viaggi nel qual se contiene la descrittione dell'Africa, e del paese del Prete Ianni, con uarii uiaggi, dal mar Rosso à Calicut, & infin all'isole Molucche, doue nascono le Spetierie, et la nauigatione attorno il mundo* (Of navigation and voyages in which is contained the description of Africa and the lands of Prester John, with various voyages, from the Red Sea to Calcutta, and finally the Moluccas, where the Spetierie was born, and the navigation around the world) (Venice: Heredidi Lucantonio Giunti, 1550). The notes give some background on the author who made five voyages from Lisbon to São Tomé between 1520 and 1545: this account was probably written in the 1540s for the Veronese Comte Rimondo della Torre. Although Portuguese secrecy about navigation was beginning to relax, the author still does not reveal how the return journey to Europe is made! The pilot is a practical guide to trade and navigation in the region and an observant commentator on island life. Sugar is the main crop, with the purpose of the pilot's voyage to bring a cargo of it back to Portugal, and he describes how it is grown and processed. Food is another of his interests: the Europeans cannot get used to the local food, and rely on what the ships bring from Europe. The slaves live on yams, palm wine and maize which they cultivate themselves on Saturdays. There are lots of pigs who eat the waste from the sugar processing and taste very good as a result; fruit trees have been introduced, not all as successfully as the coconut; fish and crabs are plentiful. The inhabitants are also described. The European population is multi-national, not just Portuguese, but also Genoese, French and Castilian. Slaves come from Guinea, Benin and the Congo and miscegenation is commonplace with merchants turning to black women when their white wives die. There is also a prosperous black class. The pilot notes some of the drawbacks to island life. Flies, ants and rats are a problem and houses are built on stilts to avoid these plagues. Everyone suffers from fever, which can be fatal on first arrival and dysentery and syphilis are also widespread. The life-expectancy for a European is rarely over 50, but the Africans can apparently reach the age of 110. This account is an indispensable source for the 16th-century history of São Tomé. Francisco Tenreiro uses it for his 'Descrição da ilha de S.Tomé no século XVI' (Description of the island of São Tomé in the 16th century) (*Garcia de Orta*, vol. 1, no. 2 [1953], p. 219-28).

17th-19th century

100   **A general history of the pyrates.**
      Daniel Defoe, edited by Manuel Schonhorn.   London: J. M. Dent, 1972. 3 maps.

First published in 1724, this edition has been prepared from the 1726 fourth edition. São Tomé and Príncipe both feature in 'A description of the islands of St. Thome, Del Principe and Annobono' (p. 177-93). São Tomé is notorious for the thefts committed there against traders, but Príncipe is apparently 'a pleasant and delightful spot to the grave and thoughtful disposition of the Portuguese, an improvement to country retirement, in that, this may be a happy and uninterrupted retreat from the whole world' (p. 180). Topics of interest such as fish, birds, plants, crops, festivals and the ravages of venereal disease are all remarked upon. The account continues with the story of Captain Howel Davis, a pirate, who arrived at Príncipe and tricked the governor into believing his ship to be an English Man of War. He managed to obtain supplies on credit, attacked a French ship, claiming that it had been trading with pirates, and then attempted to rape a group of women. 'His thoughts now were turned upon the main business, *viz*. the plunder of the island' (p. 192). However, his plot was discovered by a São Tomense aboard the ship, who swam ashore and warned the governor in time. Davis and most of his companions were ambushed and killed. Further evidence of pirates in the region can be found in 'A voyage to Guinea and the adjacent islands, in 1725. By the Chevalier des Marchais' (In: *A new general collection of voyages and tavels. Volume II.* Thomas Astley. London: Frank Cass, 1968, p. 457-63). The Chevalier had to call in at Príncipe to repair his leaking vessel and he took on crew who were survivors of a wrecked pirate ship. 'He had also the good luck to seize a French interloper with four thousand one hundred crusados, which served to reimburse the charges he had been at in this port' (p. 463).

101 Journal of an African cruiser.
Horatio Bridge, introduction by Donald H. Simpson.   London:
Pall Mall, 1968. 2nd ed. 179p. (Colonial History Series).

First published in 1845, this is Bridge's account of his experiences as an officer in the United States Navy serving in West Africa where his ship participated in the enforcement of the abolition of the slave trade. A short stay on São Tomé left a favourable impression despite a shark unfortunately eating the coxswain.

102 A narrative of the expedition sent by Her Majesty's government to the River Niger, in 1841.
William Allen, T. R. H. Thomson.   London: Richard Bentley, 1848.
2 vols. 2 maps.

Prince Albert sponsored this expedition whose mission was to gather information, with particular interest in the fields of natural history and the campaign against the slave trade. The islands of São Tomé and Príncipe were a welcome haven, away from the less healthy mainland coast, although the sickness amongst Europeans was noted, including the case of one young woman found lying on a couch, 'a most interesting and picturesque object'. The efforts of the evidently fascinating Madame Ferreira to develop Príncipe are described. The authors also noted the great natural beauty of the islands, including Ilha das Rolas, describing plants, birds and monkeys. In the jungle they were interested to see fetish objects made of clay or wood and fastened to sticks near to offerings of food and drink. On a subsequent visit to Príncipe to pick up news they found that Madame Ferreira had been put under house arrest on suspicion of dealing in the slave trade. Wood engravings illustrate the text. Andrew Hull Foote, a lieutenant in the United States Navy serving in the West African squadron in 1850-51, was also entertained by Madame Ferreira on Príncipe. His account of the navy's attempts to suppress the slave trade can be found in *Africa and the American flag* (London: Dawsons, 1970, 2nd ed., 390p.), first published in 1854.

20th century

103 **Chocolate isle - sweet and bitter.**
Edwin S. Munger. In: *African field reports 1952-1961*. Cape
Town: C. Struik, 1961, p. 127-30.

Munger, a geographer, made this report in his capacity as a member of the American
Universities Field Staff in February 1955. It includes his hearsay evidence about the
Batepá massacre in 1953, concluding that it was due to a zealous governor trying to
compel the indigenous population to work, and some politically aware creoles taking
advantage of this situation. Munger's assessment of the contemporary political
situation was that a strong police and army presence existed but that very little news
reached Lisbon or beyond. The Portuguese, he felt, were very committed colonialists
but the islands still urgently needed investment: profits from cocoa were immediately
taken out of the country. This report also records his visits to plantations, where he
finds conditions reasonable although there is some evidence of tuberculosis. He also
notes the presence of deported Mozambican dissidents on São Tomé.

104 **In search of São Tomé.**
Mick Delap. *Focus on Africa*, vol. 1, no. 3 (1990), p. 36-42.

Delap, as part of the BBC African Service, visited the islands in 1990. This is an
informative introduction to São Tomé and Príncipe, in which he notes its 'timeless
feel', its 'rather passive citizens' and the problem of the plantations. There are
thirteen evocative colour photographs, which convey the lushness of the vegetation,
the enormous plantation houses, the plantation workers' barracks, derelict steam
engines and abandoned aeroplanes from the Biafran airlift.

105 **Paisagens da ilha do Príncipe.** (Landscapes from the island of
Príncipe.)
João Tendeiro. *Garcia de Orta*, vol. 4, no. 3 (1956), p. 429-30.

The landscape of forest, palm-fringed beaches and dramatic mountains and valleys
does not seem to have enchanted Tendeiro as much as might have been expected. He
notes that it is often cloudy and that on hazy days there is a heavy and suffocating
atmosphere. The text is followed by twelve full-page black-and-white photographs.

Viagem a S.Tomé e Príncipe: encontro com o equador.
See item no. 97.

A ilha de S.Thomé e o trabalho indigena.
See item no. 275.

Labour in Portuguese West Africa.
See item no. 278.

A modern slavery.
See item no. 280.

History

General

106 **Africa and Africans in the making of the Atlantic world, 1400-1680.**
John Thornton. Cambridge, England: Cambridge University Press, 1992. 309p. 5 maps. (Studies in Comparative World History).
The early history of São Tomé and Príncipe is mentioned within the context of the enormous changes taking place on both sides of the Atlantic. Thornton focuses on slavery and the slave trade.

107 **The Atlantic slave trade: a census.**
Philip D. Curtin. Madison, Wisconsin: University of Wisconsin Press, 1969. 338p. 24 maps. bibliog.
This constitutes a remarkable attempt to measure the westward flow of slaves across the Atlantic from Africa. At various times the islands of São Tomé and Príncipe were important both as an entrepôt for the trade and as an importer.

108 **Emerging nationalism in Portuguese Africa: a bibliography of documentary ephemera through 1965.**
Ronald H. Chilcote. Stanford, California: Hoover Institution on War, Revolution and Peace, 1969. 114p. (Hoover Institution Bibliographical Series, no. 39).
Covers material issued by the Portuguese African nationalist movements and their militants which was collected and stored on microfilm at the Hoover Institution library between 1959 and 1965. A companion volume is Chilcote *Emerging nationalism in Portuguese Africa: documents* (Stanford, California: Hoover Institution Press, 1972. 646p.). This contains English translations of some of the documents covered in the bibliography. Mário de Andrade, under the pseudonym

Buanga Fele, wrote about the events at Batepá in 1953 (*Présence Africaine*, nos. 1-2 [April-July 1955], p. 146-52) in an article which appears in this volume under the title 'Massacres in São Tomé' (p. 298-301). Miguel Trovoada, as the president of the Comité de Libertação de São Tomé e Príncipe (Committee for the Liberation of São Tomé and Príncipe, the former name of the MLSTP), made a presentation to the United Nations Special Committee on Territories under Portuguese Administration on 4 September 1962, which is reproduced here under the title 'The liberation of São Tomé and Príncipe' (p. 323-26). He asks for the implementation of the United Nations General Assembly resolution of 14 December 1961 on the granting of independence to colonies. He also asks that UN inquiries to be held into labour conditions on the plantations and into the islands' high rates of mortality.

109 **The northern Gabon coast to 1875.**
K. David Patterson. Oxford: Clarendon Press, 1975. 167p. bibliog. 2 maps. (Oxford Studies in African Affairs).

From the early 16th century until the later decades of the 19th century there were continuing links between São Tomé and Príncipe and Gabon. The principal connection was the slave trade. Small ships would sail across from the mainland to the islands, which acted as an entrepôt for larger ships crossing to Brazil. In the 1860s and 1870s there was a demand for Gabonese slaves from the islands' plantations, until they were replaced by Angolan contract labourers. French efforts to stop the traffic in slaves were ineffectual. See also Robert Reynard 'Notes sur l'économie des côtes du Gabon au début du XVIIIᵉ siècle' (Notes on the economy of the Gabonese coast at the beginning of the 18th century) (*Bulletin de l'Institut d'Etudes Centrafricaines*, vol. 13-14 [1957], p. 49-54. bibliog.).

110 **Portugal in Africa: the last hundred years.**
Malyn Newitt. London: C. Hurst, 1981. 278p. 6 maps. bibliog.

Covering the period from the 'scramble for Africa' until the revolution in Portugal in 1974, this is a clear account of Portugal's colonial policy and activity in Africa. São Tomé and Príncipe is specifically covered in a brief section which focuses on the cocoa plantations and the question of labour (p. 204-11).

111 **Portuguese rule on the Gold Coast 1469-1682.**
John Vogt. Athens, Georgia: University of Georgia Press, 1979. 266p. map. bibliog.

São Tomé and Príncipe was a safe haven for the Portuguese, especially when compared to the turbulent history of the trading forts on the Gold Coast. The islands had important links with the fort of São Jorge da Mina, in present day Ghana, during the period of this study. They supplied large numbers of slaves to the fort and were a reliable channel of communications to Lisbon. This book, which has a good bibliography, offers a useful picture of Portuguese exploration and trade in the region, and also of their conflicts with other European powers. See also Vogt 'The early São Tomé-Príncipe slave trade with Mina, 1500-1540' (*International Journal of African Historical Studies*, no. 6 [1973], p. 453-67).

112 **The Portuguese seaborne empire 1415-1825.**
Charles Ralph Boxer, introduction by J. H. Plumb. London:
Hutchinson, 1969. 426p. 7 maps. bibliog. (The History of Human
Society).

An account of the discovery and settlement of the islands of São Tomé and Príncipe
has its place within a broader description of the remarkable Portuguese expansion
down the coast of West Africa and beyond. Plumb's introduction labels this empire as
'one of the great enigmas of history' (p. xx). The second half of the text discusses the
Portuguese methods of colonization, covering administration, trade and racial
attitudes. See also Bailey W. Diffie, George D. Winius *Foundations of the Portuguese
empire 1415-1580* (Minneapolis, Minnesota: University of Minnesota Press, 1977,
533p. 17 maps. bibliog. [Europe and the World in the Age of Expansion, vol. 1]) and
A. de Mantero Velarde *L'espansione politica e coloniale portoghese con special
riguardo alle isole di São Tomé e Príncipe* (Portuguese political and colonial
expansion with special attention to the islands of São Tomé and Príncipe) (Rome:
Instituto Cristoforo Colombo, 1925, 181p. 2 maps).

113 **Trade relations between the Bight of Benin and Bahia from the
17th to 19th century.**
Pierre Verger, translated from the French by Evelyn Crawford.
Ibadan, Nigeria: Ibadan University Press, 1976. 629p. 8 maps. bibliog.

São Tomé and Príncipe's role in the slave trade can be seen in the context of the
considerable trans-Atlantic commerce between Brazil and the Gulf of Guinea.

114 **Yankee traders, old coasters and African middlemen: a history of
American legitimate trade with West Africa in the nineteenth
century.**
George E. Brooks. [Boston, Massachusetts]: Boston University
Press, 1970. 370p. bibliog. 3 maps.

São Tomé and Príncipe seems to have been used relatively frequently as a stopping
point for American ships engaged in trade in West Africa. Vessels called in for
repairs and refitting, and copper coins were made in New York which were designed
specially for trade with the islands. This text is a good source for accounts written by
ships captains. Appended is 'Captain Samuel Swan's memoranda on the African
trade' (p. 313-43) dated around 1810, which gives advice on trading in Príncipe.

**The third Portuguese empire 1825-1975: a study in economic
imperialism.**
See item no. 240.

The islands

115 **Actas da Câmara de Santo António da ilha do Príncipe. I (1672-1777).** (Acts of the town council of Santo António, Príncipe. I [1672-1777].)
Edited by Fernando Castelo Branco, preface by A. da Silva Rego.
Lisbon: Centro de Estudos Históricos Ultramarinos, 1970. 801p.

Castelo Branco has transcribed and annotated the oldest documents to be found in the islands. They largely cover aspects of administrative life such as official appointments, but also include some information on economic and religious matters. The prefatory sections discuss the state of the islands' historical archives. Despite fears about the effects of the climate, insects, neglect, and an edict of 1891 to send documents earlier than 1834 to Lisbon, plenty of material was found. There were, however, difficulties in transcribing them because, as Rego puts it in his preface, the authors were men of action not of letters. This volume was originally intended as the first of a series which would complete the transcription of the *actas* and then tackle the documents relating to São Tomé and Príncipe held in the Arquivo Histórico Ultramarino in Lisbon.

116 **Cabo Verde e S.Tomé e Príncipe - esquema de uma evolução conjunta.** (Cape Verde and São Tomé and Príncipe - outline of an evolution in common.)
Francisco Tenreiro. [Praia]: Imprensa Nacional, Divisão de Propaganda, [1956]. 16p.

The settlement, colonization and social history of these two colonies are compared in this text. Despite vastly different physical environments they showed remarkable similarities up until the 19th century. Sugar was an early source of wealth for the two groups of islands, and in both cases African slaves were brought over to cultivate it. Creole societies soon emerged with the offspring of Africans and European settlers and both archipelagos suffered the same economic decline in the 17th and 18th centuries. Their paths diverged with the advent of the coffee and cocoa boom in São Tomé and Príncipe, when the new plantations re-segregated society on racial lines.

117 **O ciclo de açúcar em São Tomé nos séculos XV e XVI.** (The sugar cycle in São Tomé in the 15th and 16th centuries.)
Isabel Castro Henriques. In: *Portugal no mundo*. Edited by Luís de Albuquerque. Lisbon: Publicações Alfa, 1989, vol. 1, p. 264-80, 2 maps.

The economic history of São Tomé during this period is almost synonymous with the fortunes of the sugar industry. The plant was introduced around 1493 and cultivation increased rapidly, with vast amounts being exported, and playing their part in the emerging capitalist world system. The need for cheap labour led to the import of Africans as slaves, and information is supplied on their origins, numbers, dates and living conditions. Land ownership, mills and the system of production are also described. The problems facing the industry towards the end of the 16th century are covered: internal instability from slave uprisings; external threats from the French, the Dutch and pirates; plant diseases and pests; and the low quality of the product.

Colour photographs and reproductions of drawings and maps illustrate the text. See also H. A. Gemery, J. S. Hogendorm 'Comparative disadvantage: the case of sugar cultivation in West Africa' (*Journal of Interdisciplinary History*, vol. 9, no. 3 [Winter 1979], p. 429-49, 4 maps). The authors suggest that technical reasons caused the eventual failure of the crop in the region and that drainage, acidity and salinity were to blame.

118   **A colonização de São Tomé e Príncipe: os capitães do século XV.**
(The colonization of São Tomé and Príncipe: the 15th century captains.)
Luís de Albuquerque.   In: *Portugal no mundo*.   Edited by Luís de Albuquerque, 1989, vol. 2, p. 171-97, 4 maps.

This is a clear synthesis of events during the first years following the islands' discovery in 1470-71. The system of land grants to 'captains' is discussed, whereby the recipients were obliged to live in the islands and to people their lands. This proved an effective way of settling the previously uninhabited Atlantic islands. There is some detail on the activities and interests of the Portuguese crown, and on the figure of Álvaro de Caminho who was captain of São Tomé from 1493 until his death in 1499. His will is examined for the information it yields about contemporary economic and religious affairs. Albuquerque regrets the introduction of governors in the 16th century: these men were only administrators, whereas the captains had been intimately concerned with the settlement and development of the islands. The text is illustrated with beautiful colour photographs and reproductions of antique maps.

119   **Conflitos de europeus em S.Tomé e Príncipe em 1910.** (Conflicts among Europeans in São Tomé and Príncipe in 1910.)
Augusto Nascimento.   *Revista Internacional de Estudos Africanos*, nos. 12-13 (January-December 1990), p. 57-98.

The declaration of the Portuguese republic in October 1910 was the catalyst for insurrection and challenge to the colonial authorities from within the European community on both islands. Even before October, 1910 had been a turbulent year in São Tomé and Príncipe. A republican party had been founded, which lost elections in August by ten votes amidst accusations of electoral irregularities. This article describes the conflicts of that year in admirable detail. The Europeans seemed to fall into two camps, with the planters and officials on one side and the salaried workers on the other, although on Príncipe the conflict had a more personalized nature. At the root of the problem was the centuries-old corruption of public office holders. In a European community containing a large number of immigrants determined to make their fortunes this inequitable division of wealth, power and opportunity no doubt rankled more than ever. One consequence of events was a blossoming of journalistic activity in such papers as *O Africano* (The African) owned by Américo Augusto Mendes (São Tomé: Francisco Lança Júnior, 1909-10), *A Ilha de S.Tomé* (The Island of São Tomé) edited by Ezequiel de Campos (São Tomé: F.Trindade, 1910) and the republican and radical *A Voz de S.Thomé* (The Voice of São Tomé) which was edited by Fernando Augusto Dantas (São Tomé: [s.n.], 1910). Nascimento also notes that the indigenous São Tomense and the contract workers were barely involved in these events, although the treatment of the latter was used in the arguments between the factions. There is a summary in English.

120 **Contribuição para a história de S.Tomé e Príncipe.** (Contribution towards the history of São Tomé and Príncipe.)
Carlos Espírito Santo. Lisbon: [s.n.], 1979. 88p. bibliog.
Covers the islands' history from the arrival of the Portuguese to the early 1970s. The final chapter on resistance to colonization is of particular interest. It covers slave revolts from the 16th to the 18th centuries, mutinies of soldiers, Angolar uprisings from the 16th century attack on the city of São Tomé to late 19th century resistance to the land seizures, and the Batepá massacre of 1953.

121 **Corographia historica das ilhas de S.Thomé, Príncipe, Anno Bom e Fernando Pó.** (Historical chorography of the islands of São Tomé, Príncipe, Annobon and Fernando Pó.)
Raimundo José da Cunha Matos. Porto, Portugal: Typographia da Revista, 1842. 133p.
A highly readable and lively history and description of São Tomé and Príncipe, where Matos spent some time as an official of the Portuguese government. It contains many observations on human nature and criticisms of the actors in the islands' unedifying history. One such actor was the cruel 17th-century governor Antonio de Souza de Carvalho who, apparently, used to fake mortal accidents in order to hear the comments of those around him. When he finally died everyone found it difficult to believe, despite obvious signs of physical decay. Matos' history of Príncipe concentrates on the French invasion of 1799 when the island could only muster 25 men to counter the 400 French, and was forced to pay a heavy ransom. In addition to historical information the book contains a description of the coastline for the benefit of shipping and notes on contemporary government, society and religion. However, Fernando Castelo-Branco identifies many errors and discrepancies in this book in his article 'O valor historiográfico da obra de Cunha Matos sobre S.Tomé' (The historiographical value of Cunha Matos' work on São Tomé) (*Stvdia*, no. 35 [December 1972], p. 45-52). He recommends that it should no longer be treated as the basic work on the islands' history. In compiling his chorography, Matos made heavy use of Manuel Rosário Pinto's work, and where possible this earlier source should be used in preference to the later work - see *Manuel Rosário Pinto (a sua vida)* (q.v.). Anything in the later work for which corroboration is not possible should be treated with caution and a critical spirit. Matos was also the author of *Compêndio histórico das possessões de Portugal na Africa* (Historical compendium of the Portuguese possessions in Africa) (Rio de Janeiro, Brazil: Ministério da Justiça e Negócios Interiores, Arquivo Nacional, 1963, 364p.), which was first published in 1834.

122 **Esboço histórico das ilhas de S.Tomé e Príncipe.** (Historical outline of the islands of São Tomé and Príncipe.)
São Tomé: Imprensa Nacional, 1975. 25p.
This is a simple account of the islands' history, with a sprinkling of class analysis and anti-colonialism.

123 **Os franceses e as ilhas do Golfo da Guiné.** (The French and the Gulf of Guinea islands.)
Fernando Castelo-Branco. Paris: Fundação Calouste Gulbenkian, 1971. [4p.]

A letter from the magistrate Caetano Bernardo Castro de Mesquita to the Count of Oeiras, dated 1772, indicates the French interest in these islands. Castelo-Branco notes the French attacks on Príncipe in 1702 and 1799 and on São Tomé in 1709. He suspects that they had long wanted to occupy both São Tomé and Príncipe, and also the island of Fernando Pó.

124 **Os fundamentos históricos da nação são-tomense.** (The historical foundations of the São Tomense nation.)
Armindo Aguiar. In: *A construção da nação em África: os exemplos de Angola, Cabo Verde, Guiné-Bissau, Moçambique e S.Tomé e Príncipe.* Bissau: Instituto Nacional de Estudos e Pesquisa, 1989, p. 313-22.

This is a history of resistance to colonialism, with the issue of cultural and national identity to the forefront. The slave uprisings of the 16th century, and particularly that of King Amador in 1595, are seen as the first revolutionary acts in the islands' history with the reluctance of indigenous São Tomense to work on the cocoa plantations in the 19th and 20th centuries portrayed as another act of resistance. The author notes that attempts were made to suppress manifestations of cultural identity: some dances were prohibited, as was the use of creole in public places. Nevertheless, the indigenous languages, songs and proverbs continued to be an instrument of unity and nationhood. The Batepá massacre in 1953 is regarded as marking a watershed between spontaneous and organized resistance. The indiscriminate nature of the massacre, Aguiar suggests, revealed that the distinctions between imported plantation workers, indigenous São Tomense and other social groups were artificial divisions created amongst the exploited by the exploiters. After independence Cape Verdeans, Angolans and Mozambican workers were given the status of São Tomense, and can now hold land, take public office and have equal access to education. The islands, Aguiar claims, are free of ethnic tensions, and the São Tomense identity is one built on integration.

125 **A history of São Tomé island, 1470-1655: the key to Guinea.**
Robert Garfield. San Francisco: Mellen Research University Press, 1992. 327p. 18 maps. bibliog.

An extensive revision of his doctoral dissertation in the light of previously unavailable documents, this is an extremely valuable, comprehensive and readable piece of research. It relates a sorry and unedifying history of slavery, lawlessness and decline although Garfield describes it as 'a laboratory for an experiment in tropical civilization and in inter-racial and inter-cultural historical existence' (p.xii). From the arrival of the first settlers of Jewish children, Portuguese criminals and African slaves a society conscious of racial divisions developed. The first recorded slave revolt took place in 1517, the first Angolar attack on the city in 1574, and in 1616 free blacks revolted. By this time the island had already gone from sugar boom to bust. Islanders' supremacy in the slave trade was similarly short-lived, after initial importance in the affairs of the kingdom of Kongo and links with São Jorge da Mina (Ghana) and the kingdom of Benin. There were external as well as internal threats to the European colonists' security. The Dutch looted and burnt São Tomé city in 1599 and raided it again over the years. The Dutch superiority in seapower meant that they could virtually blockade the Gulf of Guinea, and as part of their attempt to replace the Portuguese in Brazil and Luanda they invaded and occupied the city of São Tomé between 1641 and 1644. Any pretence of solidarity amongst the colonists that might have been stimulated by the invasion was short-lived. Garfield sheds painstaking light on the feuds and internal strife within the island's elite and the clergy. The latter seem to have been extremely liberal in dispensing wholesale excommunication. Public office became almost the only secure source of income, which may explain the violent competition for posts. Garfield rather wearily suggests another reason, 'in São Tomé after the early years little was going on, and perhaps the islanders fought among themselves over trivia simply because there was nothing else to do to relieve the sense of boredom and futility' (p. 296). This book portrays some of the formidable men of the era - Álvaro de Caminho, João de Mello, João Barbosa da Cunha, Luis de Barros, Luis de Abreu, Lourenço Pires de Tavora - and exposes their excesses and ambitions. Garfield is planning a sequel to cover the period up to independence, in which he suspects history may have repeated itself, 'great land-owning barons [...], huge plantations, exploited labor and international complications all recur with a disquieting echo of earlier centuries' (p. xii).

126 **A ilha de S.Tomé como centro experimental do comportamento do Luso nos trópicos.** (The island of São Tomé as an experimental centre for Portuguese behaviour in the tropics.)
Carlos Alberto Garcia. *Stvdia*, no. 19 (December 1966), p. 209-21.

If the island had been used in the first years of settlement for anything as scientific as an experimental acclimatization centre, one of the first observations would undoubtedly have been the extremely high mortality rate amongst Europeans. Even, Garcia notes, the darker-skinned Portuguese and the transported Jewish children were not immune. Miscegenation was encouraged instead as a method for populating the islands. Little evidence is offered for Garcia's other theory that people were seasoned for missions in Brazil and the African mainland by a stay on São Tomé. This article is very much within the tradition of lauding the humane and colour blind Portuguese colonizing mission.

127 **A luta dos escravos em S.Tomé no século XVI.** (The slaves' struggle in São Tomé in the 16th century.)
José Maianga. *África: Literatura, Arte e Cultura*, vol. 2, no. 9 (July-September 1980), p. 437-43.

The 16th century was a golden age of sugar and the slave trade for São Tomé and Príncipe, and as Maianga points out, the two cannot be separated. In São Tomé slaves were 'warehoused' before making the journey to Brazil and the Americas; others were employed on the island's sugar plantations. The aim of this article is to refute any idea of passivity amongst the slaves in the face of the undoubted horrors of their condition and there is a list of their uprisings. The first large-scale revolt began on the plantation of one Senhor Lobato and quickly spread to other slaves and *mestiços*. Landowners were given the power to execute and dismember slaves and many became fugitives, living in well-organized communities in remote parts of the islands. These same slaves attacked São Tomé city in 1547 followed by the Angolars in 1574. They too attacked the city, destroying plantations on the way, but were repelled by fire-arms. The most important of the uprisings was that led by Amador in 1595. A fugitive himself, he created a force of 5,000 men and the attack began in Trindade and spread right across the island. Since the rebels had control of the surrounding area they decided to attack São Tomé city, but were eventually overwhelmed by guns and artillery. Amador fled, but was later captured and hung. Subsequent revolts were isolated, although the figures of Damião Lopes and João Roiz Gato (Yon Gato) stand out. See also 'A repressão contra os escravos de São Tomé (1595) e a guerra em Ceilão (1587-1617)' (The suppression of the São Tomense slaves [1595] and the war in Ceylon [1587-1617]) by Carlos Agostinho das Neves, Jorge Manuel Flores and Artur Teodoro de Matos (In: *Portugal no mundo* vol. 5, edited by Luís de Albuquerque. Lisbon: Publicações Alfa, 1989, p. 100-12).

128 **Manuel Rosário Pinto (a sua vida).** (Manuel Rosário Pinto [his life].)
    António Ambrósio.   Lisbon: Centro de Estudos Históricos
    Ultramarinos, 1970. 125p. bibliog.

História da ilha de S. Tomé (History of the island of São Tomé), written by Dean Manuel Pinto in 1734, is transcribed by Ambrósio and published in complete form for the first time (p. 27-125). This is an extremely important document, covering the years 1471 to 1734. Ambrósio describes the manuscript, its place in the islands' bibliographical history and its use by Raimundo José da Cunha Matos in his *Corographia historica das ilhas de S.Thomé, Principe, Anno Bom e Fernando Pó* (q.v.). He also provides a biography of Pinto (c.1666-1734), who seems to have been both intelligent and a troublemaker, and thus fully-equipped for a life spent amongst the feuding clerics of São Tomé. Born on the island, Pinto spent some of the first years of his ecclesiastical career in Lisbon. Here he managed to be sent to prison over a dispute with the church authorites about his biretta. He returned to São Tomé as a canon in 1699, and although never made bishop he was always an important figure. Rarely not involved in some conflict, either between civil and religious authorities or an internal church dispute, he is suspected of having incited a rift between black and *mestiço* clerics: at one point the Cathedral was used as a fort and the lay clergy took up arms. He even managed to attract the attention of King João V, who wrote to him in 1715 to complain that his 'pride disturbs and agitates the people in great disservice to God and to me' (p. 10). The death or incapacitation by illness of so many of the bishops and governors sent to the island can only have contributed to the disorder. Bishop João de Sahagum however, survived from 1719 to 1730, during which period events calmed down and Pinto prospered.

129 **Mixed race groups in the early history of Portuguese expansion.**
    Malyn Newitt.   In: *Studies in the Portuguese discoveries I.*   Edited
    by T. F. Earle, Stephen Parkinson.   Warminster, England: Aris &
    Phillips in association with the Comissão Nacional para as
    Comemorações dos Descobrimentos Portugueses, 1992, p. 35-52.

This article has a fascinating approach to the 16th- and 17th-century history of Portuguese expansion, and focuses on family, kinship and the mixed-race communities so typical of Portuguese overseas settlement. The first region under consideration is the Upper Guinea Coast, and although the majority of the *lançados* (Europeans or people of European descent who traded and settled on the mainland) were from Cape Verde, he notes one family from São Tomé who settled at the mouth of the Pongo river in 1594 and after three generations had established a town of 3,000 inhabitants. Of greater relevance is the section entitled 'São Tomé, the Kongo and Angola' (p. 43-47), which makes clear the island's important role in regional trade.

The mixed-race islanders penetrated the interior of the Kongo and were a conduit for trade which by-passed the monopolies so delicately negotiated between the Portuguese and the Mwissicongo, the ruling clan. It was the islanders who first settled permanently at Luanda in order to control the shell fisheries there. The governors of São Tomé and Príncipe never managed to establish much authority over these powerful Afro-Portuguese families, not least because the life-expectancy of a European in fever-ridden São Tomé was so short. A further twist in relations was São Tomé's status as a see, with religious authority over the kingdom of Kongo between the years of 1534 and 1596. The same wealthy island families provided most of the clergy, and many of the ecclesiastical disputes between island and mainland were connected to the struggle for control of the slave trade. As Newitt summarizes, 'Thus trade was officially controlled by royal factors in Kongo casting the mixed-race São Tomeans in the role of contraband traders, while in ecclesiastical affairs the centre of authority was in the island and the Kongo was the outpost that threatened to get out of control' (p. 45). Even the Dutch conquest of São Tomé and Luanda between 1640 and 1648 did not affect these families who retrenched into their trading networks 'to survive in the African half of their world when the European half collapsed'. This study also discusses the powerful role of Afro-Portuguese women, who often owned property and wielded political power. The figure of Ana de Chaves, who led the fight against the Dutch on São Tomé, is mentioned. Further information on the history of the Kongo between the 15th and the 17th centuries can be found in Anne Hilton *The kingdom of Kongo* (Oxford: Clarendon Press, 1985, 319p. 11 maps. bibliog. [Oxford Studies in African Affairs]).

130 **Le naufrage des caravelles: études sur la fin de l'empire portugais (1961-1975).** (The shipwreck of the caravels: essays on the end of the Portuguese empire [1961-1975].)
René Pélissier. Orgeval, France: Éditions Pélissier, 1979. 297p. 8 maps.

The section covering São Tomé and Príncipe contains the two essays 'São Tomé ou le poids des siècles' (São Tomé or the weight of the centuries) (first published in *Revue Française d'Études Politiques Africaines* no. 25 [January 1968]), and 'La "guerre" de Batepá (São Tomé février 1953)' (The 'war' of Batepá [São Tomé February 1953]) (first published in *Revue Française d'Études Politiques Africaines* no. 73 [January 1971]). The first is a chronological history of the two islands. An appendix gives the author's account of his visit to four plantations in the 1960s: he refers to them as 'dinosaurs'. The second essay is an extremely valuable attempt to understand the murky events of February 1953, as well as to establish a chronology for them. He describes the social and racial divisions which explain Batepá better than any political or nationalist interpretations. At the heart of the problem was the reluctance of indigenous São Tomense to work on the plantations, a reluctance which the governors Ricardo Vaz Monteiro (1933-41) and Carlos de Sousa Gorgulha (1945-53) had tried to overcome. The author sees Batepá as a riot against conscription into work brigades, fuelled by rumour, which was met by disproportionate repression. The genuinely oppressed immigrant plantation workers took no part, except when armed by the owners of their plantations. The authorities in Lisbon quickly took action against the officials involved. Pélissier feels that the number of dead is much exaggerated at 1,032-2,000 and suggests a figure of 50-100 dead.

131 **A navegação da metrópole para S.Tomé nos meados do século XVI.** (Shipping from Portugal to São Tomé in the mid-16th century.) Fernando Castelo-Branco. *Stvdia*, nos. 30-31 (August-December 1970), p. 71-80.

This is an analysis of ship movements based on two contemporary documents: the *Navigation de Lisbonne à l'île São Tomé par un pilote portugais anonyme (vers 1545)* (q.v.), and a 1552 shipping census covering the ports of northern Portugal. São Tomé was an extremely important destination because of its sugar industry. The article also discusses the length of voyages, stop-overs and ships' supplies.

132 **I Reunião Internacional de História de África: relação Europa-África no 3º quartel do século XIX.** (First International Conference on the History of Africa: relations between Europe and Africa in the third quarter of the 19th century.) Edited by Maria Emília Madeira Santos. Lisbon: Centro de Estudos de História e Cartografia Antiga, 1989. 618p. maps. bibliogs.

Amongst these thirty conference papers are two which are of specific interest to São Tomé and Príncipe: Armindo Aguiar, 'As migrações na génese da nacionalidade santomense' (Migrations in the formation of São Tomense nationality) (p. 441-50); and William Gervase Clarence-Smith, 'Creoles and peasants in São Tomé, Príncipe, Fernando Póo and Mount Cameroun, in the nineteenth century' (p. 489-99).

133 **1º Barão d'Água Izé e seu filho Visconde de Malanza.** (The first Baron of Água Izé and his son the Viscount of Malanza.) Manuel Ferreira Ribeiro. Lisbon: Papelaria Estevão Nunes, 1901. [113p.]

These represent uncritical biographies of the baron, João Maria de Sousa e Almeida, and his son Jacintho Carneiro de Sousa e Almeida. The baron is best known for his pioneering introduction of cocoa to the islands and this volume reprints his article detailing his system for planting, harvesting, processing and storing cocoa. 'As plantações de cacau nas ilhas de S.Thomé e Príncipe em 1851 a 1858' (Cocoa plantations in the islands of São Tomé and Príncipe from 1851 to 1858) was first published in the *Boletim Oficial* (q.v.) in January 1858. Also included is the Visconde de Malanza's catalogue of island products sent to the Exposição Insular e Colonial (Exhibition of the Islands and Colonies) held in Porto in 1894.

134 **Rebelião e sociedade colonial: 'alvoroços' e 'levantamentos' em São Tomé (1545-1555).** (Rebellion and colonial society: 'tumults' and 'uprisings' in São Tomé [1545-1555].) Rui Ramos. *Revista Internacional de Estudos Africanos*, nos. 4-5 (1986), p. 17-74.

Using correspondence between the islands and the authorities in Portugal this is a very detailed study of the numerous instances of internal unrest in the mid-16th century. The 1553 rebellion led by the blind *mestiço* João Rodrigues Gato is one of the better known events of this turbulent time. The disturbances are taken to be a symptom of a divided social structure and flawed political institutions. Divisions were on geographic and ethnic lines. A white Portuguese oligarchy existed in the city with officials appointed and sent by Lisbon. Outside the city were the sugar plantations owned by *mestiços* and worked by slaves. The official powers were incapable of exercising any authority outside the city and the plantation owners' armed bands of slaves were the only real source of power.

135 **Revoltas de escravos em São Tomé no século XVI.** (Slave revolts in São Tomé in the 16th century.)
Isabel Figueiredo de Barros, Maria Arlete Cruz. *Leba*, no. 7 (1992), p. 373-88. bibliog.
This is a study of the revolts which took place in this turbulent and violent century. From the 1530s onwards attacks on plantations by fugitive slaves living in the interior of the island were an almost constant occurrence, and the authorities never had the material resources to definitively crush them. Many disturbances were, however, caused by feuding settlers using their slaves as private soldiers, rather than slave uprisings in the strictest sense. The authors suggest that even the 1553 revolt led by João Gato had its origins with the settlers rather than the slaves. The uprising of 1595 led by Amador was, on the other hand, genuinely the work of plantation slaves, and is a refutation of the myth that they were well-treated. Although the uprising was brutally suppressed many of the participants fled to the traditional refuge of the forest interior, adding to the settlers' 'constant sense of danger'. When the Dutch invaded in 1599 there was a fear that they would form an alliance with the fugitives. Nevertheless, the decline in the sugar industry was caused by a number of factors, with the slave revolts probably not as important as the outbreak of a disease of the sugar cane in 1580.

136 **Rotas Atlânticas, o caso da carreira de S.Tomé.** (Atlantic itineraries, the case of the São Tomé route.)
Maria Emília Madeira Santos. Lisbon: Instituto de Investigação Científica Tropical, 1990. 9p. map. (Série Separatas, no. 226).
São Tomé and Príncipe's role in the history of early 16th-century trade routes is described in this paper. Initially the islands were a base for African trade within Africa rather than the intercontinental entrepôt they were soon to become. They had very close links with the Portuguese fort and trading post at São Jorge da Mina on the Gold Coast whose role was to provide for the safe export of gold to Portugal, with slaves becoming a type of currency in the region to facilitate the purchase of gold. Many São Tomense became involved in this trade which the Portuguese crown attempted to regulate with varying degrees of futility. By 1519 São Jorge da Mina was thought to be too unsafe a location for the conduct of slave trading and this function was transferred to São Tomé. A miniature trade triangle was established: cowry shells and armlets were used to purchase slaves in Benin who were transported to São Tomé and thence to São Jorge da Mina where they were sold for gold. This trade was not in fact of great benefit to São Tomé and Príncipe since the gold invariably ended up in Lisbon. From the 1520s, however, a new trade route developed from São Tomé and Príncipe to the Antilles.

137 **S.Tomé a primeira cidade portuguesa nos trópicos.** (São Tomé the
first Portuguese city in the tropics.)
António Ambrósio. *História,* no. 81 (July 1985), p. 26-51. map.
This history of the city of São Tomé is largely drawn from 16th-century documents.
A number of buildings within the city are described. These include the seminary, the
cathedral, forts and hospital, and indicate the importance which the city had at that
time.

138 **S.Tomé e Príncipe: do colonialismo à independência.** (São Tomé
and Príncipe: from colonialism to independence.)
Carlos Benigno da Cruz.   Lisbon: Moraes Editores, 1975. 159p.
(Actualidade Portuguesa).
This selective collection of documents from the recent history of São Tomé and
Príncipe provides an interesting flavour of the times. The pre-independence
documents are all related to plantation work and the first section contains material on
wage rates from 1928 to 1974. The Curadoria Geral (General Curator), which was
responsible for the well-being of the workers, produced a number of documents
concerned with complaints about such things as food, hygiene and unfair dismissals.
Their recommendation for medical inspections to stop the damage being done to the
good name of the colony by the poor physical condition of repatriated workers is also
included. Recommendations made in 1954 by the Sociedade de Emigração para S.
Tomé e Príncipe (Society for Emigration to São Tomé and Príncipe) for more humane
treatment of Cape Verdean workers suggest a hitherto less acceptable regime: for
example, it advises that workers' heads should not be shaved, hats should be allowed,
meals should be served on plates and with cutlery rather than on banana leaves,
workers should be given beds, Sunday should be a day of rest and worship, and
corporal punishment should be applied with prudence. In 1967 the Instituto do
Trabalho, Previdência e Acção Social (Institute of Labour, Welfare and Social
Action) felt the need to publish a cautionary document warning Cape Verdeans
against leaving the 'hospitable land of plenty' (São Tomé) for the ruinous temptations
of Luanda. The section covering the time around independence is mostly concerned
with the MLSTP and its sister organization, the Associação Cívica pró-MLSTP (Civic
Association for the MLSTP), their programme and broadcasts in 1974. A final
collection of very interesting documents deals with the disagreements between the
MLSTP and the transitional government and the general unrest of early 1975. This
eventually led to the exile of two ministers, Pedro Umbelino and Gastão Torres, and
some members of the Associação Cívica pró-MLSTP and revealed the MLSTP to be
somewhat out of touch with the islands after so many years abroad.

139 **S.Tomé e Príncipe. Do descobrimento aos meados do século XVI:
desenvolvimento interno e irradiação no Golfo da Guiné.** (São
Tomé and Príncipe. From discovery to the mid-16th century: internal
development and diffusion in the Gulf of Guinea.)
Celso Batista de Sousa.   Masters thesis. University of Lisbon, 1990.
559 leaves. 14 maps. bibliog.
The period covered in this expansive study (1473-1550) is that of São Tomé and
Príncipe's early wealth, which was derived from sugar and slaves. A wide range of
social and economic issues are the focus of this illuminating work, which draws
heavily on contemporary accounts. The vast amounts of information, figures and

detail included in the text do not detract from an overall readability. De Sousa begins by looking at the influences of an inhospitable geography on the process of settlement, from the enervating climate, to the destructive plagues of black ants. Public administration, the judicial system, public finance, defence and government are all dealt with, followed by a study of the settlement of the islands by slaves and Europeans. This chapter contains considerable detail on the 2,000 Jewish children who were brought to the islands in 1493 to be brought up as Christians. Despite Captain Álvaro de Caminho's solicitude, and the assignment of two slaves to care for every five children, by 1506 it is estimated that at least 1,400 had died. Demography and living conditions are described and issues such as housing, food and health are also covered: rats the size of large rabbits were a common food stuff, and Europeans were particulary vulnerable to fever, venereal disease and scabies. The first hospital was founded in 1504. The social framework within the islands was not based on any sort of legislation and this instability and lawlessness is highlighted by the author. Many slaves were freed comparatively early and had already begun to ascend the social and economic ladders, while those still-enslaved were fleeing to the interior and the white elite remained isolated and arrogant. Agriculture is treated next: all food plants had to be introduced, so this was a time of interesting experiments. The cultivation of wheat and beans failed, but yams, corn, bananas and sugar cane were more successful. The islands' developing role in regional trade is analysed. Sugar and slaves were the principal commodities and prices, cargoes and regulations are well-documented. The final chapter covers the history of the Catholic Church. A substantial bibliography is appended (p. 537-59): it is an excellent guide to archival resources as well as to published works.

140 **S.Tomé e Príncipe na segunda metade do século XVIII.** (São Tomé and Príncipe in the second half of the 18th century.)
Carlos Filomeno Azevedo Agostinho das Neves.   Funchal, Madeira:
Secretaria Regional do Turismo, Cultura e Emigração; Lisbon:
Instituto de História de Além-Mar, 1989. 478p. 10 maps. bibliog.
(Colecção Memórias, no. 2).

Generally thought of as a period of stagnation between the sugar and cocoa booms, little has been written about this period of the islands' history. Neves has therefore relied very heavily on primary sources in this interesting, well-presented and well-researched book. It begins by setting the islands in an international context, noting the importance of the slave trade to European interests in West Africa and discussing Pombal's colonial policy. A look at the organization of power on the islands follows: public administration was in a chaotic state and the islands were almost ungovernable, with conflict between officials, the church and economic interests. Neves includes a section on the military, and the threat posed by the English and French: the latter launched a successful attack on Príncipe in 1799 and imposed humiliating terms of surrender. It was during this time that the Portuguese colonies seemed particularly vulnerable: Neves enters into some detail on the transfer of the other Guinea islands, Annobon and Fernando Pó, from Portugal to Spain. The economic situation is thoroughly examined, from the slave trade to agriculture and soap-making. International trade and shipping is studied, and the relative unimportance of Portugal is revealed. A shortage of coin hampered trade for the islanders and led to the economic ruin of some, who used their jewels and slaves in its place. The final chapter looks at São Tomense society, and considers race and class, slavery, the church, and rural and urban issues. The move of the capital from São Tomé to the town of Santo António on Príncipe took place in 1753, and the claim that this was for motives of public health is analysed. Some of Neves' conclusions about the trends emerging during this period are worth repeating: although the islands were not in such complete decadence as is sometimes thought, the final quarter of the century was indeed a time of decline. Trade with Baía, Brazil, was decreasing and islanders were selling goods in order to purchase luxuries and were not investing in agriculture. It was a period of social and administrative instability, with increasingly poor relations with Lisbon. At the same time blacks and *mestiços* were becoming more important in public life. A substantial appendix (p. 199-465) contains 157 transcriptions of documents from this era. These include contemporary descriptions of the islands, instructions to officials, public accounts and censuses. There are also reports on plantations, the French invasion of Príncipe, the 1795 revolt of black soldiers, false passports, and an attack on Príncipe in 1793 by an English frigate.

Descobrimento e cartografia das ilhas de S.Tomé e Príncipe.
See item no. 23.

Engenhos de água na ilha de São Tomé no século XVI.
See item no. 24.

O manuscrito 'Valentim Fernandes'.
See item no. 98.

Navigation de Lisbonne à l'île São Tomé par un pilote portugais anonyme (vers 1545).
See item no. 99.

A general history of the pyrates.
See item no. 100.

Os Angolares: da autonomia à inserção na sociedade colonial (segunda metade do século XIX).
See item no. 146.

Da origem dos Angolares habitantes da ilha de S.Tomé.
See item no. 148.

São Tomé e Príncipe: uma arqueologia para a identidade.
See item no. 149.

Subsídios para o estudo dos 'Angolares' de S.Tomé.
See item no. 150.

Os Barbadinhos italianos em S.Tomé e Príncipe de 1714 a 1794.
See item no. 168.

D. João Baptista, O.P., Bispo de S.Tomé?
See item no. 169.

Estado religioso de S.Tomé e Príncipe em meados do século XVIII.
See item no. 170.

Monumenta missionaria africana. África ocidental.
See item no. 171.

Public Christians, secret Jews: religion and political conflict on São Tomé in the sixteenth and seventeenth centuries.
See item no. 172.

Subsídios para a história de S.Tomé e Príncipe.
See item no. 176.

Vivência religiosa em S.Tomé no século XIX.
See item no. 177.

Anas de Chaves.
See item no. 191.

Maria Corrêa: a princesa negra do Príncipe (1788-1861).
See item no. 192.

Mary and misogyny. Women in Iberian expansion overseas, 1415-1815: some facts, fancies and personalities.
See item no. 193.

O comércio externo de S.Tomé no século XVII.
See item no. 235.

Boletim.
See item no. 383.

Fontes para a história do antigo ultramar português. Volume II São Tomé e Príncipe.
See item no. 385.

Guia de fontes portugueses para a história de África.
See item no. 386.

Population

141 **Aspectos demográficos das ilhas de São Tomé e do Príncipe.**
(Demographic aspects of the islands of São Tomé and Príncipe.)
Maria Albertina Pinto da Rocha Coelho. In: *Conferência
Internacional dos Africanistas Ocidentais 6ª Sessão. Volume V.*
[Lisbon]: Commission for Technical Co-operation in Africa South of
the Sahara; Scientific Council for Africa South of the Sahara, 1956,
p. 127-32.

The increasing birth rate is noted, and a distinction is made between that part of the
population which is foreign-born and that which is indigenous to the islands. A
summary in English is appended.

142 **Comparação de alguns caracteres antropológicos entre nativos de
S.Tomé.** (Comparison of some anthropological characteristics between
natives of São Tomé.)
Leopoldina Ferreira Paulo. Lisbon: Trabalhos do Centro de Estudos
de Etnologia do Ultramar, 1959. 50p. bibliog.

Reports on the findings of anthropometric studies carried out on one hundred
Angolars, measuring height, weight, thorax and muscularity. These results were
compared to an earlier study carried out on the descendants of Angolans and
Mozambicans living on the island and it was found that the Angolars were generally
larger. They were also compared to various ethnic groups from Guinea-Bissau and
Angola, and some affinities were found with the latter. There is a summary in
English.

143 **Contribuição para o estudo da antropologia física dos 'Angolares'**
(ilha de São Tomé). (Contribution to the study of the physical
anthropology of the Angolars [island of São Tomé].)
António de Almeida. In: *Conferência Internacional dos Africanistas*
Ocidentais 6ª Sessão. Volume V. [Lisbon]: Commission for
Technical Co-operation in Africa South of the Sahara; Scientific
Council for Africa South of the Sahara, 1956, p. 11-21. bibliog.

Almeida obtained height, cephalic and nasal indexes from one hundred Angolars and
found that there were similarities with ethnic groups from Angola. This volume of
conference papers contains several anthropometric studies of the inhabitants of São
Tomé and Príncipe. Maria Emília de Castro e Almeida contributes 'Estatura-
perímetro torácico e sua correlação em indígenas da ilha de São Tomé' (Stature and
thoracic perimeter and their correlation in the indigenous population of São Tomé) (p.
29-40) based on a study of Angolars and descendants of Mozambican and Angolan
workers; and 'Contribuição para o estudo dos caracteres descritivos dos nativos -
'Tongas' and 'Tonguinhas' - da ilha de São Tomé' (Contribution to the study of
descriptive characteristics of the indigenous population - Tongas and Tonguinhas - of
São Tomé) (p. 41-54) which is mainly concerned with the facial features of the
descendants of Mozambican and Angolan workers. Alfredo Athayde writes on
'Relações da capacidade vital, estatura e peso em nativos da ilha de São Tomé'
(Relationship between strength, stature and weight in the natives of São Tomé) (p.
55-58); and 'Robustez dos nativos da ilha de São Tomé avaliada pelo índice de
Pignet' (Strength of natives from São Tomé according to the Pignet index) (p. 59-77).
Leopoldina Ferreira Paulo's piece 'Alguns caracteres antropológicos em nativos da
ilha de São Tomé' (Some anthropological characteristics of the natives of São Tomé)
(p. 361-96) measures stature, weight and thoracic perimeter. 'Volume, corpulência e
constituição dos nativos da ilha de São Tomé' (Volume, corpulence and constitution
of the natives of São Tomé) (p. 399-409) by the same author finds that the Angolars
have a distinctively greater volume than other ethnic groups on the island. Most of
these studies have bibliographies and English summaries.

144 **Contribuição para o estudo do problema demográfico de S.Tomé e**
Príncipe. (Contribution to the study of the demographic problem of
São Tomé and Príncipe.)
Nuno Alves Morgado. *Garcia de Orta*, vol. 5, no. 4 (1957),
p. 633-58. bibliog.

The islands' continuing reliance on immigrant plantation labour is examined from a
demographic perspective. Using the limited statistical data available Morgado
presents a history of the population from settlement onwards. Between 1844 and 1909
there was an astonishing 500 per cent increase in population, leaping from 12,753
inhabitants to 64,221, due to the import of labour for the cocoa plantations. A gradual
decline to 57,644 in 1954 is commensurate with a decline in cocoa production, but as
the number of foreign workers was decreasing the indigenous population was
increasing at an annual rate of 1.4 per cent. The population's age and sex distribution
is studied, as are its high natality and mortality rates. There is an attempt to forecast
the future availability of agricultural labour under various hypotheses of
demographical behaviour. In assessing the economic implications of these forecasts
the author suggests that the indigenous population will eventually have to offer
themselves as plantation labour, as the number of men of working age increases. A
summary in English is provided.

145 **1º recenseamento geral da população e da habitação.** (First general census of population and housing.)
São Tomé: Ministério do Plano, Direcção de Estatística, 1987. 2 vols.
This is the first post-independence census. Earlier censuses, from 1914, 1921, 1940, 1950 and 1960, are listed in *African population census reports: a bibliography and checklist*, edited by John Pinfold (Oxford: Hans Zell, 1985, 100p.).

Ensino secundário básico 1989/90. Educação em matéria de população e para a vida familiar. Livro de referência.
See item no. 293.

Angolars

In 1693 Matheus Pires came to an accord with the Angolars which allowed them to be left alone by the São Tomense authorities. The 19th-century expansion of the plantations however, ended this tranquility. In 1878 Governor Estanislau Xavier de Almeida installed troops in Santa Cruz. This was an attempt to subjugate the Angolars to Portuguese law and integrate them into colonial society by means of schools and continued evangelization. Perhaps more serious was the expropriation of adjacent lands for the plantations although the Angolars maintained as far as possible their autonomy and refused to become plantation labourers. Similar ground is covered in Fernando Ferreira da Costa 'Crónica do fim de um reino' (Chronicle of the end of a kingdom) (*História*, no. 68 [June 1984], p. 2-16) which also treats Angolar religion, social structure and economic activities. Fernando de Macedo has compiled a collection of material about the Angolars entitled *O povo angolar* (The Angolar people) ([São Tomé]: The Author, 1990, 6 maps).

Most of the Angolar forenames and surnames are found to be of Christian and Portuguese origin, although they have altered phonetically. A minority of names are of Bantu origin. The text is summarized in English.

148   **Da origem dos Angolares habitantes da ilha de S.Tomé.** (On the origins of the Angolars living on the island of São Tomé.)
António de Almeida.   Lisbon: Academia das Ciências de Lisboa, 1962. 21p. bibliog.

The first half of this study evaluates the existing historical sources on the Angolar population, commonly believed to be the ancestors of survivors of a shipwrecked slaver from the 1540s. The events of the 19th century are a little better documented, from the military occupation of the Angolar village of Santa Cruz in 1878 to the amicable entente between the Angolar king and the governor of the islands. The second half is based on Almeida's anthropological research in Angola in 1950 and São Tomé in 1954. Angolar physiognomy, diet, skills, economic activity, architecture, language and religion are all covered. Almeida concludes that there has been a long-standing process of acculturation taking place, leading to cultural and physical similarities with the rest of the indigenous population of São Tomé. He is able, however, to suggest that the Angolars have strong affinities with the Mussurongo people from the former kingdom of Kongo on the left bank of the River Zaire and points to physical resemblances and traces of Umbundu in the Angolar language.

149   **São Tomé e Príncipe: uma arqueologia para a identidade.** (São Tomé and Príncipe: archaeology for identity.)
Armindo Aguiar.   *Leba*, no. 7 (1992), p. 41-46.

No archaeological work has been carried out on the islands, but Aguiar suggests that a study of the islands' languages and oral traditions might shed some light on the ethnic origins of the population. He is particularly interested in the origins of the Angolars, which he feels merits marine archaeological research to investigate the existence of the shipwreck which is thought to have brought them to São Tomé.

150   **Subsídios para o estudo dos 'Angolares' de S.Tomé.** (Contributions to the study of the 'Angolars' of São Tomé.)
Fernando Castelo-Branco.   *Stvdia*, no. 33 (December 1971), p. 149-59.

This is a review of the literature on the subject of the Angolars, covering early descriptions and anthropological, religious and linguistic studies. The author is particularly pleased to have found perhaps the earliest description extant, from 1712-18.

Comparação de alguns caracteres antropológicos entre nativos de S.Tomé.
See item no. 142.

Contribuição para o estudo da antropologia física dos 'Angolares' (ilha de São Tomé).
See item no. 143.

Resultados de um inquérito sobre o estado de saúde e de nutrição dos 'Angolares' da ilha de São Tomé.
See item no. 187.

Anguéné: gesta africana do povo Angolar de S.Tomé e Príncipe.
See item no. 312.

Egoísmo castigado: fábula angolar.
See item no. 368.

O galo, a galinha e o falcão: fábula angolar.
See item no. 370.

Language

151 **Africa do Sul e Portugal.** (South Africa and Portugal.)
Marius F. Valkhoff. In: *Miscelânea luso-africana.* Edited by
Marius F. Valkhoff. Lisbon: Junta de Investigações Científicas do
Ultramar, 1975, p. 87-101.

The revised text of a speech made in São Tomé in 1963, it begins by describing the
Portuguese influence in South Africa, their expansion around the world and the creole
languages which emerged in their wake. It goes on to mention the early publications,
writings and research on the languages of São Tomé and Príncipe - the
communication between Manuel João da Silva Costa and Alfredo Coelho in the
1880s; Almada Negreiros in the 1890s; the poet Francisco Stockler. There is an
appendix of São Tomense proverbs and sayings.

152 **African influences on Principense creole.**
Luiz Ivens Ferraz. In: *Miscelânea luso-africana.* Edited by Marius
F. Valkhoff. Lisbon: Junta de Investigações Científicas do Ultramar,
1975, p. 153-64. bibliog.

Phonological and grammatical features of the creole of Príncipe are used to show the
influence of 'substratum' Bantu and Kwa languages. Some of the grammatical
features selected for study are the use of ideophones, the absence of the passive
transformation, the absence of articles and the marking of negation at the conclusion
of utterances. See also Ferraz and A. Traill 'The interpretation of tone in Principense
creole' (*Studies in African Linguistics,* vol. 12, no. 2 [1981], p. 205-15).

153 **Algumas notas sobre o falar dos nativos da ilha de São Tomé.**
(Some notes on the speech of the natives of the island of São Tomé.)
Alda do Espírito Santo. In: *Conferência Internacional dos Africanistas Ocidentais 6ª Sessão. Volume V.* [Lisbon]: Commission for Technical Co-operation in Africa South of the Sahara; Scientific Council for Africa South of the Sahara, 1956, p. 141-48.

This article provides some examples of creole expressions, which serve as a window on São Tomense life. There is also a summary in English.

154 **The article systems of Cape Verde and São Tomé creole Portuguese: general principles and specific factors.**
Dante Lucchesi. *Journal of Pidgin and Creole Languages*, vol. 8, no. 1 (1993), p. 81-108. bibliog.

This is a study of the article systems of the creole languages of the two countries, which tests Derek Bickerton's 'bioprogramme' theory of creole language evolution and human language acquisition in general, and Tore Janson's theory that the article systems of creole languages have been transmitted from the lexifying language. Portuguese is the lexifying language for the creole languages of Cape Verde and São Tomé and Príncipe. In São Tomense creole (often referred to as *Forro*) there is no definite article, although there is an indefinite article and demonstrative adjective. The use of the indefinite article is extended so that it can, in some contexts, take on the role of the definite article. In São Tomé there is a strong influence from 'substratum' African languages which may affect the article system. Another possible reason for the disappearance of the Portuguese definite article may be its lack of a first consonant. Lucchesi concludes that 'the researcher must take into account a complex network in which general principles and specific factors intersect' (p. 104).

155 **Cape Verde, Guinea-Bissau and São Tomé and Príncipe: the linguistic situation.**
Jorge Morais-Barbosa, translated by J. Carter. In: *Miscelânea luso-africana.* Edited by Marius F. Valkhoff. Lisbon: Junta de Investigações Científicas do Ultramar, 1975, p. 133-51.

An overview of all the languages spoken in the three countries, which points out some of the distinguishing features of the creole languages. Morais-Barbosa boldly suggests that the creole of São Tomé 'lacks temporal distinctions, it has only aspectual distinctions' (p. 140). He also notes the increasing influence of the Portuguese language in São Tomé and Príncipe. An intriguing, and disappointingly undeveloped, remark about the creole spoken on Príncipe is that 'although not significantly affected by contact with Portuguese shows a marked tendency towards rapid disappearance owing to increasing neglect by its speakers who tend to use Portuguese instead' (p. 149). This is a translation of the chapter which appeared in *Cabo Verde, Guiné, São Tomé e Príncipe: curso de extensão universitária, ano lectivo de 1965-1966,* (q.v.).

156 A comparative study of São-Tomense and Cabo-Verdiano creole.
Luiz Ivens Ferraz, Marius F. Valkhoff. In: *Miscelânea luso-africana*.
Edited by Marius F. Valkhoff. Lisbon: Junta de Investigações
Científicas do Ultramar, 1975, p. 15-39. bibliog.
The creole languages of São Tomé and Príncipe, Barlavento and Sotavento (Cape
Verde) are compared and the various differences discussed. The creole languages of
Cape Verde have a fuller temporal system of verbs than those of São Tomé and
Príncipe, which use an aspectual system. The lexicon is another area of comparison
which reveals differences between the two countries. This can largely be attributed to
the greater contact with the Portuguese language that has occurred in Cape Verde.
The creole languages of São Tomé and Príncipe contain many more words of African
origin, and also retain a greater number of items from archaic Portuguese. The article
lists a number of parallel sentences in the four languages and Portuguese, with notes
on the differences. See also José Gonçalo Herculano de Carvalho 'Deux langues
créoles: le criôl du Cap Vert et le forro de São Tomé' (Two creole languages: the
Criôl of Cape Verde and the *Forro* of São Tomé) (*Biblios*, no. 57 [1981], p. 1-16).

157 **The creole of São Tomé.**
Luiz Ivens Ferraz. Johannesburg: Witwatersrand University Press,
1979. 122p. bibliog.
Ferraz has produced an exemplary study of a creole language, and a highly-
recommended starting point for any study of the São Tomense language. Prefatory
chapters speculate on the history and evolution of the language, and include a survey
of previous research into the languages of São Tomé and Príncipe. Relationships
between the four Gulf of Guinea creole languages (São Tomense, Angolar,
Principense and Annobonese) are discussed. They share significant proportions of
their lexicon and may all have originated from one creole, to which Angolar probably
has the closest resemblance. Phonology, however, varies a great deal. There is strong
evidence of an African substratum in São Tomense, provided mainly by the Bini and
Kishikongo languages. Bini, sometimes known as Edo, is a Kwa language from
Benin. Kishikongo is a Bantu language and was spoken in the kingdom of the Kongo.
The earliest import of slaves into São Tomé was from these two areas of West Africa,
although Ferraz warns that the available documentary evidence for this is less than
adequate. He suggests that the language was formed within the first eighty years of
the island's settlement. During this crucial period of initial contact between
Portuguese and African language speakers there was much intermarriage and a
mixed-race generation soon emerged who took the Portuguese language as a model.
The exodus of Europeans towards the end of the 16th century probably accounts for
the language's strong African component. The main body of the book constitutes a
description of São Tomense which attempts to establish, where possible, its links with
the languages of the West African coast. The chapter on phonology, which includes
orthographic suggestions, concludes that it is 'African-based rather than Portuguese-
based' (p. 54). Other chapters cover word grammar and compounding, which
embraces morphology and inflexional devices; and the grammar itself, which includes
ideophones, phrase structure and syntax. The chapter on the lexicon is particularly
interesting. Although Portuguese-derived words are 'an open-ended inventory, and
the items of African origin are a closed inventory with only a few hundred items' the
African words are not limited to specifically African concepts. They include such
basic terms as parts of the body, food, plants, and animals. Many terms are also
derived from an archaic form of Portuguese. Recent changes have seen the

Language

introduction of more Portuguese terms, but there is no indication of a large-scale relexification taking place. A concluding chapter notes that São Tomense shows a balance between substratum influences, linguistic universals, and features common to creole languages as a family. The appendix describes the complex forms of address of the social idiom.

158 **Os dialectos românicos ou neo-latinos na África, Ásia e América.**
(The Romance or neo-Latin dialects in Africa, Asia and America.)
F. Alfredo Coelho. In: *Estudos linguísticos: crioulos. Reedição de artigos publicados no Boletim da Sociedade de Geografia de Lisboa.*
Introduction by Jorge Morais-Barbosa. Lisbon: Academia Internacional da Cultura Portuguesa, 1967, p. 1-234.

First published in the *Boletim da Sociedade de Geografia de Lisboa* in three parts in 1880, 1882 and 1886, this was one of the very first studies of Portuguese-related creole languages. It includes poetry and proverbs in São Tomense creole, with Portuguese translations provided. Almost simultaneously Hugo Schuchardt was engaged in similar research. His publications include 'Kreolische Studien 1: über das Negerportugiesische von S. Thomé (West-afrika)' (Creole studies 1 : on the black Portuguese language from São Tomé [West Africa]) (*Sitzungsberichte der Wiener Akademie der Wissenschaften: Philosophisch-Historisch Klasse*, no. 101 [1882], p. 889-917) and 'Beiträge zur Kenntnis der Kreolischen Romanisch 4: zum Negerportugiesische der Ilha do Príncipe' (Contributions to knowledge about the Romance creoles 4: on the black Portuguese language of the island of Príncipe) (*Zeitschrift für Romanische Philologie*, no. 13 [1889], p. 463-75).

159 **Kabuverdianu - Elementaria seiner TMA-Morphosyntax im lusokreolischen Vergleich.** (Kabuverdianu - contributions towards a tense-mode-aspect morphosyntax in Portuguese creole languages.)
Petra Thiele. Bochum, Germany: Universitätsverlag Brockmeyer, 1991. 151p. 4 maps. bibliog. (Bochum-Essener Beiträge zur Sprachwandelforschung, no. 12).

The tense-mode-aspect (TMA) systems of the creole languages of Cape Verde, Guinea-Bissau and São Tomé and Príncipe are investigated and post-verbal as well as pre-verbal TMA elements are found. These markers are often polyfunctional and the majority are syntactically 'bound' rather than free. Thiele contrasts these features with the TMA model prepared by Derek Bickerton in *Roots of language* (Ann Arbor: Karoma, 1981) and then goes on to apply this research to the debate on the origins of creole languages, specifically in the area of substratal transfer. She concludes that the TMA systems of these particular creole languages are not simplifications of the Portuguese tense system since it was never adopted. Rather, the fundamental grammatical characteristics of West African languages were preserved and the verbal system of these creoles is a synthesis of Portuguese lexical items and substrata grammar from West African languages. There is a useful summary in English. A related work by the same author is 'Zur Spezifizierung von Substrateinflüssen auf die Entwicklung der portugiesisch-basierten Kreolsprachen Westafrikas' (Specifics of substratum influences in the development of West African Portuguese-based creole languages), (*Linguistische Studien. Reihe A Arbeitsberichte*, no. 172 [1987], p. 79-91. bibliog.).

160   **The liquid in the Gulf of Guinea creoles.**
Luiz Ivens Ferraz.   *African Studies*, vol. 46, no. 2 (1987), p. 287-95.
bibliog.

The four languages of the Gulf of Guinea under consideration are São Tomense, Angolar, Príncipense and Annobonese. These are generally regarded as mutually unintelligible, but with much in common in terms of phonology, lexicon and syntax. Ferraz, however, quotes G. de Granda's interesting observation that 'The mutual intelligibility of the speakers of São Tomense and Annobonese was confirmed to me by several Annobonese informants and one from São Tomé whom I met in Malaba. But all agreed that "the old" understood each other better than the present day "young"' (p.288). This article is concerned with one aspect of the comparative phonology of these languages, that of liquid clusters. Tables are prepared to demonstrate examples of liquids in the four languages, together with etymology and English meanings. Only Príncipe has both the 'l' and 'r' liquids: the others have only 'l'. Angolar has greater similarities with Príncipe and Annobon than with São Tomense, which in turn is markedly different from the others in favouring consonant clusters including 'l'. The influence of Kwa and Bantu languages on phonology is also noted. Ferraz suggests that the four creoles have a common origin and 'that the declustering pattern was the original one', with the distinctiveness of São Tomense developing subsequently.

161   **Das portugiesische Kreolisch der Ilha do Príncipe.** (The Portuguese
creole language of the island of Príncipe.)
Wilfried Günther.   Marburg an der Lahn, Germany: Im Selbstverlag,
1973. 277p. map. bibliog. (Marburger Studien zur Afrika- und
Asienkunde. Serie A: Afrika-Band 2).

The introduction to this valuable study of the creole language spoken on Príncipe covers the island's history, the creole languages spoken in the other islands of the Gulf of Guinea, and touches briefly on the author's thoughts on the existence of a Bini substrata to the Príncipense creole. Bini is a member of the Kwa family of languages and is spoken in parts of Nigeria. The first section of the book is a grammar of the creole, covering phonology, morphology and syntax. The second section, grandly entitled 'Chrestomathy', is a collection of materials from the oral literature of Príncipe. There are five *swá* (oral narratives), each transcribed in an orthography dependent on the use of phonetic symbols and accompanied by a translation in German. The first text also has a literal German translation. The five stories are 'Swá tetúga ki kõpwé agbé' (The story of turtle and godfather mud-turtle); 'Swá tetúga ki mígu sé' (The story of turtle and his friend); 'Swá tetúga ki ína mínu sé' (The story of turtle and his children); 'Swá micá máshi moci deké vedadi' (The story of a lie which was worth more than the truth); 'Swá pédu ki aré ki zwá' (The story of Pedro, the king and João). There are sixty-one *pyáda* (riddles), each with a German translation and explanations. The section concludes with two *kãcíga* (songs), one an anthem to the town of Santo António, another an improvisation. The book concludes with an extremely useful glossary. Each entry has a German translation and a note on etymology: although the overwhelming majority of words have a Portuguese origin, Günther has occasion to refer to Angolar, Bini, Ewe, São Tomense creole, Fulani, Hausa, Igbo and archaic and Brazilian Portuguese. Many entries also give examples of usage and other contextual notes. The entry for one of the many words referring to workers, *tabaladó*, for example, gives a fascinating glimpse of Príncipe's history and culture, 'a word that occurs in the chorus line of an invocation. According to my

Language

informant it is a word which stems from the littoral creole of Angola and means worker. All this suggests that indigenous sorcery has been strongly influenced by the contract workers. The word is only used in the context of sorcery'.

162 **Situação actual da língua portuguesa nas ilhas de S.Tomé e Príncipe.** (Current situation of the Portuguese language in the islands of São Tomé and Príncipe.)
Carlos Espírito Santo.   In: *Congresso sobre a situação actual da língua portuguesa no mundo. Actas: volume II.*   Lisbon: Instituto de Cultura e Língua Portuguesa, 1987, p. 253-60.

Presented at the conference held in 1983, this paper first outlines the islands' linguistic situation and justifies the choice of the colonizer's language as the official language of the independent state. The government's language policy is to promote the coexistence of the three creole languages alongside the Portuguese language. In practice, however, Portuguese is the language of education, commerce, the media, literature, politics and of government. Portuguese, the author explains, is a 'structured' language and has dictionaries and grammars. He makes the interesting point that there is such a thing as 'São Tomense Portuguese', which is influenced in its phonetics, syntax, morphology and lexicon by borrowings from the creole languages. Other papers of interest from the same conference are Manuel Ferreira 'Numa perspectiva sociocultural. Que futura para a língua portuguesa em África?' (From a socio-cultural perspective. What future for the Portuguese language in Africa?) (Volume I, p. 248-72); and Jean-Michel Massa, Marie Françoise Bidault, A.-M. Conas, F. Massa 'La lusographie africaine - un project de dictionnaire bilingue de particularités en Afrique de la langue portugaise (écrite)' (African written Portuguese - a project for a bilingual dictionary of special characteristics in Portuguese-speaking Africa) (Volume I, p. 188-93).

163 **Sobre a terminologia anatómica no crioulo de S.Tomé e Príncipe.**
(On anatomical terminology in the creole of São Tomé and Príncipe.)
António de Almeida.   *Anais da Junta de Investigações Coloniais,* vol. 4, no. 5 (1949), p. 49-61. bibliog.

Lists creole terms for 141 parts of the body, but without making any distinction between the languages of the two islands.

164 **The social context of creolization.**
Edited by Ellen Woolford, William Washabaugh.   Ann Arbor, Michigan: Karoma, 1983. 149p. bibliog.

The essays brought together in this volume share 'the notion that social forces are the crucial factor in determining whether or not pidginization and/or creolization will occur' (p. 1). Two essays contain reflections on the creoles of São Tomé and Príncipe: William Washabaugh and Sidney M. Greenfield in 'The development of Atlantic creole languages' (p. 106-19) pay particular attention to the role played by the sugar plantations in the formation of the creole languages of Cape Verde and São Tomé and Príncipe in the 15th and early 16th centuries. Luiz Ivens Ferraz's 'The origin and development of four creoles in the Gulf of Guinea' (p. 120-25) provides illustrations of the African substratum of the creoles of Annobon, São Tomé and Príncipe. The strength of the substratum can be attributed to the exodus of Portuguese settlers in the 16th century.

strength of the substratum can be attributed to the exodus of Portuguese settlers in the 16th century.

165   **Studies in Portuguese and creole with special reference to South Africa.**
Marius F. Valkhoff.   Johannesburg: Witwatersrand University Press, 1966. 282p. bibliog.

Although primarily a study of the role of Portuguese creole in the evolution of Afrikaans in South Africa in the 16th and 17th centuries, this text does contain material on the creoles of São Tomé and Príncipe as possible living ancestors of this historical creole. There is a chapter on the Gulf of Guinea creoles, 'Outline of the creole of St Thomas, Príncipe and Annobón' (p. 77-115), which describes the social background to the formation of these languages, including Angolar, and their phonologies, grammars, verbal systems, aspectual systems and vocabulary. There are also two appendixes, 'Twenty-five proverbs and sayings in St Thomas and Príncipe creole' (p. 248-52) and 'Parallel sentences in St Thomas and Príncipe creole' (p. 253-60).

166   **Towards a functional identification of moneme categories in the Portuguese creole of São Tomé.**
Jorge Morais Barbosa.   In: *Actas do colóquio sobre 'Crioulos de Base Lexical Portuguesa'*.   Edited by Ernesto d'Andrade, Alain Kihm.   Lisbon: Edições Colibri, 1992, p. 177-89.

Through the analysis of sentences of differing complexity this study attempts to identify the syntactic functions and morphological classes of different categories of word. It concludes that São Tomense creole has 'a fairly simple grammatical structure' (p. 187).

Nomes crioulos e vernáculos de algumas plantas de S.Tomé e Príncipe.
See item no. 46.

Contribuição para o estudo da antroponímia dos Angolares (S.Tomé).
See item no. 147.

Auswahlbibliographie zu Sprache und Literatur São Tomés und Príncipes.
See item no. 409.

Religion

167 **O Apóstolo Brinkmann na África ocidental.** (Apostle Brinkmann in West Africa).
Arminn Brinkmann. *Pequena Nossa Família*, [1990?], p. 8-10.
Brinkmann's account of his visit to Africa in 1990 includes São Tomé and Príncipe, where there is a thriving branch of the Igreja Nova Apostólica (New Apostolic Church).

168 **Os Barbadinhos italianos em S.Tomé e Príncipe de 1714 a 1794.**
(The Italian Capuchins in São Tomé and Príncipe between 1714 and 1794.)
F. Leite de Faria. *Portugal em África*, vol. 11, no. 62 (March-April 1954), p. 69-85; vol. 11, no. 66 (November-December 1954), p. 390-404; vol. 12, no. 67 (January-February. 1955), p. 46-55.
The first section is a general history of the Capuchin missionary activity in the islands. The remainder is a transcript of documents from the order's archives. This takes the form of a list of the missionaries who were sent, with some brief notes. Faria's own annotations are more extensive, and include interesting snippets of information about such things as the putative missionary who had to be substituted after failing, in a test, to distinguish between bigamy and polygamy.

169 **D. João Baptista, O. P., Bispo de S. Tomé?** (D. João Baptista, O. P., Bishop of São Tomé?)
António Brásio. *Portugal em África*, vol. 8, no. 47 (September-October 1951), p. 275-87.
Using and transcribing some of the original documents, Brásio tries to establish the identity and dates of the comings and goings of the mid-16th century bishops of São Tomé. See his other articles in *Portugal em África* 'D. Pedro de Sousa Bispo de S.Tomé?' (D. Pedro de Sousa Bishop of São Tome?) (vol. 4, no. 22 [July-August

1947], p. 235-38) and 'Dom Frei Bernado da Cruz, Bispo de S.Tomé' (Dom Fra Bernado da Cruz, Bishop of São Tomé.) (vol. 6, no. 36 [November-December 1949], p. 321-33).

170   **Estado religioso de S.Tomé e Príncipe em meados do século XVIII.**
       (The state of religion in São Tomé and Príncipe in the mid-18th century.)
       António Brásio.   *Portugal em África*, vol. 3, no. 14 (March-April 1946), p. 100-09.

Brásio provides a brief description of the clergy present on the islands, plus transcripts of three contemporary letters on the subject. These letters are preoccupied with the inadequacy of the missionary activity taking place.

171   *Monumenta missionaria africana.* **Africa ocidental.** (*Monumenta missionaria africana*. West Africa.)
       António Brásio.   Lisbon: Agência Geral do Ultramar, 1953-88.
       15 vols.

A truly remarkable, and monumental, collection of documents concerning the Catholic Church's activities in that part of West Africa which fell within the Portuguese sphere of influence. The documents in the fifteen volumes of the first series date from 1471 to 1885, although the 18th and 19th centuries are lightly covered in comparison to the earlier centuries. The geographical scope stretches from Rio de Santo André (Liberia/Ivory Coast) to the Cape of Good Hope. The early diocese of São Tomé encompassed the northern half of this zone. Brásio's aim has been to make these documents as usable as possible. This is reflected in the style of transcription which he has adopted, and by the provision of brief summaries and indexes of name, subject and place. Not all the documents are exclusively of a religious nature: many are of interest to the region's history from a broader perspective. Volumes 12-15 (1981-88) were published by the Academia Portuguesa da História in Lisbon.

172   **Public Christians, secret Jews: religion and political conflict on São Tomé island in the sixteenth and seventeenth centuries.**
       Robert Garfield.   *Sixteenth Century Journal*, vol. 21, no. 4 (1990), p. 645-54.

Many Jews expelled from Castille in 1492 fled to Portugal, but in 1493 2,000 of their children under the age of ten were taken by Álvaro da Caminho to settle on São Tomé. They were baptized and brought up as Christians and 600 were reported to have survived into the 16th century. During the years of economic prosperity Jewish origins were occasionally remarked upon as a curiosity, but there is every indication that the São Tomense of European origins were all practising Catholics. This article traces the increasing use of accusations of Judaism as a standard means for discrediting political opponents. In the early 17th century the exodus of planters to Brazil would have included most of the population which had Jewish origins, although it was at this time of economic decline that the accusations became more frequent. Newly-appointed bishops were told that their main tasks were to eliminate the Jews and ensure that no 'New Christian' (Jews who had converted to Christianity) was given civil or ecclesiastical appointments. In 1621 the newly-arrived Bishop

Pedro da Cunha Lobo thought he saw a procession of Jews carrying a golden calf, and fled back to Portugal on the next ship. African religious practices - which the bishop might in fact have witnessed - were not understood, whereas the fear of Judaism was well-established in the Iberian peninsula. The Catholic establishment in Portugal did not, however, think that these charges merited formal investigation by the Inquisition. The article concludes that the struggle for economic and political power was probably at the root of these accusations.

173 **A religiosidade entre os Forros.** (Religiosity amongst the Forros.)
Carlos Espírito Santo. *África: Literatura, Arte e Cultura*, vol. 2, no. 10 (October-December 1980), p. 590-93.

Espírito Santo offers some interesting thoughts on the two religious systems, one Christian, one animist, adhered to by the indigenous population. Firstly, he looks at the supernatural beings of São Tomense faith. These include Sum d'Océ (Lord of the Heavens), who is both the Christian creator and the controller of weather and people. The Nén ké Mu (the dead) are São Tomense ancestors, who are respected and feared and can provide protection for their descendants. Offerings of food, wine and clothing are regularly made to the Nén ké Mu. The Djábu (devil) and Santissimu (saints) are of Christian origin. The article concludes with some examples of oaths, which are of great importance, and often seem to be of a medical nature: for example 'Jiba cumé mu món' (May elephantiasis rot my hands).

174 **San Men Dêçu: a senhora Mãe de Deus em S. Tomé e Príncipe.**
(Our Lady Mother of God in São Tomé and Príncipe).
Francisco Vaz. Lisbon: Província Portuguesa da Congregação dos Missionários do Coração de Maria, 1989. 293p. 7 maps.

Vaz was a priest in the islands for nearly twenty years, and has remained entranced by this country where he finds the Roman Catholic faith to be firmly rooted. The early chapters cover the arrival of the Catholic Church in the islands and the formation of the enormous diocese of São Tomé, which stretched from the Gulf of Guinea to the Cape of Good Hope. Vaz quotes liberally from *Monumenta missionaria africana: África ocidental* (q.v.). The main body of the work is a description of those island churches which are dedicated to Mary. The buildings' history, construction and contents are explored and some black-and-white photographs are included. Feast days and processions associated with these churches are also mentioned. One of the more entertaining aspects of the book is its collection of legends and miracles. Several accounts of miracles performed by Mary in the islands and the surrounding ocean are quoted from the 1721 manuscript of Frei Agostinho de Santa Maria, 'Santuário mariano' (Marian shrines). Local legends are also recorded. These explain, for example, why the cathedral building has never been finished, or describe how Mary's intervention saved a man who had been stashed in an underwater larder by a shark in the seas off Ilhéu das Cabras.

175 **Sobre alguns costumes de S.Thomé.** (About some of the customs of
São Tomé.)
Francisco R. da Silveira Magalhães. *Boletim da Sociedade de
Geographia de Lisboa*, no. 3 (March 1903), p. 113-16 and no. 8
(August 1903), p. 316-19.

Using previously unpublished material from the early 19th century Magalhães makes
some disparaging comments about the superstitious practices of all classes of São
Tomense society. These seem to have made some inroads into Catholic religious
practices on the island. A distressing account of the persecution and murder in 1800
of three women accused of witchcraft is included: even the priest refused to let them
take sanctuary in his church. The article also contains some comments on language,
education and race.

176 **Subsídios para a história de S.Tomé e Príncipe.** (Contributions
towards the history of São Tomé and Príncipe.)
António Ambrósio. Lisbon: Livros Horizonte, 1984. 253p. 8 maps.
(Colecção Horizonte Histórico).

Ambrósio has transcribed a number of documents relating to the history of the
Catholic Church on São Tomé and Príncipe from the 18th century up until 1980.
During this period the indigenous clergy were supplemented at various times by
members of religious orders from Brazil, Italy and Portugal. Ambrósio himself was a
missionary on the islands between 1963-73, and the material included reflects his
interest in evangelism, missionary work and social action. The collection begins with
a general historical introduction and information on the archival sources. The Arquivo
Diocesano and the Arquivo Histórico de S.Tomé have both been sources of material
and the *Boletim Oficial* (q.v.) was another useful resource. The first part of the book is
entitled 'A relação nominal dos eclesiásticos em S.Tomé e Príncipe. 1820-1975' (List
of names of clerics in São Tomé and Príncipe. 1820-1975) (p. 29-126). The second
part of the book is a miscellaneous collection of material, including a number of
extracts from books and periodicals as well as previously unpublished documents.
There are a number of interesting descriptions of the islands. 'O estado da Diocese de
S.Tomé e Príncipe em 1897' (The condition of the Diocese of São Tomé and Príncipe
in 1897) (p. 209-23) by Monsignor José António Pereira, for example, describes a
booming economy but a church in decline. Church buildings were in such poor repair
that the roof of one actually collapsed on Christmas day, and cemetery walls were so
inadequate that animals could enter and exhume the corpses. A final report describes
the state of the Catholic faith in 1983: 'A profoundly religious people, but in their
own manner: baptism, festivals, processions, funeral masses, obsequies. In general
they don't appreciate Sunday, nor live by Holy Communion' (p. 249). Another source
on the Catholic Church in São Tomé and Príncipe is José Gonçalves Pereira *Os
mensageiros da paz* (Messengers of peace) (Lisbon: Edição Colégio Universitário Pio
XII, 1984, 181p.).

177 **A vivência religiosa em S.Tomé no século XIX.** (Religious life in São Tomé in the 19th century.)
Augusto Nascimento.   In: *Congresso Internacional de História: Missionação Portuguesa e Encontro de Culturas. Actas: volume IV. Missionação: problemática geral e sociedade contemporânea.*
Braga, Portugal: Universidade Católica Portuguesa, 1993, p. 37-53. bibliog.

Religious institutions, like many other aspects of the island, had entered into a profound decadence before the cocoa boom of the second half of the 19th century. Nascimento finds that they did not improve with the island's prosperity either. This paper also looks at the divisions between European and São Tomense priests. The 'recolonization' of the island caused a 'Europeanization' of religious life. The Europeans would not tolerate the indigenous priests and were extremely critical of their lax ways. The traditional religious processions and festivals also came under official disapproval. Missionaries from Europe came in a steady stream, but the Catholic Church was never as powerful here as in the other colonies of Portuguese Africa.

Manuel Rosário Pinto (a sua vida).
See item no. 128.

Society and Social Issues

Development projects

178　**Micro-hydro in São Tomé.**
Julie Tilling. *Proceedings of the Institution of Civil Engineers: Civil Engineering*, vol. 92, no. 3 (August 1992), p. 138-43. 2 maps.
This is a prize-winning account of a Voluntary Services Overseas' project to investigate the possibilities for small-scale hydro-electric power generation on four cocoa plantations in southern São Tomé. The problems encountered were both technical and social. Hydrological information was difficult to obtain, although Tilling eventually found some rainfall data collected over several years by a Russian team. Many sites were inappropriate because small-scale hydroschemes cannot store water and evidence had accumulated that rainfall seasonality had an effect on some watercourses. There was also a problem with the 'ownership' of the project. It was very much the plantation owner's idea, and Tilling felt some doubt about his workers' committment to it and the quality of maintenance which they would provide. In the end she recommended postponement, and seems to have left the island with some strong feelings about the living conditions endured by the plantation workers.

179　**São Tomé & Príncipe and Guinea-Bissau.**
Steve Carter, Mireille Flowerdew, Phillip Scarr, Stephen Turner.
Orbit, no. 44, (1992), p. 15-19. map.
The role of Voluntary Services Overseas in São Tomé and Príncipe and Guinea-Bissau is described. There are also accounts of the experiences of two of the volunteers in São Tomé: Scarr worked at a vehicle repair and machine shop and Flowerdew was a laboratory technician at the Monte Café plantation hospital.

180 **O serviço social em Cabo Verde, na Guiné e em S.Tomé e Príncipe.**
(Social services in Cape Verde, Guinea and São Tomé and Príncipe.)
Maria Palmira de Moraes Pinto Duarte. In: *Cabo Verde, Guiné, São
Tomé e Príncipe: curso de extensão universitária, ano lectivo de
1965-1966.* Lisbon: Universidade Técnica de Lisboa, Instituto
Superior de Ciências Sociais e Política Ultramarina, 1966, p. 377-440.

The section on São Tomé reports on some perhaps rather naïve social development
projects carried out in the villages of Santana and Angra Toldo (an Angolar fishing
community) between 1962 and 1965. The projects were mostly of an educational
nature, with women's domestic skills a high priority.

Health

181 **Assistência médica à criança nos meios nativos da ilha de São
Tomé.** (Medical care for children amongst the natives of the island of
São Tomé.)
Maria de Jesus Neves. In: *Conferência Internacional dos
Africanistas Ocidentais 6ª Sessão. Volume V.* [Lisbon]: Commission
for Technical Co-operation in Africa South of the Sahara; Scientific
Council for Africa South of the Sahara, 1956, p. 327-32.

Traditional methods of care for pregnancy, childbirth and infants are described as an
amalgam of herbal medicine and 'superstition'. There is a summary in English.

182 **A case of *Schistosoma intercalatum* infection from Sao Tome.**
M. Corachan, R. Romero, J. Mas, A. Palacin, R. Knowles. *Tropical
and Geographical Medicine*, vol. 40, no. 2 (1988), p. 147-50. bibliog.

This is the case study of a young girl from Pantufo, São Tomé, who was heavily
infected by the *Schistosoma intercalatum* parasite. The species, associated with the
disease bilharzia, was probably carried to the islands by workers from Central Africa.
The possibility of its hybridization is discussed. See also Romero, Corachan, M. Luis
'Schistosomiasis in São Tomé. A pilot study' (*Transactions of the Royal Society of
Tropical Medicine and Hygiene*, vol. 83, no. 1 [1989], p. 81-82. map). A survey of
school children and villagers showed that *Schistosoma intercalatum* was widely
disseminated. The intermediate host of this parasite is probably the freshwater snail
Bulinus forskalii: see D. S. Brown, M. A. Gracio, P. J. Moore, D. Rollinson, Romero,
V. R. Southgate 'The snail host of schistosomiasis in São Tomé' (*Transactions of the
Royal Society of Tropical Medicine and Hygiene*, vol. 83, no. 6 [1989], p. 812-13.
bibliog.); and 'Freshwater snails of São Tomé, with special reference to *Bulinus
forskalii* (Ehrenberg), host of *Schistosoma intercalatum*' (q.v.).

183 **Man against tsetse - struggle for Africa.**
John J. McKelvey Jr.   Ithaca, New York; London: Cornell University
Press, 1973. 306p. 11 maps. bibliog.

This history of public health campaigns against the tsetse fly includes an account of
the measures taken in Príncipe (p. 113-24) from the first identification of bacterium in
1901, through the 1907-08 commission headed by Dr. Corrêa Mendes, and the
successful campaign of 1911-14 described in *Sleeping sickness. A record of four
years' war against it in the island of Príncipe* (q.v.). The return of the tsetse in the
1950s (although this time without the trypansome parasites which cause sleeping
sickness) is also covered. The fly was eradicated by the use of traps and DDT. The
latter had to be used with care however, because a programme of scale insect control
using insect predators was taking place concurrently. See also H. Harold Scott *A
history of tropical medicine* (London: Edward Arnold, 1942. 2 vols.) for his chapter
on the history of medical knowledge and practice regarding sleeping sickness, which
includes a passage (p. 503-11) covering the history of the disease on Príncipe.

184 **Medicina tradicional.** (Traditional medicine.)
E. Sardinha dos Santos.   *Cultura em Movimento: Revista Cultural,*
vol. 1 (August 1989), p. 23-27.

The paper stresses the importance of collecting and recording oral knowledge about
medicinal plants in order that they can enter the world of scientific research. The
therapeutic use and methods of preparation for five plants from São Tomé and
Príncipe are described. These plants are *Bryophyllum pinnatum, Euphorbia serpens,
Gynbopogon citratus* (DC) Stapf, *Achyrantes aspera* Linn. and *Jatropa curcas* L.

185 **A provincia de S.Thomé e Principe e suas dependencias ou a
salubridade e insalubridade relativa das provincias do Brazil, das
colonias de Portugal e de outras nações da Europa.** (The province
of São Tomé and Príncipe and its dependencies or the relative
salubrity and insalubrity of the provinces of Brazil, the colonies of
Portugal and of other nations of Europe.)
Manuel Ferreira Ribeiro.   Lisbon: Imprensa Nacional, 1877. 705p.
map.

Ribeiro resided in São Tomé during the 1870s in order to study the condition of
public health. His resulting book is a veritable compendium of information, ranging
from descriptions of all the countries south of the equator to the question of human
evolution. However, its main purpose is to be a 'reliable and indispensable guide' to
São Tomé and Príncipe. There is an emphasis on issues relating to public health,
which he reports on with regard to the capital city and the work being carried out by
the authorities. He suggests improvements such as widening roads, draining swamps
and channelling the Água Grande river which flows through the city. Figures for
births, deaths and illnesses are provided and some comparative material from other
Portuguese colonies is also included. The islanders' way of life is described, covering
such topics as diet, clothing and religion. Ribeiro also considers the islands'
topography, climate, natural history and plantations. One glorious feature of the book
is its map, entitled 'Mappa medico geographico da região guineana equatorial na qual
se comprehende a provincia de S.Thomé e Principe e suas dependencias' (Medico-
geographical map of the equatorial Guinean region which includes the province of
São Tomé and Príncipe), which stretches from Gabon to Lake Chad. It is shaded to

show the areas of influence of various European powers and is annotated with the names of European 'discoverers'. The medical content consists of areas being labelled as 'healthy', 'unhealthy' or 'very unhealthy'. Ribeiro also published *Saneamento da Cidade de S.Thomé* (Sanitation in São Tomé City) (Lisbon: Typographia de Vicente da Silva, 1895).

186 **República Democrática de São Tomé e Príncipe: uma experiência no domínio de saúde.** (The Democratic Republic of São Tomé and Príncipe: an experience in the field of health.)
Bologna, Italy: Gruppo Volontariato Civile, 1985. 50p.
Reports on health care undertaken by a non-governmental organization.

187 **Resultados de um inquérito sobre o estado de saúde e de nutrição dos 'Angolares' da ilha de São Tomé.** (Results of a survey into the health and nutritional status of the 'Angolars' of the island of São Tomé.)
Jorge G. Janz, Luiz N. Garcia.   In: *Conferência Internacional dos Africanistas Ocidentais 6ª Sessão. Volume V.* [Lisbon]: Commission for Technical Co-operation in Africa South of the Sahara; Scientific Council for Africa South of the Sahara, 1956, p. 219-31.
A survey of the health and diet of the Angolars confirms the important role of bananas and fish in the islands' cuisine. Some recipes are included along with a summary in English.

188 **Seroprevalence of human parvovirus B19 infection in Sao Tomé and Principe, Malawi and Mascarene Islands.**
T. F. Schwarz, L. G. Gürtler, G. Zoulek, F. Deinhardt, M. Roggendorf. *Zentralblatt für Bakteriologie*, vol. 271, no. 2 (July 1989), p. 231-36. bibliog.
The B19 infection is associated with a wide range of diseases in humans. Antibodies to it were found in 51.5 per cent of a sample group from São Tomé and Príncipe. This indicates that it is slightly less prevalent than results show is the case in Malawi (58.4 per cent) and Mauritius (55 per cent).

189 **Sleeping sickness. A record of four years' war against it in the island of Principe.**
Bernardo F. Bruto da Costa, J. F. Sant'Anna, A. C. dos Santos, M. G. de Araujo Alvares, translated from the Portuguese by J. A. Wyllie.   London: Baillière, Tindall & Cox for the Centro Colonial, Lisbon, 1916. 261p. 6 maps.
Between 1911 and 1914 a medical mission was based on Príncipe to combat trypanosomiasis (sleeping sickness), which had been a serious problem for the previous twenty years. This is the mission's final report, divided into five parts. The first section fills in the background to the disease on the island: Trypansomes are the parasites which cause the disease, hosted in Príncipe by pigs and other animals. The tsetse fly (*Glossina palpalis palpalis*) is the vector which then transports the parasite

from the host to victim. The tsetse was probably first brought to the island with cattle imported in the 1820s, although the disease was not recorded until some years later. The authors attempt to calculate the financial cost of the high mortality rate amongst the plantation workers. The next section describes the sanitary measures enforced in 1911. Pigs, dogs and civet-cats were slaughtered as potential hosts of the trypansomes, and swamps were drained and undergrowth cleared to deprive the tsetse of its natural environment. Atoxyl was given to people stung by the fly. The costs and administrative problems of this campaign are presented and its success is demonstrated by the figures, included in the next section, for the number of tsetse caught and the mortality and infection rates amongst humans: both became negligible by 1914. The fourth section considers the methods for preventing a return of the disease and general improvements in public health - important given the high mortality rates for a predominantly adult population. The authors are not, however, critical of conditions on the plantations. The high level of malaria amongst Cape Verdean workers is noted, as is the unhealthy state of the indigenous population 'upon whom alcoholism, paludism and syphilis have placed their indelible mark'. The final section is a biological study of the trypansomes and hematophagous insects found on Príncipe. The 1915 regulations to prevent re-infestation are appended to the main text and two 1:50,000 maps show, respectively, the distribution of the fly and the areas where sanitary work has drained and filled swamps and felled forest. Four smaller-scale maps show the zones affected by the disease in 1909, 1911, 1913 and 1914. The volume includes a number of photographs of plantations, scenery and the work of the campaign. The report was published in Portugal in the *Archivos de Hygiene e Pathologia Exoticas*, vol. 5 (March 1915).

190 **Sleeping sickness in the island of Principe. Sanitation, statistics, hospital services and work of official conservancy brigade.**
Bernardo F. Bruto da Costa, translated from the Portuguese by J. A. Wyllie. London: Baillière, Tindall & Cox for the Centro Colonial, Lisbon, 1913. 90p.

Da Costa, a health official and chief of the Sleeping Sickness Commission sent to Príncipe, covers similar ground as *Sleeping sickness. A record of four years' war against it in the island of Principe* (q.v.). This volume contains some interesting insights into the administration of Príncipe, 'We have known the island ever since 1905, and still we fail to discover any but the most insignificant improvements effected by the Municipal Commissioners, unless it be the building of a town hall costing many thousand dollars, far too fine for a town whose streets are fringed with weeds, sweepings and filth, not even paved for the most part, and, last but not least, whose houses in the great majority of cases are not worthy the name' (p. 82-83). Da Costa explains how he had to bypass the council completely in order to rebuild the hospital. There had been no ward for women, but the male patients had been little better catered for, in an old cattle shed.

Plantas úteis da flora de S.Tomé e Príncipe - medicinais, industriais e ornamentais.
See item no. 53.

Sobre os vectores da malária em S.Tomé e Príncipe.
See item no. 86.

Women

191 **Anas de Chaves.** (Annas of Chaves.)
Manuel Braga da Cruz. *Boletim da Sociedade de Geografia de Lisboa*, (January-March 1964), p. 97-101.

A large number of São Tomense toponyms are named after women, and the name of Ana de Chaves is particularly frequent. This article suggests two women from the islands' history who might have inspired the naming of a mountain, a river and the bay around which São Tomé city is built. The first died in 1566, leaving evidence of grants to charities and religious institutions and the author indulges in romantic speculation on her relationship with King João III, either as mistress or illegitimate daughter. The second candidate lived in the mid-17th century and was married to Lourenço Pires de Távora, hero of the struggle against the Dutch occupation of São Tomé.

192 **Maria Corrêa: a princesa negra do Príncipe (1788-1861).** (Maria Corrêa: the black princess of Príncipe [1788-1861].)
José Brandão Pereira de Melo. Lisbon: Agência Geral das Colónias, Divisão de Publicações e Biblioteca, 1944. 22p. (Colecção pelo Império, no. 104).

Maria Correia Salema Ferreira was the wealthiest landowner on Príncipe. Her first husband, the Brazilian José Ferreira Gomes, introduced cocoa to the island in 1822. He was also a shipowner and can be assumed to have had dealings in the slave trade. Popular legend has it that Maria Corrêa diverted the British navy from apprehending cargoes of slaves by inviting the officers to lavish dinners and entertainments at her two palaces. After her husband's death, and feeding the legends which surround her, she married a man who, at thirty-three, was twenty-six years her junior. Her will is used to establish the extent of her wealth and fulfilment of religious and civic duties. See also *A narrative of the expedition sent by Her Majesty's government to the River Niger, in 1841*, (q.v.).

193 **Mary and misogyny. Women in Iberian expansion overseas, 1415-1815: some facts, fancies and personalities.**
Charles Ralph Boxer. London: Duckworth, 1975. 142p.

Within a wider picture of the position of women in the Portuguese overseas expansion, some vignettes from their history in São Tomé and Príncipe are assembled (p. 16-23). Boxer notes the small number of women of European origin on the islands and the relationships formed by European men with women of African origin throughout this period. Slave women were given to the early settlers by the Crown and powerful creole families were born from them. When a daughter of one of these families was carried off and forcibly married in 1545 the weakness of royal authority in the face of the creole elite and their armed slaves was demonstrated (for a full account of this incident see 'Rebelião e sociedade colonial: "alvoroços" e "levantamentos" em São Tomé [1545-1555]', [q.v.]). Women must have been toughened by this environment: in 1664 Captain Robert Holmes reported that an armed force of women had been formed to protect the islands from attack. Boxer also notes 16th-century complaints about prostitution, immorality and immodest dress in women. This book is published in the USA under the title *Women in Iberian expansion overseas, 1415-1815: some facts, fancies and personalities* (New York: Oxford University Press, 1975, 142p.).

194 **Notas sobre a posição moral e social da mulher na ilha de São Tomé.** (Notes on the moral and social position of women on the island of São Tomé.)
Martinho Pinto da Rocha. In: *Conferência Internacional dos Africanistas Ocidentais 6ª Sessão. Volume V.* [Lisbon]: Commission for Technical Co-operation in Africa South of the Sahara; Scientific Council for Africa South of the Sahara, 1956, p. 425-29.

Da Rocha, a priest, establishes a patronizing moral hierarchy for three groups of São Tomense women. The indigenous women are religious and take good care of their families; the Tongas (children of foreign-born plantation workers) have benefited from their contact with civilized people and aspire to be like the indigenous women; but the Angolars are slovenly, backward and superstitious. There is a summary in English.

Politics and
Government

Colonial government

195 **Estatuto político-administrativo da província de S.Tomé e
Príncipe.** (Political-administrative statute for the province of São
Tomé and Príncipe.)
Ministério do Ultramar. Lisbon: Agência-Geral do Ultramar, 1972.
45p.

This document sets out the regime which was to be in force from 1973 for São Tomé
and Príncipe, at that time an autonomous region within the Portuguese republic. The
three bodies of government are heavily dominated by the Governor, who is the
executive arm and representative of the Portuguese government. The Assembleia
Legislativa (Legislative Assembly) is largely a rubber-stamping instrument. It has
sixteen members, six elected by Portuguese citizens, two from the public
administration, three from business organizations, three from labour organizations
and two from moral and cultural interests (one of whom must be a Roman Catholic
clergyman). The Junta Consultiva Provincial (Provincial Consultative Council) is an
advisory body consisting of six elected members, one from the public administration,
one from moral and cultural bodies and two each from labour and business
organizations, plus three officials and members nominated by the governor. The
document also covers local government, administrative services and issues of finance,
credit and budget policy.

196   **Organização político-administrativa: os conselhos legislativos e os
       conselhos do governo.** (Political and administrative organization:
       legislative councils and government councils.)
       Armando M. Marques Guedes.   In: *Cabo Verde, Guiné, São Tomé e
       Príncipe: curso de extensão universitária, ano lectivo de 1965-1966.*
       Lisbon: Universidade Técnica de Lisboa, Instituto Superior de
       Ciências Sociais e Política Ultramarina, 1966, p. 617-48.

Administrative and constitutional legislation applicable to the colonies of Cape
Verde, Guinea-Bissau and São Tomé and Príncipe is set out for the period between
1811 and 1966. This publication also contains numerous other articles of relevance to
São Tomé and Príncipe (q.v.).

197   **Para um futuro melhor: discursos e mensagens no governo de
       S.Tomé e Príncipe 1963-1966.** (For a better future: speeches and
       communications in the government of São Tomé and Príncipe
       1963-1966.)
       António Jorge da Silva Sebastião, introduction by José Maria de
       Castro Salazar.   São Tomé: Câmara Municipal de S.Tomé, 1967.
       404p.

This is a wide-ranging collection of the governor's speeches, many of which
acknowledge some of the islands' political, economic, social and financial problems.

198   **Relatório do governo da província de S.Tomé e Príncipe
       respeitante aos anos de 1948 a 1951.** (Government report for the
       province of São Tomé and Príncipe for the years 1948 to 1951.)
       Carlos de Sousa Gorgulho.   São Tomé: Imprensa Nacional de
       S.Tomé, 1952. 389p. map.

Some of the 20th-century governors of the islands were reasonably conscientious in
publishing these annual reports: see also Gorgulho *Relatório do governador da
colónia de S.Tomé e Príncipe referente aos anos de 1946 a 1947* (Governor's report
for the colony of São Tomé and Príncipe for the years 1946 to 1947) (1948); Ricardo
Vaz Monteiro *Colónia de São Tomé e Príncipe: relatório do ano de 1936* (Colony of
São Tomé and Príncipe: report for the year 1936) (1937) and *Colónia de S.Tomé e
Príncipe: relatório anual do Governador Ricardo Vaz Monteiro, 1935* (Colony of São
Tomé and Príncipe: annual report of Governor Ricardo Vaz Monteiro, 1935) (1936).

Boletim Oficial.
See item no. 394.

1974-1991: MLSTP

199 **Boletim do Militante. Edição especial.** (The Militant's Bulletin.
Special edition.)
São Tomé: Comité Central do Movimento de Libertação de São Tomé
e Príncipe, 1985. 30p.

The first issue of a periodical aimed at being bi-monthly and intended to provide
information to the MLSTP activists. This special issue coincides with the tenth
anniversary celebrations of independence. The first item is entitled 'Circulo de
estudos - a mensagem presidencial de 12 de Julho no âmbito de programa de
actividades da segunda etapa do ano do décimo aniversário' (Study circle - the
presidential message of the 12th of July within the ambit of the programme of
activities for the second phase of the tenth anniversary), p. 6-22. It is a rather strange
document in which the text of the president's speech seems to have been intercut by
questions from a 'militant'. The purpose of this less than naturalistic script is to
stimulate understanding of the speech in MLSTP study circles. The speech is an
assessment of the past ten years' achievements and problems. The nationalizations are
defended, but nevertheless even here the country's economic problems cannot be
ignored. The second item is 'Contributo à reflexão sobre a política económica e social
de S. Tomé e Príncipe à luz do Conselho Nacional' (Contribution to reflections on the
economic and social policy of São Tomé and Príncipe in the view of the National
Committee), p. 23-30. Again, this is in question and answer format. It does not enter
into any great detail, but is of interest for the great symbolic importance attached to
the nationalization of the plantations.

200 **Discursos.** (Speeches.)
Manuel Pinto da Costa. São Tomé: Arquivo Histórico de S. Tomé e
Príncipe, Ministério da Informação e Cultura, 1978-79. 2 vols.

The first volume of this selection of speeches by the former president and leader of
the MLSTP contains sixteen speeches, radio broadcasts and interviews from August
1974 to December 1975. This period covers the move from the first post-colonial
transitional government to full independence in July 1975. The second volume
contains twenty speeches from February 1976, the twenty-third anniversary of the
Batepá Massacre, to December 1977. Many of the institutions of MLSTP rule were
being set up during this time - the army, youth movements, Organizacão das
Mulheres de São Tomé e Príncipe (Women's Organization of São Tomé and Príncipe)
- and the speeches reflect this. The close links with Angola are also mentioned. The
first volume contains a preface by Alda Espírito Santo. A further collection of the
president's speeches can be found in *Retrospectiva em análise política, económica e
social* (Retrospective with a political, economic and social analysis) (Luanda: Gráfica
Popular, 1983).

201 **Documentos do Comité Central do M.L.S.T.P. emanados da sessão
de Abril de 1988.** (Documents of the Central Committee of the
MLSTP from the April 1988 session.)
MLSTP. São Tomé: Empresa de Artes Gráficas, 1988. 56p.

These internal MLSTP reports make suggestions for significant changes in the party's
political and economic strategies. They propose increased democracy in political life

and a clearer distinction between the MLSTP and the political organs of the state. The implications of the International Monetary Fund and World Bank structural adjustment programmes are discussed and the withdrawal of the state from productive activity is proposed. A report is made on the invasion attempt of March 1988 by the Frente de Resistência Nacional Renovada (Front for Renewed National Resistance). The translation of the MLSTP proposals into government programme is effected in *Programa de governo 1988-1990* (Government programme 1988-1990) (São Tomé: Edição do Gabinete do Primeiro-Ministro, 1988, 55p.).

202 **Documentos orientadores para os círculos de estudo. (Baseados nos discursos do Camarada Presidente do M.L.S.T.P. Dr. Manuel Pinto da Costa).** (Guiding documents for the study circles. [Based on the speeches of the Comrade President of the MLSTP Dr. Manuel Pinto da Costa].)
MLSTP. São Tomé: Empresa de Artes Gráficas, 1986. 53p.

This publication is interesting as an illustration of the MLSTP's centralist style of government and party organization. The first document is the president's New Year message of 1986 (p. 4-11) which, according to its introduction, should be analysed 'for the proper understanding of the tasks which will have to be taken on and internalized by party militants at all levels, by workers in all fields of labour activity and by the population as a whole' (p. 4). The second document is derived from the Plano de Economia Nacional (National Economic Plan) and the Plano Perspectivo 1986-90 (Projected Plan), which sets out party policy in economic, political and social fields (p. 12-27). The final document is the president's account of government activity rendered to the National Assembly in April 1986 and introduced by the slogan 'Cumprir de maneira eficiente aquilo colectivamente aprovamos' (Carrying out in an efficient manner that which we have collectively approved). The document is edited in question and answer format. It includes some detail on economic performance, providing not only the percentage fulfilled in cocoa production quotas (61.7 per cent), but also in philately quotas (60.7 per cent).

203 **Interview: Manuel Pinto da Costa, President, the Democratic Republic of São Tomé and Príncipe.**
Tony Hodges. *Africa Report*, (January-February 1986), p. 57-60.

The interview begins with Pinto da Costa emphasizing the scale of the problems facing the country after independence. There were only four doctors who stayed, there were insufficient teachers and trained administrators, and no means of communication even between the two islands of São Tomé and Príncipe, 'The Portuguese did not leave us a single ship' (p. 58). And, of course, the islands were totally dependent on cocoa. The president feels that, given this start, the subsequent achievements in education, health care, transport and communications are praiseworthy. Clothing and ceramics factories and a brewery have been set up when previously there was no industry at all. There are plans ahead for palm oil, soap and rum factories. Nationalization was forced on the new government by circumstances, 'After independence, one could say that there were no native São Tomeans with the initiative, stimulus, or money to invest' (p. 58), but the private sector and joint ventures are being encouraged. The president's view of domestic politics is that the MLSTP is not a political party on Western lines, but a broad 'democratic front' in which all citizens regardless of their opinions should be able to participate. He denies that the opposition politicians Carlos da Graça and Miguel Trovoada are exiles, and says they are free to return. The president also discusses foreign relations with the Economic Community of Central African States, with the other four Portuguese-speaking African nations and with the United States of America. He denies that the islands were a Soviet military base and explains that Angolan troops were only invited to the islands in 1978 in order to protect the sovereignty of São Tomé and Príncipe after an attempted invasion. See also 'Sao Tomé and Principe: interview with President Manuel Pinto da Costa' (*The Courier*, no. 85 [May-June 1984], p. 35-39).

204 **Mozambique. São Tomé and Príncipe. Economics, politics and society.**
Jens Erik Torp, L. M. Denny, Donald I. Ray.   London, New York: Pinter Publishers, 1989. 204p. 2 maps. bibliog. (Marxist Regime Series).

Although the multi-party elections of 1991 have rendered this less of a handbook and more of a historical document, it is an interesting account of the workings of the MLSTP regime and an evaluation of its policies (p. 119-94). There is a fairly detailed history of the MLSTP from its inception in 1960 as the Comité de Libertação de S.Tomé e Príncipe (Committee for the Liberation of São Tomé and Príncipe). The authors describe the years of exile in various African countries, the independence negotiations and problems with the more radical sister organization on the islands, the Associação Cívica Pró-MLSTP (Civic Association for the MLSTP). The political system and developments since independence are fairly comprehensively covered, including the political trials and exiles, the party structure and its prominent members, and the concentration of power in President Manuel Pinto da Costa's hands - at one point in 1985 he was President of the MLSTP, President of the Republic, Minister of Defence and National Security, Minister of Foreign Affairs, Minister of Planning and Commander-in-Chief of the Armed Forces. The economic system and the influence of the International Monetary Fund and World Bank since 1985 on economic policy are considered, with education and cultural policy judged to have been more successful than economic policy. Foreign policy and relations with Portugal, France, Gabon, Angola, Cuba and what was the USSR are also covered. Denny and Ray's conclusion illustrates their reluctance to see the islands' slip out of the Marxist fold: economic pragmatism is compared to Lenin's New Economic Policy and 'to declare that the MLSTP has abandoned socialism would seem premature' (p. 192).

205 **Relação entre o M.L.S.T.P. e o estado.** (The relationship between the MLSTP and the state.)
[São Tomé]: [MLSTP], [n.d.] 10p.

This pamphlet, now of historical curiosity, and produced during the MLSTP's period of government, tries to elucidate the constitutional and practical relationship between the party and the state. The roles of the party, the party member and the administrative organs of the state are set out. It is clearly an area which is delicate and difficult to define, particularly given that the state is 'the main instrument through which the MLSTP carries out its objectives' (p. 3).

206 **Selecção de textos sobre S.Tomé e Príncipe (período
pós-independencia) 1975-1977.** (A selection of texts on São Tomé
and Príncipe [post-independence period] 1975-1977.)
Carlos Agostinho das Neves. São Tomé: Arquivo Histórico de
S.Tomé e Príncipe, 1978. 85p.

The preface states that this is the third volume in a series devoted to national history
and culture. Thirteen documents have been selected: the MLSTP's provisional
constitutional law, dated 12 July 1975, which covered the first months after the party
took power but before the constitution was finalized (p. 8-15); legislation, dated 27
August 1975, setting up the Fundo de Reconstrução Nacional (National
Reconstruction Fund) into which all workers were to contribute a sum equivalent to
one day's wages (p. 17-18); Miguel Trovoada's speech of admission to the United
Nations of 19 September 1975 (p. 19-20); the decree nationalizing the plantations on
30 September 1975 (p. 21-22); the constitution of 5 November 1975, with its
characteristic interweaving of party and state (p. 23-31); a speech made by Henrique
Costa on 30 September 1976 on the subject of the plantations, their nationalization
and the social and power structures which they had created (p. 33-36); the speech
made by the Minister of Foreign Affairs, Leonel Mário de Alva, at the United Nations
General Assembly in 1976 (p. 37-47) expressing the country's non-aligned and anti-
imperialist stance; a MLSTP document describing the work of local party committees
- they do not replace the administrative authorities, but complement the work of
government particularly in their role as information providers (p. 49-54); the final
report, dated 11 June 1977, of a national conference of political and technical cadres
(p. 55-61); the new local administrative structure, dated January 1977 (p. 63-66); the
final report of a national conference of the Organização das Mulheres de São Tomé e
Príncipe (Women's Organization of São Tomé and Príncipe) held on 18 and 19
September 1977 which seems to have been more concerned with the organization
itself than with any wider issues concerning the islands' women (p. 67-68); a patriotic
speech made by Miguel Trovoada on 8 September 1977, inspired by the launch of the
new national currency, the dobra (p. 69-73); finally, there is another speech by Leonel
Mário de Alva to the United Nations General Assembly, made in October 1977 (p.
75-85).

207 **Teses, programa e resoluções da 1ª Assembleia do MLSTP.**
(Theory, programme and resolutions from the First Congress of the
MLSTP.)
[São Tomé]: [MLSTP], [1978], 39p.

This pamphlet proclaims the party's slogan as 'Frente revolucionária de forças
democráticas anti-neocolonialistas anti-imperialistas' (Revolutionary front for anti-
neocolonial and anti-imperialist democratic forces) and something of these large aims
carries over into the three documents contained within it. The first, 'Teses para a
Assembleia' (p. 3-12) (Theory for the Congress) sets out the party line on such
subjects as socio-cultural alienation, the hindrance to an immediate socialist
revolution caused by the pre-existing socio-economic structure, and the non-capitalist
road to development. The next document, 'Programas do MLSTP' (MLSTP
programmes) (p.13-33) outlines the party's far-reaching aims. Finally, the
'Resoluções da 1ª Assembleia do MLSTP' (Resolutions of the First Congress of the
MLSTP) (p. 35-39) contains amongst its resolutions some very ambitious
recommendations, such as the elimination of illiteracy within one year. See also *2ª
Assembleia Ordinária do M. L. S. T. P.: relatório e resoluções* (The Second Ordinary

Assembly of the M L S T P : report and resolutions) (São Tomé: Empresa de Artes Gráficas, 1986. 55p.).

S.Tomé e Príncipe: do colonialismo à independência.
See item no. 138.

The political economy of micro-communism.
See item no. 227.

Multi-party elections and beyond

208 **Anteprojecto de constituição da República de São Tomé e Príncipe.** (Draft of the constitution of the Republic of São Tomé and Príncipe.)
Jorge Miranda. *Africana*, no. 7 (September 1990), p. 183-212.
The final text of the constitution which ushered in multi-party democracy differs little from this draft. It was approved by referendum in September 1990.

209 **Arquipélagos da alternância; a vitória da oposição nas ilhas de Cabo Verde e de São Tomé e Príncipe.** (Archipelagos of change: the victory of the opposition in the islands of Cape Verde and São Tomé and Príncipe.)
Michael Cahen. *Revista Internacional de Estudos Africanos*, nos. 14-15 (1991), p. 113-54.
The post-independence political and economic conditions experienced by the two countries are covered in some detail. Cahen points out that the defeat of the MLSTP in the 1991 multi-party elections was not a reaction against Marxism since the MLSTP was not a Marxist party. The party's nationalization of the plantations was not Marxist, but the product of a centralist, technocratic and bureaucratic style of government. Economic liberalization had been a long-standing process, with recourse made to the International Monetary Fund as early as 1977. The analysis of the political crisis is an interesting one: by 1985 the tiny São Tomense elite was so depleted by exile that reuniting it had become 'sociologically indispensable' (p. 134). Gestures towards liberalization were made with this end in mind. The party attempted to institutionalize three internal wings, Marxist, social-democratic and liberal. However, with a background of malnutrition, malaria and inflation, the regime showed itself incapable of uniting the elite and in 1989 initiated the process towards a new constitution and elections. The electoral results are analysed. Cahen denies that there was a vote for a change of policy or a new political culture. Many of the new Partido de Convergência Democrática (Party for Democratic Convergence) ministers had been MLSTP ministers between 1975 and 1985. It is perhaps not a good omen for future political stability that the electoral victors are simply the other half of a schism within the elite. Also published in French in *L'année africaine 1991* (Bordeaux, France: CEAN/CREPAO, 1992, p. 347-92, bibliog.) and in abridged form in *Politique Africaine*, no. 43, (October 1991), p. 63-78, under the title 'Vent des îles: la victoire

de l'opposition aux îles du Cap-Vert et à Sâo Tomé e Príncipe'. See also Gerhard Seibert 'Demokratische Transformation in São Tomé und Príncipe' (Democratic transformation in São Tomé and Príncipe) (*DASP-Hefte*, no. 29 [1991], p. 11-19). The democratic system has been discussed at two seminars held on São Tomé since the 1991 election. *A compreensão do processo democrático* (Understanding the democratic process) (São Tomé: Consultoria e Projectos, [1994]) contains papers delivered by Patrick Chabal, Armindo Fernandes, José Vicente Lopes and Aristides Salvaterra. The seminar was held between 25 November and 1 December 1992. *Seminário sobre separação de poderes e o papel dos parlamentos na consolidação da democracia* (Seminar on the separation of powers and the role of parliaments in the consolidation of democracy) ([São Tomé]: Consultoria e Projectos, 1994. 47p.) contains papers by Leonel Mário d'Alva, Ângelo Bonfim, Oscar Alexandre Silva Gomes, Paulo Jorge Espírito Santo and Roger Bennett da Cunha Lopes. The seminar was held in April 1994.

210 **Eleições e sistemas eleitorais - os casos de S.Tomé e Príncipe e de Cabo Verde.** (Elections and electoral systems - the case of São Tomé and Príncipe and Cape Verde.)
José de Matos Correia. *Politica Internacional*, vol. 1, no. 4 (Summer 1991), p. 115-33.

Both countries held multi-party elections in 1991, marking the first successful transition to democracy in sub-Saharan Africa. The first part of this article describes the São Tomense and Cape Verdean electoral legislation, systems and results. The second section makes a comparative analysis between the two. The factors leading to the democratic transition are similar: the influence of events in Eastern Europe and the USSR; a desire for change; the ruling party's lack of solutions to entrenched problems; the abuses of uninterrupted power; internal party disputes; and the parties' primary function to be agents of decolonization long since fulfilled. Neither country is ideologically or ethnically polarized, and opposing political parties proffer very similar policies. The small milieu probably contributes to a homogeneous social fabric. Relationships between the electoral system and the party system are closely examined: contrary to commonly-held electoral theory, proportional representation did not preclude the emergence of a two-party system rather than a fragmented multi-party system. Also, the party which received the most votes was not most rewarded: in both countries the second party (the former ruling party) benefited. The article concludes that social structure and political history are of more importance in determining electoral outcomes than the mechanics of an electoral system and is summarized in English. A report of the presidential election of 1991 can be found in Mark Gleeson 'New team in power' (*West Africa*, no. 284 [May 1991], p. 19).

211 **Guia político dos PALOP.** (Guide to the politics of the countries of Portuguese-speaking Africa.)
Fernando Marques da Costa, Natália Falé. Lisbon: Editorial Fragmentos; Fundação de Relações Internacionais, 1992. 209p. 5 maps.

This reference work is a by-product of a larger research project being carried out by the Fundação de Relações Internacionais (Foundation for International Relations) and the Instituto de Estudos para o Desenvolvimento (Institute for Development Studies) into the process of democratization in the five countries of Portuguese-speaking

Africa. The chapter on São Tomé and Príncipe (p.183-208) is a very useful source of information. The history and economy of the islands from 1960-91 is discussed first and this is followed by brief descriptions of current legislation on foreign investment, the constitution, elections, political parties, referenda and local elections. The history, structure and programmes of the four political parties extant at the time of publication - the Frente Democrata Cristã (Christian Democratic Front), MLSTP/Partido Social Democrata (MLSTP/Social Democratic Party), Partido da Convergência Democrática/Grupo de Reflexão (Party for Democratic Convergence/Think Tank) and Partido Democrática de São Tomé e Príncipe/Coligação Democrática de Oposição (Democratic Party of São Tomé and Príncipe/Opposition Democratic Coalition) - are also covered.

212 **Time for a change.**
Tikum Mbah Azonga. *West Africa*, no. 3,960 (16-22 August 1993), p. 1442-43.

News of political trends and MLSTP hopes of forming a coalition with the Partido da Convergência Democrática (Party for Democratic Convergence) are conveyed in this article.

Foreign relations

213 **Africa's new island republics and U.S. foreign policy.**
Laurie S. Wiseberg, Gary F. Nelson. *Africa Today*, vol. 24, no. 1 (January-March 1977), p. 6-30. map.

The Cold War is the backdrop for this study of US foreign policy towards the newly-independent island republics of Cape Verde, the Comoros Islands, São Tomé and Príncipe and the Seychelles. Both Cape Verde and São Tomé and Príncipe decided not to allow either Soviet or American foreign military bases. However, American policy towards Africa is perceived to have been hardening as Soviet imperialism is suspected at every turn.

214 **Die Kooperation der portugiesischsprachigen Staaten Afrikas.**
(Co-operation between the Portuguese-speaking African states.)
Jutta Merkes, Bernhard Wiemer. *DASP-Hefte*, no. 17 (1989), p. 7-23. bibliog.

Covers economic, political and cultural co-operation between the five Portuguese-speaking African nations, and their relations with Portugal. The impact of Portugal's adhesion to the European Community on her co-operation with Africa is discussed in *Portugal - países africanos - CEE: cooperação e integração. Workshop realizado no Centro de Estudos da Dependência* (Portugal - African countries - EEC: co-operation and integration. A workshop which took place at the Centre for Dependency Studies), edited by Eduardo Sousa Ferreira and Paula Fernandes dos Santos (Lisbon: Gradiva; CEDEP, 1985, 174p.).

215 **The perils of being a microstate: São Tomé and the Comoros Islands since independence.**
Malyn Newitt. In: *The political economy of small tropical islands: the importance of being small.* Edited by Helen M. Hintjens, Malyn Newitt. Exeter, England: University of Exeter Press, 1992, p. 76-92.
The island microstate as well as having dubious economic viability is also politically vulnerable. This most illuminating comparative study analyses the very different political fortunes of the Comoros Islands and São Tomé and Príncipe. Both countries became independent quite suddenly in 1975, just in time to face a world recession for which their heavy dependence on one or two export commodities made them singularly ill-prepared. Both suffer from a shortage of land for food crops, and for both independence has limited the opportunites for emigration, although in São Tomé and Príncipe this was only ever of importance to the elite families. Both are too small to generate a worthwhile internal market or investment funds and are isolated from international shipping. Post-independence political experience has been very different however. The Comoros Islands have suffered coups, invasions by mercenaries, and the predatory interests of France and South Africa. In contrast São Tomé and Príncipe appears politically stable. The two invasion threats posed no real danger. The first, in 1978, may have been nothing more than a rumour about mercenaries from Benin. The second, in 1988, was organized by Afonso dos Santos, a dissident. Forty-six exiles invaded in canoes and fishing boats and were rounded up within a day. The different experiences of the two countries seem to depend on the quality of their international relations. The Comoros Islands were isolated and friendless. São Tomé and Príncipe, despite until recently having poor regional relations with Gabon, Cameroon and Equatorial Guinea, has strong links with the other Portuguese-speaking African nations. These relationships pre-date independence, and have their origins in the Conferência das Organizações Nacionalistas das Colónias Portuguesas (Conference of Nationalist Organizations of Portuguese Colonies). CONCP instilled a degree of political discipline and may have helped prevent the kind of government corruption that developed in the Comoros Islands. Perhaps of greatest importance has been the relationship with Angola, who, for no apparent benefit to itself, for many years supplied the islands with a garrison of troops and a lifeline of cheap oil. This has not, however, solved chronic economic problems and São Tomé has had to balance the security provided by this relationship with the need to turn to the West for aid.

216 **Sao Tome et Principe ou le charme discret de l'occident.** (São Tomé and Príncipe or the discreet charm of the West.)
P. Decraene. *Afrique et l'Asie Modernes*, no. 157 (1988), p. 64-69.
Decraene looks at post-independence São Tomé and Príncipe's foreign relations, particularly with the West. The account begins with the murky events of March 1988 when a boat from Cameroon with South Africans aboard was intercepted, perhaps in the process of attempting a coup d'etat. The incident fuelled a climate of suspicion. In 1978 and 1979 West-leaning politicians were arrested, imprisoned or exiled, including the then Prime Minister Miguel Trovoada, as President Manuel Pinto da Costa concentrated power in his own hands. In the second half of the 1980s attitudes became more liberal and attempts were made to invite exiles back. Links to the Soviet bloc have been exaggerated, although aid did come from the USSR, Cuba and East Germany until 1987. The islands have close relations with Angola, who used to supply them with cheap oil and a garrison of soldiers. São Tomé is eager to turn to the West, and now receives aid from France, Japan, the United Nations and the European

Community amongst others. Gabon has been used as an intermediary in approaches to France. South Africa has invested in the airport, perhaps to reduce their dependence on the international airport on Sal in Cape Verde, and the hotel industry.

217 **São Tomé und Príncipe: Ausbruch aus der Isolation.** (São Tomé and Príncipe: escape from isolation.)
     Martin Schumer.   Bonn: Forschungsinstitut der Deutschen
     Gesellschaft für Auswärtige Politik, 1987. 78p. map. bibliog.
     (Arbeitspapiere zur Internationalen Politik, no. 45).
Looks at foreign relations and economic policy, with a summary of the discussion in English.

CEE, que cooperação: o caso dos países africanos de expressão oficial portuguesa.
See item no. 218.

Economy

General

218 **CEE, que cooperação: o caso dos países africanos de expressão oficial portuguesa.** (EEC, what co-operation: the case of the African countries whose official language is Portuguese.)
António Abecasis. *Economia e Socialismo*, no. 61, (April-June 1984), p. 93-130. bibliog.

São Tomé and Príncipe was a signatory to the Lomé Convention in 1978 and this article includes a section on relations between the islands and the European Community (p. 102-08). The projects financed by the EC are listed: these include palm oil cultivation, fisheries development, transport and hospital facilities. In 1983 EC states were granted important fishing licences, linked to aid as well as a payment of 20 ecu for every tonne caught. See Neil Crumbie 'Cooperation with the EEC' (*The Courier*, no. 136 [November-December 1992], p. 22-23) and 'EEC-Sao Tomé and Principe cooperation' (*The Courier*, no. 85 [May-June 1984], p. 48-51) for summaries of EEC aid and co-operation projects for São Tomé and Príncipe since 1976.

219 **Combating cocoa colonialism.**
Tony Hodges. *Africa Report* (January-February 1986), p. 61-66.

Gives the background to the islands' economic problems, and the policies adopted by the government. In 1985 sweeping economic reforms and liberalization measures were put into effect. Attempts at diversification away from dependency on cocoa are also described. In an earlier article Hodges assesses the economic challenges facing the new MLSTP government of the time 'Sao Tome starts the climb out of poverty' (*New African Development*, no. 127 [March 1978], p. 35-36).

220 **Comércio externo de São Tomé e Príncipe.** (External trade of São Tomé and Príncipe.)
Alfredo de Sousa.   Lisbon: Junta de Investigações do Ultramar, 1963. 83p. (Estudos de Ciências Políticas e Sociais, no. 63).
These trade figures are, unsurprisingly, largely concerned with cocoa exports.

221 **Development problems and prospects in Portuguese-speaking Africa.**
Jean Mayer.   *International Labour Review*, vol. 129, no. 4 (1990), p. 459-78. bibliog.
A short section on São Tomé and Príncipe (p. 472-74) follows a brief history and statistical review of the five Portuguese-speaking African nations. Mayer gives a succint review of the post-independence economy, from the nationalization of the plantations to the 1986-90 development plan. The plan's ambitions to privatize the plantations, promote small-scale industry, double cocoa production, become self-sufficient in food, develop the timber industry and improve transport are set against the many other problems the country is experiencing: 'pressure on the land and demographic growth (2.6 per cent a year) in the two islands - which, unlike Cape Verde, have no tradition of emigration - are flooding the capital city with young people of working age, and the number of potential jobseekers, male and female, is likely to rise from 45,000 to 100,000 within the next generation' (p. 473).

222 **L'evolution économique de Sao Tomé et Principe.** (The economic evolution of São Tomé and Príncipe.)
Septime Martin.   *Afrique Contemporaine*, no. 166 (1993), p. 45-51.
This article looks at the islands' economic situation between 1990 and 1992 with the aid of some useful statistics. The period is midway into the programme of structural adjustment agreed between the government and the World Bank in 1987. Although tax revenue has increased and public expenditure decreased, the current account is still in deficit. The interest paid on external debt accounts for this deficit. The weakness of the agricultural sector, with the gross domestic product continuing to fall, is another serious problem. Although the rate is decreasing, inflation is still high, due to the islands' dependence on imports coupled with the devaluation of the dobra and the deficit in the balance of trade has continued to increase. The stabilization measures are summarized, and although some of these have taken effect, the situation remains worrying. Martin, a technical advisor to the São Tomense Ministry of Finance, considers the islands' economic prospects and offers some advice.

223 **Investimento estrangeiro em São Tomé e Príncipe.** (Foreign investment in São Tomé and Príncipe.)
Miguel Teixeira de Abreu.   *Revista ELO*, vol. 3, no. 15 (April-June 1993), p. 52-53.
The 1992 law on investment is explained as it applies to foreign investors.

224 **Mesa redonda dos parceiros de desenvolvimento.** (Roundtable of development partners.)
São Tomé: Ministério da Cooperação, 1985.
This is the report from a conference of organizations involved in São Tomé and Príncipe's economic development and economic policy. A report of a more recent meeting can be found in *3ª confèrence de table ronde pour le République Démocratique de Sao Tome et Principe: programme d'ajustement structurel a moyen terme, 1992-1994: problème de l'endettement et scénarios pour la renégociation de la dette* (3rd round table conference for the Democratic Republic of São Tomé and Príncipe: structural adjustment programme for the medium term, 1992-1994: the debt problem and scenarios for debt renegotiation) (Geneva: PNUD, 1992, 138p.). See also *Conferência das organizações não governmentais: dossier de apoio* (Conference of non-governmental organizations: supporting document) (São Tomé: Ministério dos Negócios Estrangeiros e da Cooperação, 1986, 160p.).

225 **Orçamento geral do estado para o ano económico de 1992.**
(General national budget for the fiscal year of 1992.)
São Tomé: Ministério de Economia e Finanças, 1992. 320p.
Sets out the national budget, appropriations and expenditure.

226 **Pobreza absoluta e ajustamente estrutural na República de São Tomé e Príncipe.** (Absolute poverty and structural adjustment in the Republic of São Tomé and Príncipe.)
Manuel Ennes Ferreira. *Revista Crítica de Ciências Sociais*, no. 33 (October 1991), p.25-41. bibliog.
This interesting article begins with a survey of economic conditions, together with background facts and figures on population, education, housing, nutrition and employment. The economic problems of the 1980s are quite shocking: cocoa production at 3,957 tonnes in 1987 is a third of the 1973 figure; the world price has declined from US$3,492 per tonne in 1979 to a mere US$1,392 in 1989; the external debt in 1986 was 174 per cent of the gross domestic product. The government's 1987 structural adjustment programme is summarized and despite insufficient statistical resources, income distribution and poverty levels are quantified: agricultural workers and rural areas come off worst. Poverty is measured against the ability to satisfy the nutritional requirements of four diets. A diet rich in fish and meat is found to be beyond the means of 86 per cent of the population in 1988, especially when black market prices are taken into consideration. During the period 1978-88 this diet has been increasingly unattainable: however, two less rich diets have become more accessible. The impact of structural adjustment, Ferreira argues, will harm the least-favoured classes in the short and medium term. The devaluation of the dobra has caused inflation of 32 per cent in food prices and workers on plantations have struck in protest against unpaid salaries. The English summary concludes, 'The application of "adjustment with a human face" coupled with the establishment of democracy would contribute to the reduction of existing social inequalities'. Another version of this article appears under the title 'Pobreza absoluta e desigualdades sociais, ajustamento estrutural e democracia na R. D. São Tomé e Príncipe' (Absolute poverty and social inequalities, structural adjustment and democracy in the Democratic Republic of São Tomé and Príncipe) (*Revista Internacional de Estudos Africanos*, nos. 12-13 [1990], p. 137-66, bibliog.).

227   **The political economy of micro-communism.**
       Frederic L. Pryor.   *Communist Economies*, vol. 2, no. 2 (1990),
       p. 223-49.

A fascinating, if depressing, account of the economy during the MLSTP years
emerges from this comparative study of the economic policies of four Marxist micro-
states - Cape Verde, Grenada, the Seychelles and São Tomé and Príncipe.
Background political information reveals a certain degree of instability in the
government of São Tomé and Príncipe. Despite, in 1990, retaining the same president
since independence, the average term of a cabinet minister was only 2.7 years, and
there has always been intra-party conflict. Another potentially influential factor is the
initial situation at independence. São Tomé was unfortunate in witnessing the exodus
of around two thousand Portuguese and their skills at this time and the abandonment
of the plantations '"condemned" São Tomé to follow a Marxist path' (p. 229). Even
after nationalization, however, agriculture was neglected by the government, which
failed to provide sufficient investment or credit. This contributed to the 7 per cent
annual decline in agricultural exports between 1970 and 1986. Of all these countries
only São Tomé and Príncipe tried to circumvent international market forces, which
led to a black market in foreign currency and official prices for agricultural goods
being perhaps only a third of their free market value. External economic policy has
been similarly unfortunate with its international debt service to exports ratio of 69 per
cent the worst of all four countries. The aid São Tomé and Príncipe managed to
obtain has not, perhaps, been used wisely: it 'received $12 million [$127 per person]
to construct a Congress Palace to serve as an international conference centre for over
1,000 foreign visitors; unfortunately, the country only has 50 hotel rooms with
running water' (p. 241). Pryor concludes that 'São Tomé has had the worst of the East
and West' (p. 242). It failed to attract Western aid because of its public commitment
to Marxism-Leninism and low geostrategic value; failures of domestic economic
policy do not attract private lenders; its weak economy and insufficient enthusiasm
for Soviet foreign policy did not even attract aid from that quarter; and its
incompetence in administering aid projects does not attract the international lending
agencies. Comparisons with Cape Verde's success are inevitable. This original piece
of work is enhanced by the efforts made to find statistical data.

228   **Rapport annuel sur l'assistance au développement à Sao Tomé et
       Principe.** (Annual report on development aid to São Tomé and
       Príncipe.)
       São Tomé: United Nations Development Programme, Office of the
       Resident Representative in São Tomé and Príncipe, 1977- . annual.

This is an annual report on the United Nations Development Programme's activities
on the islands, presented largely in tabular form. Technical, financial and investment
assistance from other external sources, including non-governmental organizations, is
listed by sector.

229 **S.Tomé e Príncipe e o futuro da sua economia.** (São Tomé and Príncipe and the future of its economy.)
Eurico D. Baltazar. *Boletim Informativo Trimestral da Repartição Provincial dos Serviços de Economia de S.Tomé e Príncipe*, vol. 7, no. 31 (July-September 1970), p. 1-4.

Baltazar outlines some ideas for the islands' economic development. He expresses concern about the small landholdings, many of which are not properly cultivated and are not terribly productive. He is also worried about the labour surplus: in an ironic reversal of the centuries of labour moving westwards, he suggests that São Tomense should emigrate to Angola.

230 **Sad legacy, difficult future: the search for viability.**
The Courier, no. 85 (May-June 1984), p. 40-45. map.

At a time when the government was still following the path of a planned economy, several ministers discuss the 1982-85 development programme. The men and their portfolios are Agapito Mendes Dias (Minister for Planning), Tomé Dias da Costa (Minister for Agriculture and Livestock), José Fret Lau Chong (Minister for Industry and Construction, with responsibility for tourism), Aurelio do Espirito Santo (Minister for Fisheries) and Celestino Rocha da Costa (Minister for Trade).

231 **Sao Tome & Principe: an alternative to cocoa?**
The Courier, no. 136 (November-December 1992), p. 11-21. map.

The search for economic viability for São Tomé and Príncipe continues. Attempts have been made to rehabilitate the plantations and restore their productivity with funding from the World Bank, the Caisse Centrale de Coopération (Central Office for Co-operation) the African Development Bank and contracts with European firms. Diversification into food crops, fishery exploitation and palm oil is also being tried. Technical difficulties, however, have plagued the palm oil processing plant provided by EC aid. Tourism is the big hope and the experience of the Seychelles is much cited. The article includes two illuminating interviews by Amadou Traore with Prime Minister Norberto da Costa Alegre and MLSTP-PSD opposition leader Carlos Graça. Traore broaches the subject of the business interests of Christian Herringer - involved in the Bom Bom holiday complex and the former national airline - and the 'white elephant' development projects of the past. One of these projects was the scandal of the $100,000 prefabricated houses: Graça disarmingly quotes the advice given the MLSTP government by Manuel dos Santos, the Minister of the Economy for Guinea-Bissau, 'No problems. Officially, there is a price which is far more than the houses are worth, but you don't pay anything. You sign and a year later you tell the Italian government that you can't pay' (p. 20). The interviews also cover some of the political difficulties accompanying the new government.

232 **São Tomé e Príncipe: estruturas económicas e contabilidade nacional 1963/1969.** (São Tomé and Príncipe: economic structures and national accounting 1963/1969.)
Missão de Estudo do Rendimento Nacional do Ultramar.   Lisbon: [Junta de Investigações do Ultramar], 1973. 123p. 2 maps. bibliog.

The economic situation is described, the national accounts are set out, and monetary and financial statistics are provided.

233 **São Tomé e Príncipe 1975-1990: evolução da economia e das relações económicas com Portugal.** (São Tomé and Príncipe 1975-1990: developments in the economy and in economic relations with Portugal.)
Paulo Brito. In: *Portugal-PALOP: as relações económicas e financeiras.* Edited by Adelino Torres, preface by Jorge E. Costa Oliveira. Lisbon: Escher, 1991, p. 173-213, map. bibliog. (Colecção Estudos sobre África, no. 2).

Well-supported by statistical data, this is a very clear account from a macroeconomic perspective of the post-independence economy. It is described as being a small open-economy characterized by a dualism between the cash crop sector and the internal supply sector which closely corresponds to the division between rural and urban zones. Brito describes the changes in all aspects of economic policy over this fifteen year period. Development strategy had been based on increasing export production, but entered into crisis in the 1980s with the fall in world cocoa prices, compounded by the plantations being within the public sector. Structural adjustment and some privatization followed. There is a detailed analysis of the balance of payments, which, as Brito notes, is highly irregular from one four-year period to the next. Holland, East Germany and West Germany have all been more important destinations for exports than Portugal. Major suppliers of imports have been Portugal, East Germany, the European Community and Angola. Also covered are sources of aid, amongst whom France stands out, and information on external debt and its servicing. The bilateral relationship with Portugal is examined in some detail, encompassing trade and technical co-operation. The conclusion states that the price of cocoa affects everything, that the internal sector is in need of investment, manufacturing is stagnant and external debt is a problem. Unemployment and inflation are the signs of disequilibrium which are being revealed by the new policy of liberalization. The solution to these problems lies in increased diversification and efficiency which are not necessarily achievable by macroeconomic policy. Portugal could assist by granting credit on favourable terms, and relations between the two countries will almost certainly benefit by the withdrawal of economic relations between São Tomé and Príncipe and the countries of Eastern Europe.

234 **Towards an alternative development policy for São Tomé and Príncipe.**
Henrique Pinto da Costa. In: *The political economy of small tropical islands: the importance of being small.* Edited by Helen M. Hintjens, Malyn Newitt. Exeter: University of Exeter Press, 1992, p. 112-22.

The economic and social problems caused by the islands' reliance on their cocoa plantations are described along with the MLSTP government's attempts to cope with these problems: structural adjustment and privatization have been the main instruments of economic policy. The plantations, however, seem to operate under their own dynamic regardless of ownership. The government has tried to stimulate citizen participation through a policy of *envolvimento* (involvement), but there are powerful social factors impeding *envolvimento*, not least of which is the passivity engendered by life as a landless plantation labourer. Possibilities for regional and international co-operation are considered, external support being seen as the key to São Tomé and Príncipe's economic survival.

Interview: Manuel Pinto da Costa, President, the Democratic Republic
of São Tomé and Príncipe.
See item no. 203.

Mozambique. São Tomé and Príncipe. Economics, politics and society.
See item no. 204.

Die Kooperation der portugiesischsprachigen Staaten Afrikas.
See item no. 214.

History

235 **O comércio externo de S.Tomé no século XVII.** (São Tomé's
foreign trade in the 17th century.)
Fernando Castelo Branco. *Stvdia,* no. 24 (August 1968), p. 73-98.

The view that the islands were in economic stagnation after the decline of their sugar
industry is countered by the suggestion that there were other, less-documented,
sources of economic activity. Using some interesting documents besides those of
Portuguese origin, Castelo Branco finds that sugar continued to be of importance, as
were slaves, soap made from palm oil and cotton. The islands were not, however,
much used as a port of call for shipping in need of supplies as the winds were not
favourable.

236 **Descrição das moedas de Angola e S.Tomé e Príncipe.** (Description
of the coins of Angola and São Tomé and Príncipe.)
Luís Pinto Garcia. *Nvmmvs: Boletim da Sociedade de Portuguesa de
Numismática,* vol. 7, no. 3 (January 1965), p. 179-215. bibliog.

The islands did not have their own coinage until 1813. These are listed here with
substantial annotations. Garcia makes a number of critical references to an earlier
work by Kurt Prober, 'Moedas de cobre para "S. Tomé e Príncipe"' (Copper coins for
'São Tomé and Príncipe') (*Nvmmvs,* no. 5 [1954], p. 21-28). Prober then continues
the dispute with some astonishingly angry correspondence, published under the same
title as Garcia's article (*Nvmmvs,* vol. 8, no. 3 [December 1966], p. 167-78). See also
St. Thomas and Prince islands: numismatic analysis of a developing political system
by Ora W. Eads (Nashville, Tennessee: Practical Behavioral Studies Institute, 1974,
71p., bibliog.). Coins available for sale are frequently listed in *Moeda: Revista
Portuguesa de Numismática e Medalhística* (Coin: Portuguese Numismatic and
Medallic Review) (Lisbon: Publinummus, 1975- . quarterly).

237 **A ilha de S.Thomé. A questão bancaria no ultramar e o nosso problema colonial.** (The island of São Tomé. The question of banking in the overseas territories and our colonial problem.)
A. Francisco Nogueira, preface by J. P. Oliveira Martins.   Lisbon: Typographia do Jornal *As Colonias Portuguezas*, 1893. 191p. 3 maps.

The first chapters offer a general geographical description of the island, moving on to discuss labour issues and agricultural activity. Nogueira looks beyond cocoa and coffee to other tropical products such as quinine, sugar, vanilla, rubber, annatto dye, palm oil, timber and livestock. He alludes to areas requiring public intervention: roads, plantation boundaries, rural police, administrative reform and, of course, labour. A substantial part of the book is devoted to commerce, finances, the colonial economy and banking. In this last area the role of the Banco Nacional Ultramarino is of great importance. Nogueira concludes with some thoughts on the agricultural future of the islands. On similar themes see Nogueira 'A ilha de São Thomé, sob o ponto de vista da sua exploração agrícola' (The island of São Tomé from the point of view of its agricultural exploitation) (*Boletim da Sociedade de Geographia de Lisboa*, 5th series, no. 7 [1885]).

238 **As nossas colonias.** (Our colonies.)
Gomes dos Santos.   Lisbon: Empreza do *Portugal em Africa*, 1903. 201p.

The chapter on São Tomé and Príncipe (p. 97-129) focuses mainly on labour, agriculture and trade, and contains some statistics. It is principally of interest because of the long-lost optimism it expresses, being written at the height of the islands' cocoa prosperity.

239 **Le rôle du capital bancaire dans les colonies portugaises de l'Angola et de St.Thomé de 1864 au début du XXe siècle.** (The role of bank capital in the Portuguese colonies of Angola and São Tomé and Príncipe from 1864 to the beginning of the 20th century.)
Adelino Torres.   *African Economic History*, no. 12 (1983), p. 227-40.

The Banco Nacional Ultramarino, founded in 1864, played a powerful role in the Portuguese colonies. It was responsible for monetary circulation and, except in Macau, had a monopoly of banking operations. Torres sets out the regulations governing the bank and identifies its shareholders in Portugal. He then goes on to describe the bank's activities in Angola and São Tomé and Príncipe. It rapidly began to acquire land from defaulting creditors, including the Água Izé plantation on São Tomé and was heavily criticized by the other agricultural interests - who could hardly compete with this powerful institution - for failing to provide credit with which to develop the colonies. Other extra-banking activities in which the bank was involved were transport, commercial intermediation, and the supply of labour to the islands' cocoa plantations. The Banco Nacional Ultramarino exported capital from the colonies and served the interests of the Lisbon mercantile bourgeoisie, concludes Torres, and 'was an obstacle and one of the causes of the backwardness of Portuguese colonization' (p. 238).

240   **The third Portuguese empire 1825-1975: a study in economic imperialism.**
Gervase Clarence-Smith.   Manchester, England: Manchester University Press, 1985. 246p. 8 maps. bibliog.

Clarence-Smith has produced an economic history of the last 150 years of the Portuguese empire, in which São Tomé's cocoa boom based on forced labour from Angola seems to have been a rare incident of prosperity. From the involvement of São Tomé and Príncipe's creole elite in the slave trade, through the rise of the planter class and forced plantation labour, to the effects of Salazar's fiscal probity and colonial policy, the islands' recent economic history can be seen within the broader context of events in Brazil, Portugal, Angola and the rest of the Portuguese colonies. See also R. J. Hammond *Portugal and Africa 1815-1910: a study in uneconomic imperialism* (Stanford, California: Stanford University Press, 1966. 384p. 7 maps), in which the labour issue in São Tomé and Príncipe is covered specifically (p. 313-24).

Agriculture

General

241 **L'agriculture à San Thomé.** (Agriculture in São Tomé.)
António Lôbo de Almada Negreiros. *La Science pour Tous*, no. 10
(1901), p. 201-16.
An illustrated description of plantation agriculture and life at the turn of the 19th
century.

242 **The ecology of swidden agriculture and agrarian history in São
Tomé.**
Pablo B. Eyzaguirre. *Cahiers d'Études Africaines*, vol. 26,
nos. 101-02 (1986), p. 113-29. 3 maps. bibliog.
Swidden agriculture is the shifting cultivation of forest zones. Once an area is cleared
and burnt it is planted with a variety of crops for around three years, after which time
fruit trees may be planted, but otherwise secondary forest is allowed to regenerate.
Unlike the shifting agriculture of traditional subsistence economies in Amazonian
communities, in Africa shifting agriculture is associated with cash crops and
squatting. In São Tomé it is the fastest growing sector within the food-producing
economy. The fortunes of the plantations have exerted a considerable influence on
the development of this type of agriculture. Their rise deprived the indigenous
population of land to cultivate, but their fall has left land unused and an economy
deprived of hard currency with which to import food for its growing population.
Swiddens in São Tomé are associated with mountainous areas where uncultivated
land is abundant. Although these swiddens are only 3 per cent of the total area
cultivated, they are an extremely important supplier of vegetables and tubers sold on
the urban market, and represent 40 per cent of the land used for growing annual food
crops. This study also looks at the social and cultural aspects of swiddens. Sixty
farmers were surveyed: coming from a variety of social and ethnic backgrounds, all
had previously been salaried employees. Of those who began farming before

independence 59 per cent were Tongas (children of foreign contracted plantation labourers), 24 per cent Cape Verdeans and 17 per cent indigenous São Tomense; after independence 17 per cent were Tongas, 35 per cent Cape Verdeans and 48 per cent São Tomense. The men control the crops produced in the first two years, which are generally destined for sale: the crops of the later years of cultivation tend to be controlled by women and destined for family consumption. There seems to have been no serious environmental degradation caused by the temporary forest clearing: ten fallow years is sufficient for regeneration to take place, and in remoter areas land may be left for considerably longer. It is only on land closer to houses and roads that soil fertility has declined due to more continuous cultivation. Eyzaguirre concludes that 'swidden agriculture represents commercial entrepreneurship in an agrarian economy where land use is constrained by social and political factors' (p. 125).

243 **A ilha de S.Thomé e a Roça Água-Izé.** (The island of São Tomé and the Água-Izé plantation.)
Conde de Sousa e Faro. Lisbon: Typographia do Annuario Commercial, 1908. 194p. map.

At the time of publication the plantations were at their zenith of modernity and profitability. Since 1895 the count had been the administrator of one of the most celebrated of the plantations, the Roça Água-Izé, and this volume is in some respects a report to the Companhia da Ilha do Principe which had taken over ownership from the Banco Nacional Ultramarino in 1898. The first chapters cover the island's physical geography, climate, transport network, population and labour situation. The final chapter consists of a detailed inventory of Roça Água-Izé, enumerating staff, machinery, buildings, infrastructure and cocoa production. The plantation covered eighty square kilometres and employed fifty Europeans and 2,500 labourers. A number of photographs are included.

244 **The independence of São Tomé e Príncipe and agrarian reform.**
Pablo B. Eyzaguirre. *Journal of Modern African Studies*, vol. 27, no. 4 (1989), p. 671-78.

In this article the agrarian problem is examined from social, political and economic perspectives. The cocoa plantations have always been a cause of social division in São Tomé and Príncipe. The arrival of the European planters in the middle of the 19th century ousted the indigenous São Tomense elite from their leading role in island society. However, the São Tomense were determined to maintain a distinction between themselves and the imported African plantation workers and their refusal to work on plantations effectively prevented any reform of what was already an inefficient method of production. The plantations were a focus of resistance to colonial government, but the indigenous São Tomense and the plantation workers were separate even in this: the former resisted any attempts to conscript them for agricultural work while the latter struck against working conditions. Reform of the plantations was central to the MLSTP's programme. Despite nationalization after independence little changed, with 'fundamental differences between the immediate goals of the labourers on the estates and the foreign exchange needs of the country' (p. 675). The São Tomense took administrative jobs - by 1982 only 60 per cent of plantation employees actually worked on the plantations - but the workers remained Cape Verdeans or the children of Angolan and Mozambican contract labourers. The social distinctions were as clear as ever. In 1986 foreign capital was invited back, but it is 'doubtful if further investment in plantation agriculture can solve the socio-economic problems that the system itself has caused' (p. 678). The plantation, Eyzaguirre suggests, is an outdated concept and cocoa can be grown more efficiently by smallholders.

245 **Mudança na paisagem das ilhas de S.Tomé e Príncipe.** (Changes in the landscape of the islands of São Tomé and Príncipe.)
Ezequiel de Campos. *Garcia de Orta*, vol. 6, no. 2 (1958), p. 263-82. 2 maps.

The history of cultivation on the islands is described in this paper, from the first crop, sugar cane, to the 19th century plantations of cocoa and coffee. The effects on the environment are also described: cutting down the primary forest led not only to a decline in humidity, but also to soil erosion. The consequence of this was a decline in soil fertility, followed in turn by a decline in cocoa production. De Campos suggests some practical measures for agricultural renewal. His article includes tables giving figures for the islands' agricultural production. On a similar theme and by the same author is 'Perturbação do meio ecológico das ilhas de São Tomé e Príncipe' (Disturbance of the environment in the islands of São Tomé and Príncipe) (in: *Conferência Internacional dos Africanistas Ocidentais, 6ª Sessão. Volume II.* [Lisbon]: Commission for Technical Co-operation in Africa South of the Sahara; Scientific Council for Africa South of the Sahara, 1956, p. 47-54) and 'A ilha de S.Tomé antiga e actual' (The island of São Tomé past and present) (*Estudos Ultramarinos*, vol. 5 [1955], p. 199-231).

246 **O presente e o futuro da agricultura de São Tomé e do Príncipe: persistir ou desistir, eis a questão!** (The present and future of agriculture in São Tomé and Príncipe: persist or desist, that is the question!)
Carlos Rebello Marques de Almeida. In: *Cabo Verde, Guiné, São Tomé e Príncipe: curso de extensão universitária, ano lectivo de 1965-1966.* Lisbon: Universidade Técnica de Lisboa, Instituto Superior de Ciências Sociais e Política Ultramarina, 1966, p. 1007-36.

A history of the islands' agriculture is followed by a description of the problems which have arisen in the 20th century. The cocoa trees are ageing, the infestation by *Selenothrips rubrocintus* was devastating, and production has been steadily declining. There are major problems at the international level as well. The island has some powerful competitors and the price of cocoa is highly volatile. Even in the 1960s the need to diversify was apparent. Numerous other topics of relevance to São Tomé and Príncipe are also treated in this publication (q.v.).

247 **A Roça Rio do Ouro: uma empresa agrícola nacionalizada em S.Tomé e Príncipe.** (The Rio do Ouro plantation: a nationalized agricultural enterprise in São Tomé and Príncipe.)
Lisbon: Centro de Informação e Documentação Amílcar Cabral, [1979]. 34p. (Cadernos CIDAC, no.3).

Almost all the plantations were nationalized between 1975 and 1978. This is the report of a 1978 study mission to the Roça Rio do Ouro, formerly owned by the Sociedade Agrícola Valle Flor, to see the effects of nationalization on labour relations and everyday life. The plantation layout, crops and technical aspects of production are described and the authors' convey their shock at finding a vast urban centre in the midst of the tropical vegetation, dominated by a palatial 600-bed hospital. Cocoa is the main crop, although coconut, palm oil, coffee and foodstuffs are also grown. It is the only plantation to have electrical drying equipment, run on hydro-electric power. In its heyday there were three thousand workers on the plantation, but this had fallen to nine hundred by 1974 and areas were slipping out of cultivation. In 1978 numbers had risen again to 1,400: 450 Cape Verdeans, 2 Angolans, 4 Mozambicans and the rest from São Tomé. This number of indigenous workers would formerly have been unusual. Wages, work duties and living conditions are detailed and the poor state of housing is noted. The social organization of plantation life is also addressed. The old union, the Sindicato Nacional dos Empregados do Comércio, Indústria e Agricultura (National Union of Commercial, Industrial and Agricultural Workers) still existed at the time of the study, although unionism was not strong. Every plantation had a branch of the MLSTP, and usually had its own militia which was supervised by the Ministry of Defence. Finally the plantation management structure and its relationship with the Ministry of Agriculture and Agrarian Reform and the centrally-planned quota system are examined. The lack of clear management direction is criticized.

248   **S.Tomé e Príncipe: um caso de concentração.** (São Tomé and Príncipe: an example of concentration.)
Alfredo de Sousa.   Lisbon: Instituto Superior de Ciências Sociais e Política Ultramarina, 1963. 21p.

More than a decade before the post-independence government's nationalization programme, the problem of land ownership was already recognized. This study shows the pattern of ownership, the crops grown and the percentage of land cultivated. The figures show the domination of the European-owned plantations: eleven plantations owned 64 per cent of the land and twenty-three plantations owned 85 per cent of the land. The larger the plantation the smaller the proportion of land which is cultivated. De Sousa believes that improvement in agricultural performance is probably dependent on reform of the agrarian structure. This work was also published in *Estudos Políticos e Sociais*, vol. 1, no. 2 (1963), p. 319-36.

249   **São Tomé e Príncipe: isolation extracts a heavy toll.**
John Ladhams.   *African Business*, no. 140 (April 1990), p. 10-13.

Ladhams presents a brief survey of the cocoa sector and a summary of some of the particular problems which it faces. The high quality of the cocoa was not reflected in the price received, since the majority of exports went to East Germany at below world prices as part of an aid-exchange agreement. Production has fallen since independence, partly through a lack of management skills, partly through a lack of foreign exchange to purchase such things as machinery, fertilizers and pesticides. Finally, the plantation system has not been adapted for modern production. This article is illustrated by excellent colour photographs of island landscapes and plantation life.

250 **São Tomé e Príncipe, sob o ponto de vista agrícola.** (São Tomé and
Príncipe, from an agricultural perspective.)
F. M. de Carvalho Rodrigues, preface by Leopoldo Carlos Carvalho do
Vale. Lisbon: Junta de Investigações Científicas do Ultramar, 1974.
174p. 12 maps. bibliog. (Estudos, Ensaios e Documentos, nos. 130,
130-A).

This is a wide-ranging survey of the islands' agriculture which has its origins in a
project to map rural property. Each island is treated individually. A background on
climate and soil is followed by notes on the principal agricultural products - cocoa,
coffee, coconut, palm oil and bananas. Also included are a short essay on the recent
agricultural history of São Tomé and some statistics derived from the mapping
procedure. Three of the maps are separately bound: there is a 1:25,000 map of
Príncipe and two 1:50,000 sheets for São Tomé. These maps are coloured to show
land use and crops.

251 **Subsídios para um trabalho de promoção sócio-economica em
S.Tomé. Avaliação de recursos naturais e extensão rural.**
(Contributions towards work on socio-economic promotion in São
Tomé. Evaluation of natural resources and rural extension.)
Daniel dos Santos Nunes. São Tomé: [Imprensa Nacional], 1975.
240p.

Nunes assesses the islands' natural and human resources, as well as the possibilities
for rural extension. The plantation sector has a culture of paternalism which the rural
extension philosophy opposes: however, the small-scale agricultural sector is
conducted in a highly individualistic and independent manner, which makes it
difficult to set up any kind of co-operative association. Agriculture of both sectors is
described, as is its role in the national economy. A low level of mechanization and
technical development is found. Small-scale agriculture is seen as inefficient and to
yield low income: fruit trees dominate and 'the selection of plants is the work of
Nature'. Forestry and threats to the forest are also covered and relevant social issues,
such as demography, rural-urban migration, agricultural education and training,
nutrition and diet, health, standard of living and housing are discussed. The
conclusions to this study take the form of a formidable list of the problems facing
agriculture and the rural population.

**A ilha de S.Thomé. A questão bancaria no ultramar e o nosso problema
colonial.**
See item no. 237.

Technical

252   **Aspectos da defesa fitossanitária do cacau armazenado em
S.Tomé.** (Aspects of the protection against fungi for cocoa
warehoused in São Tomé.)
Maria Antonieta de Freitas Barbosa, A. J. Soares de Gouveia, Maria
Elmina Soares de Gouveia, Maria Hermínia Lima, Maria José Sousa
Lobo, C. M. L. Baeta Neves, M. E. da Silva e Sousa.   *Garcia de
Orta*, vol. 16, no. 3 (1968), p. 309-66; vol. 18, nos. 1-4 (1970),
p. 131-213; vol. 19, nos. 1-4 (1971), p. 107-205. 2 maps. bibliog.

The humidity and temperature of cocoa warehouses are studied in some detail.
Recommendations for the storage, drying and fumigation of cocoa are made in an
attempt to reduce the threat of damage by fungi. Summaries in English are included.

253   **The biological problems of cacao in S.Tomé e Príncipe.**
Carl T. Schmidt.   *Garcia de Orta*, vol. 15, no. 4 (1967), p. 495-500.

Some of the underlying problems of cocoa production in São Tomé and Príncipe are
outlined in the introduction to this article. In the 1920s shade trees were removed
from the plantations which improved conditions for the insect pest *Selenothrips
rubrocinctus* Giard., standards of planting and tree quality declined and the random
planting of other crops increased the difficulty of insect control. Many of the islands'
trees at the time of writing seemed hardly worth protecting: the average crop yield
was 500kg per hectare, half the yield achieved elsewhere in the world. Schmidt goes
on to describe seven insect pests, the damage they cause and possible methods of
control. The introduction of predators might be particularly successful on small
islands. Rats are the other animal pest. See also *Entomofauna de S.Tomé: insectos do
cacaueiro* (q.v.).

254   **Contribution for the study of root system development in coffee
tree and cacao tree in some soils in São Tomé.**
J. B. Vieira da Silva.   *Garcia de Orta*, vol. 8, no. 3 (1960), p. 703-35.
bibliog.

Root systems were found in general to be evenly, if sparsely, developed throughout
the soil profile. Problems encountered with the trees could generally be ascribed to
poor planting techniques.

255   **As cultivares de bananeira de São Tomé.** (The banana cultivars of
São Tomé.)
J. Crespo Ascenso.   *Garcia de Orta*, vol. 12, no. 2 (1964). bibliog.

Bananas are grown on São Tomé for the local market only. This article, with a
summary in English, looks at ways in which they might become an export crop and at
their potential export markets. The work of the Potó agricultural research station on
São Tomé is also described. Potó has identified twenty-six different varieties of
banana found on the island, and has imported samples of other types to test their
performance. Fungal diseases are another important area of research.

256 **Dotações, épocas e frequência da rega em S. Tomé.** (Quantities, seasons and frequency of irrigation in São Tomé.)
Domingos B. Mariano. *Garcia de Orta*, vol. 15, no. 1 (1967), p. 25-40. bibliog.

Provides tables of values to indicate the frequency and quantity of irrigation needed at different times of the year and in different regions of the island in order to gain the maximum fertility from the soil. There is a summary in English.

257 **Esboço da carta de aptidão agrícola de São Tomé e Príncipe.**
(Outline from the agricultural suitability map of São Tomé and Príncipe.)
Helder Lains e Silva. *Garcia de Orta*, vol. 6, no. 1 (1958), p. 61-86. 4 maps. bibliog.

This is a study of the suitability of different regions of the islands for different tropical crops. Climate, soil (the contribution of José Carvalho Cardoso) and vegetation are described. Three maps with a scale of 1:300,000 illustrate rainfall, soil and vegetation and a 1:100,000 scale map is coloured to show where different crops could be grown; shading marks the areas where cocoa requires different water management strategies. A briefer version of this article, restricted to the treatment of cocoa, is 'Esboço da carta de aptidão cacauícola de São Tomé e Príncipe' (Outline from the cocoa suitability map for São Tomé and Príncipe) (*Garcia de Orta*, vol. 8, no. 1 [1960], p. 201-07. 5 maps.). Both articles provide summaries in English.

258 **Um estudo comparativo de resistência à secura em cacaueiros.**
(A comparative study of resistance to drought in cacao trees.)
Maria Antonieta Nunes. *Garcia de Orta*, vol. 15, no. 13 (1967), p. 361-66. bibliog.

Three types of cacao from São Tomé were tested for their resistance to water shortage. The type known locally as *amelonado vermelho* proved most resistant. The article is summarized in English.

259 **A evolução das produções de cacau nas ilhas de São Tomé e Príncipe: estudo comparativo com outras regiões produtoras do globo.** (Development of cocoa production in the islands of São Tomé and Príncipe: comparative study with other producing regions of the world.)
Carlos R. Marques de Almeida, António de Matos Morais. In: *Conferência Internacional dos Africanistas Ocidentais 6ª Sessão. Volume III.* [Lisbon]: Commission for Technical Co-operation in Africa South of the Sahara; Scientific Council for Africa South of the Sahara, 1956, p. 25-32. bibliog.

The decline of cocoa production is considered in this paper and some suggestions are made for the rehabilitation of the plantations. This volume contains four other papers by the same authors on aspects of cocoa cultivation in São Tomé and Príncipe.

260 **Manual da cultura de cacau.** (Manual for cacao cultivation.)
Agostinho Dória. [São Tomé]: The Author, 32p. bibliog.
This is a simple guide to the techniques of cacao cultivation. Its bibliography includes references to technical publications of the Ministry of Agriculture and Livestock.

261 **Notas fitopatológicas.** (Phytopathological notes.)
Maria de Lourdes Borges, Maud L. de Barros. *Garcia de Orta*,
vol. 15, no. 1 (1967), p. 61-68; vol. 15, no. 3 (1967), p. 323-28.
bibliogs.
The first of these two articles describes four of the banana-leaf fungi which can be found on the islands' banana trees and the symptoms which they cause. The second article records the first appearance of two coffee-leaf fungi and the symptoms caused. Borges discusses some of the work carried out on the islands in this field in *Nota prévia sobre a actuação, em São Tomé, do grupo de trabalho de fitopatologia da Missão de Estudos Agronómicos do Ultramar* (Note on the operations, in São Tomé, of the phytopathology working group of the Overseas Agronomic Studies Mission) (Lisbon: Missão de Estudos Agronómicos do Ultramar, 1963, 32p.).

262 **Outlines of the cacao selection and breeding programme in San Thome.**
J. Crespo Ascenso. *Economic Botany*, vol. 18, no. 2 (April-June 1964), p. 132-36. bibliog.
A history of the crop on São Tomé is followed by an account of the contemporary situation. Ascenso deals with the types of cacao grown, levels of yield, and incidence of pests and disease. In 1960 a project was undertaken to consider ways of halting the decline in production which had been affecting the industry for much of the 20th century. A cacao breeding programme was made a priority: yield was a primary aim and resistance to the fungus *Phytophthora palmivora* secondary. The programme's methods of selection and breeding are described. A longer version of this article is 'Selecção e melhoramento do cacaueiro em S.Tomé e Príncipe' (Selection and improvement of cacao trees in São Tomé and Príncipe) (*Garcia de Orta*, vol. 13, no.2 [1965], p. 305-16. bibliog.).

263 **Potencialidade bananícola da ilha de S. Tomé.** (The island of São Tomé's potential for banana cultivation.)
Domingos B. Mariano. *Garcia de Orta*, vol. 14, no. 4 (1966),
p. 579-88. bibliog.
Several factors which affect the potential for banana cultivation, such as temperature, rainfall, soil and the prevalence of disease, are used to delineate regions within the island. It was found that the northeast was the most suitable region for bananas, but that the land there was already being used for cocoa. There is a summary in English.

264 **Primeiras observações sobre o comportamento de algumas leguminosas no sul da ilha de São Tomé.** (Preliminary observations on the behaviour of some legumes in the south of the island of São Tomé.)
F. Almeida Ribeiro, J. Vieira da Silva. *Garcia de Orta*, vol. 7, no. 3 (1959), p. 501-07.
After trials certain species of legume showed potential as ground cover, hedges, mulch and food.

265 **São Tomé e Príncipe e a cultura do café.** (São Tomé and Príncipe and coffee cultivation.)
Hélder Lains e Silva, José Carvalho Cardoso. Lisbon: Junta de Investigações do Ultramar, 1958. 499p. 7 maps. bibliog. (Memórias da Junta de Investigações do Ultramar, Segunda Série, no. 1).
The purpose of this book is to provide information for the coffee grower who wishes to 'establish, improve or restore his plantation'. It is also, incidentally, a valuable geographical study of the two islands. A full description is given of geology, climate, soil (Cardoso's contribution) and vegetation and the historical and economic influences on the islands' agriculture are also examined. Technical aspects of coffee cultivation are discussed, including the selection of strains, harvesting and the preparation of the beans. Lains e Silva warns of the islands' low labour productivity. The geographical research has been channelled into the production of five maps with a scale of 1:100,000. These are coloured and shaded to show isohyetals (rainfall), climatic zones, soils, both natural and agricultural vegetation, and areas where different types of coffee might be successfully grown. In addition, the book is illustrated with 113 photographs, the bibliography contains 257 items, and there is a substantial summary in English (p. 353-87).

266 **Subsídios para o estudo dos cacaus de S.Tomé e Príncipe.**
(Contributions to the study of the cacaos of São Tomé and Príncipe.)
Jonas Silva Wahnon. Lisbon: Ministério da Economia, Direcção Geral dos Serviços Agrícolas, 1941. 84p. bibliog.
This is a technical guide for those involved in cocoa production.

Fertilité et fertilisation des sols à vocation cacaoyère de São Tomé.
See item no. 16.
Santomenses (agricultores) cuidado com a erosão.
See item no. 20.

Labour

267 **Alma negra! Depoimento sobre a questão dos serviçais de S.Tomé.**
(Black soul! Testimony on the question of the contract labourers of
São Tomé.)
Jerónimo Paiva de Carvalho.   Porto, Portugal: Tipografia Progresso,
1912. 28p.

Paiva de Carvalho was the Curador (curator of labourers) for Príncipe for five years
between 1903 and 1909 until he was sacked by the governor. This emotional account
is his version of the atrocities to which he was witness. For the Angolans, although
not for the Mozambicans or Cape Verdeans, there was no repatriation and they were
no more than *de facto* slaves. Dozens committed suicide because the only way to
return to their country was as spirits. The Curador heard the complaints of the
workers who managed to make the journey through the forest to see him: he reports
on disgusting cruelties and incivilities which were carried out on the isolated
plantation fiefdoms. The plantations were unhealthy, rife with tuberculosis and
sleeping sickness, and the work was hard and hot: the lack of roads turned workers
into beasts of burden, and the drying sheds reached temperatures of 46°C. This is a
striking document which provides a convincing context to the words of one João
Antunes from Santiago, Cape Verde, 'I will never return to Príncipe. And none of my
countrymen would wish to either. I would rather be broken by hunger at the side of
the road than descend to the shame that has dragged me down during these years of
the contract' (p. 20).

268 **The Boa Entrada plantations.**
Henrique José Monteiro de Mendonça, translated from the Portuguese
by J. A. Wyllie.   Edinburgh: Oliphant Anderson & Ferrier, 1907. 63p.

Written in response to the growing labour scandal being raised by Henry Nevison and
others, Mendonça begins by defending Portugal's record on labour law and native
rights. He goes on to describe the plantation which he himself owns. It is, of course, a
model plantation, with modern machinery and every facility for medical care, child
care and good housing. Mendonça quotes from favourably impressed foreign visitors.

The plantation's accounts are included, showing the cost of wages and other expenditures related to labour. In addition, Antonio José d'Almeida and José Antonio Salvado Matta submit medical reports, and attempt to defend an annual mortality rate of 9 per cent. The location is humid and there is a problem with geophagy and alcoholism among the labourers. Statistics for the period 1890-1905 show the numbers employed, numbers recruited, death rate, food consumption and expenditure. There are thirty-three photographs of plantation buildings, equipment, workers, processes and plants. This title was originally published in Portuguese under the title *A Roça Boa Entrada* (Lisbon: Typographia 'A Editora', 1906, 63p.).

269 **Cabindas em São Tomé.** (Cabindas in São Tomé.)
Augusto Nascimento. *Revista Internacional de Estudos Africanos,* nos. 14-15 (1991), p. 171-97.

During the second half of the 19th century and the beginning of the 20th century workers were recruited for São Tomé and Príncipe from Cabinda, an Angolan territory north of the River Congo. Unlike the Angolan contract workers, the Cabindas insisted on receiving the pay to which they were entitled and on being released at the end of their period of service. Their complaints against the planters often received the support of the mainland authorities who disapproved of the islands' poaching of this labour force.

270 **Cadburys and the dilemma of colonial trade in Africa, 1901-1910.**
Geoffrey I. Nwaka. *Bulletin de l'Institut Fondamental d'Afrique Noir. Series B,* vol. 42, no. 4 (1980), p. 780-93.

Despite the English chocolate manufacturer's embarrassment at the labour conditions on São Tomé and Príncipe, they were reluctant to implement a boycott until an alternative supply of cocoa had been secured. In 1900 55.6 per cent of their raw cocoa came from the islands, and this high-grade product was hard to replace. Experiments were unsuccessful in Trinidad, but by 1908 improved methods of processing and the presence of experts in the Gold Coast (Ghana) were yielding good results. In addition, in 1908 and 1909 there was an abundance of cocoa on the world market. Only in 1909, when they no longer needed to rely on the islands' cocoa, was the boycott implemented.

271 **Contrato colectivo de trabalho.** (Collective labour contract.)
São Tomé: Imprensa Nacional, 1967. 66p.

This book contains speeches made by the presidents of the organizations which negotiated the contract - Afonso Henriques Ferreira of the Grémio do Comércio e da Indústria (Board of Trade and Industry) and Manuel Silva Duarte of the Sindicato Nacional dos Empregados do Comércio, Indústria e Agricultura (National Union of Commercial, Industrial and Agricultural Workers). The speech made by the governor, António Jorge da Silva Sebastião, on the occasion of the signing of the contract is included. Also contained within the text are tables of the new minimum wage rates.

272 **A 'crise braçal' de 1875 em S.Tomé.** (The 'labour crisis' of 1875 in São Tomé.)
Augusto Nascimento. *Revista Crítica de Ciências Sociais*, no. 34 (February 1992), p. 317-29.
The culmination of the legislative progress towards the abolition of slavery in São Tomé and Príncipe came in 1875. Abolition would take effect within a year. To allay the planters' fears of a labour shortage it was arranged that there should be a period of obligatory paid service for former slaves. However, by the end of 1875 there was a mass exodus from the plantations and workers came to the city to protest about their conditions. Many were found not to have legally been slaves or to have already completed their original contractual obligations. There was widespread antipathy towards continuing to work for their former masters, and many contracted to different plantations instead. Diogo Vaz was the only plantation not to lose any of its labour-force because each family had been given its own plot of land. It was at this time that planters began to import contracted workers from Angola over whom they could have more influence than the freed labour of the islands. Nascimento has based his research on documents from the Arquivo Histórico Ultramarino, the Arquivo Histórico de São Tomé e Príncipe and the correspondence of Francisco Mantero, a plantation manager.

273 **From slave to servical: labor in the plantation economy of Sao Tome and Principe: 1876-1932.**
Robert Nii Nartey. PhD thesis, University of Illinois at Chicago, Illinois, 1987. 223 leaves. 3 maps. bibliog. (Available from University Microfilms International, Ann Arbor, Michigan, order no. 8712036).
The labour system on the islands' plantations is studied for the years which began with the abolition of slavery in Portugal's African colonies and ended with the birth of the Portuguese *Estado Novo* (New State). Nartey is keen to establish a continuity of practice from slave to contract worker. He also makes some comparisons with cocoa production in the British colonies of Ghana and Nigeria, and looks at the British involvement in the controversies surrounding the recruitment of labour for São Tomé and Príncipe.

274 **The hidden costs of labour on the cocoa plantations of São Tomé and Príncipe, 1875-1914.**
William Gervase Clarence-Smith. *Portuguese Studies*, no. 6 (1990), p. 152-72.
This article attempts to calculate the real cost of the plantation labour on São Tomé and Príncipe for the years of the cocoa boom. Despite the low wages paid to the workers, the costs of recruitment (or, purchase) were high. Wastage from mortality was also high and well-paid European overseers had to be employed to coerce this reluctant workforce. Given that productivity was low, the labour costs to the planters were, in fact, relatively high. Clarence-Smith concludes that the high cost and inefficiency of the forced labour system was probably the most significant reason for the uncompetitiveness of the plantations in the 20th century. The article was published in Portuguese under the title 'O papel dos custos do trabalho no florescimento e declínio das plantações de cacau em S.Tomé e Príncipe' (*Revista Internacional de Estudos Africanos*, nos. 14-15 [1991], p. 7-34).

275   A ilha de S.Thomé e o trabalho indigena. (The island of São Tomé
      and native labour.)
      Lisbon: Typographia da Livraria Ferin, 1907. 99p.

First published in the *Revista Portugueza Colonial e Maritima*, this defence of
conditions on the plantations uses Portuguese translations of the accounts of visitors
to the islands. Augusto Chevalier (p. 1-23, bibliog.) visited in 1905 and his report
includes geographical descriptions as well as praise of the efforts of the plantation
owners. Dr. Strunk (p. 25-42) was in the islands in 1904 and gives an account of the
agricultural system. Théo Masui (p. 43-92) visited in 1900 on behalf of the Belgian
Compagnie Sucrière Européenne et Coloniale. As well as describing the plantations
he provides quite an entertaining picture of the discomforts of travel: his hotel room,
for example, was plagued by mosquitoes, rats and neighbours playing music until
three o'clock in the morning. Masui also points out the ruinous exchange rates
charged by the Banco Nacional Ultramarino. The final account is by H. H. Johnston
(p. 93-99) which includes the memorable lines that 'São Tomé must be the ideal of
paradise for the blacks, and the blacks of São Tomé the happiest in the world' (p. 97).

276   A importação de libertos em São Tomé no terceiro quartel de
      oitocentos. (The import of freedmen to São Tomé in the third quarter
      of the 19th century.)
      Augusto Nascimento, Alfredo Gomes Dias. *Revista de História
      Económica e Social*, (1989), p. 47-70.

This is a study of the movement of *libertos* (freed slaves with an obligation to work
for a fixed number of years for their former masters) from Angola to the newly-
developing plantations of São Tomé and Príncipe. This was certainly in contravention
of the spirit, and probably also the letter, of the 1842 treaty between Portugal and
Britain to end the slave trade. The means which were used to exploit loopholes in the
law are described and an estimate made of the numbers of people involved. The
period studied marked a convergence of interests between the slave traders of Angola,
who were now prevented from exporting to Brazil, and the planters on the islands.
Some individuals, such as João Maria de Sousa e Almeida, the future Baron Água-
Izé, had been both slaver and planter.

277   Labour conditions in the plantations of São Tomé and Príncipe,
      1875-1914.
      William Gervase Clarence-Smith. *Slavery and Abolition*, vol. 14,
      no. 1 (April 1993), p. 149-67.

Clarence-Smith has produced a balanced and clear study of conditions for the
plantation workers based on research carried out in the Arquivo Histórico de S.Tomé
e Príncipe, the Arquivo Histórico Ultramarino and the Cadbury Papers of the
University of Birmingham Library. The year 1875 marked the abolition in law of
slavery, and the forty years covered by Clarence-Smith saw changes in the labour
system. However, it 'did not lead to lasting reforms, and the quasi-slaves of former
times were soon replaced by administratively coerced and penal labour from
Portugal's African colonies' after World War One (p. 162). Topics treated include the
quest for freedom and the right to contract to an employer of the worker's choice,
wage rates, food, clothing, housing, marriage, punishments, working hours, leisure
and access to land. The article concludes that 'material amelioration was
accompanied by an ever more regimented control of the labour process and of social

life [. . .] it would seem that workers would have preferred more leisure time, more access to land, more control over their labour, and, above all, a measure of real personal freedom' (p. 161).

278 **Labour in Portuguese West Africa.**
William A. Cadbury. London: George Routledge & Sons; New York: E. P. Dutton, 1910. 2nd ed. 87p. map.

William Cadbury, of the English confectionery firm of the same name, visited São Tomé and Príncipe and Angola in 1908 in the company of one Joseph Burtt. Their mission was to investigate labour conditions on the islands on behalf of English cocoa manufacturers: on their return in 1909 they recommended a boycott of the islands' cocoa, which the firms of Cadbury, Fry, Rowntree and the German firm of Stollwerk put into effect. Cadbury summarizes his impressions thus, 'On the one hand a brutal system of capture and supply of slave labour by a licensed agent; on the other hand, a fairly humane treatment on some of the best estates' (p. xi). He spent three weeks on the islands, reporting on many aspects of plantation life and, although this is far from an emotive or polemical work, he does make some important criticisms. The hours of work were too long and 'the effect is a dull monotony that generally appears to suppress individuality and pleasure in life and work' (p. 40). Dancing was the only entertainment. Neither was it usual for the workers to have any introduction to religion, something which was often given as a justification for slavery. It was also unusual for the children on plantations to receive any education. The high mortality rate of about 10 per cent per year, or one funeral a week on a large plantation, was also of great concern. Cadbury suggests that the debilitated state in which these people - in the prime of life - arrive on the islands after their ordeals in Angola is an important factor in this rate of mortality. An additional cause may be the lack of sanitation provided for concentrations of people living in close proximity in a tropical climate. Another serious criticism is that the wages were too low to attract freely-contracted workers. This is an important contrast with the recruitment of Mozambican men to work in the South African mines, to which the islands' labour system was often compared: the Mozambicans were eager to earn the high wages offered there. The book continues with a description of Cadbury's experiences in Angola where he received even less official co-operation than in São Tomé and Príncipe. Appended are a selection of reports and statements. A final chapter added to the second edition concerns the new labour regulations of 1909 and critical newspaper articles from Portugal, Angola and São Tomé. British newspapers played an important role in the labour issue: George Cadbury, the uncle of William, sued *The Standard* for libel in 1909 over their allegations that he was profiting from slavery: he was awarded a farthing in damages. See A. G. Gardiner *Life of George Cadbury* (London: Cassell, 1923, 324p.) and Iolo A. Williams *The firm of Cadbury* (London: Constable, 1931, 295p.).

279 **A mão d'obra em S. Thomé e Principe.** (Labour in São Tomé and Príncipe.)
Francisco Mantero. Lisbon: The Author, 1910. 200p.

This defence of the labour situation on the plantations of São Tomé and Príncipe was produced in response to the Cadbury investigations. It covers agricultural history, current methods of production and labour conditions, the provenance of workers, the method of recruiting workers, the English campaign on labour conditions, and economic relations between the islands and Portugal. Also included are translations and documents relating to the controversy. In 'S.Thomé e Príncipe' (São Tomé and

Príncipe) (in: *Questões coloniais e económicos: conclusões e pareceres, 1913-1919.* Edited by the Sociedade de Geografia de Lisboa, Lisbon: Tipografia Cooperativa Militar, 1919, p. 219-31), Mantero proposes that families from the rest of Portuguese Africa be settled on the islands as a solution to the labour problem. This later work also describes roads, railway and maritime transport in the islands, with proposals for improvement.

280   **A modern slavery.**
Henry W. Nevinson, introduction by Basil Davidson.   New York: Schoken Books, 1968. 215p. map. (Sourcebooks in Negro History).

First published in 1906, this is a vivid and passionate account of Nevinson's visit to Angola and São Tomé and Príncipe in 1904-05. Nevinson, a journalist, set out to expose the myth of voluntary labour recruitment in Angola. Not without incurring personal risks, whether from lions, the 'hungry country' of the hinterland, or the threats of Portuguese traders, he travelled by foot and ox-cart along the paths taken by the agents and victims of the slave trade alike. These paths were strewn with discarded shackles and skeletons. Nevinson himself is in no doubt that he is witnessing the slave trade, with the islands' cocoa plantations as the principal customer of the trade. The contracting formalities at the Angolan ports are described as a hypocritical farce: 'The government has "redeemed" the slaves which its own agents have so diligently and so profitably collected. They went into the tribunal as slaves, they have come out as "contracted laborers". No one in heaven or on earth can see the smallest difference' (p. 173). Following the slaves' journey to its conclusion Nevinson visits the islands and sees plantation life for himself. Except for some Cape Verdeans, who are paid more and may sometimes be repatriated, the 20 per cent annual mortality rate and a re-contracting procedure as farcical as the original contract made in Angola ensure that most never return to their homeland. Some escape into the islands' uncultivated forest, where they may be hunted down by the planters. This still-shocking book is a salutary counterweight to accounts of the islands' prosperity and agricultural efficiency at the beginning of the 20th century. Even at the end of the 20th century it remains an illuminating text on the foundations of modern São Tomense society.

281   **Native labour in West Africa.**
Lisbon: Sociedade de Emigração para S.Thomé e Principe, 1921. 24p.

This defence of labour recruitment to São Tomé and Príncipe was made in response to a report sent to the British government by the British Anti-Slavery Society. It points out that the labour is recruited for the islands in exactly the same way as it is from Mozambique for the Witwatersrand mines and emphasizes the new protections enshrined in the labour law of 1914. It also states that proper statistics are now being kept and published in the *Boletim Oficial* (q.v.), and reproduces some tables of figures. Annexed are several favourable reports of conditions on the islands. Finally, there is a rather pathetic listing of all the cruel attacks against the beleaguered planters, which has a hint of a paranoid conspiracy theory, 'These campaigns are due to the leading chocolate manufacturers in England as well as to individuals who during the world war turned out to be notoriously pro-German' (p. 18). The tract was originally published in French in Geneva in 1920 under the title *La main d'oeuvre indigène dans l'ouest africain.*

282 **Nouveaux documents sur la main d'oeuvre a St.Thomé et a l'île du Prince: réponse aux accusations contre le Portugal.** (New documents on labour in São Tomé and Príncipe: response to accusations against Portugal.)
Alfredo Augusto Freire d'Andrade.   Berne, Switzerland: Imprimerie Neukomm & Zimmermann, 1913. 112p.

A collection of letters and articles has been put together which defend the labour situation in São Tomé and Príncipe; most are written by Freire d'Andrade of the Portuguese Colonial Ministry. He responds to the criticisms of, amongst others, William Cadbury, Jerónimo Paiva de Carvalho and the British Foreign Office's *White Book* of 1912. He also makes favourable comparisons with labour conditions in Peru, and points out the successful campaigns against sleeping sickness in Príncipe.

283 **The people of the Cape Verde islands: exploitation and emigration.**
António Carreira.   London: C. Hurst; Hamden, Connecticut: Archon Books, 1982. 224p. 2 maps. bibliog.

Cape Verdeans were, and are, a significant proportion of the labour force on the plantations of São Tomé and Príncipe. Accordingly, a substantial portion of this book is devoted to the theme of their 'forced migration' to the cocoa islands. This began with the 1863-66 famine in Cape Verde, when the government suggested to the São Tomense planters that they recruit workers from Cape Verde. At the same time, every obstacle was put in the way of Cape Verdeans leaving the stricken islands for destinations other than São Tomé. This recruitment continued throughout the 20th century, as the painstakingly-gathered statistics show. Between 1941 and 1970 a remarkable 56,000 Cape Verdeans left for São Tomé and Príncipe. As well as statistical analyses, this study covers the evolution of legislation and regulations governing recruitment, contracts, wage rates and conditions on the plantations. The role of recruiting agencies, such as the Sociedade de Emigração para S. Tomé e Príncipe (Society for Emigration to São Tomé and Príncipe), is also scrutinized. Carreira finds few redeeming features in the Cape Verdeans' experience of migration to 'the South', unless it be the literature, both written and oral, which it has inspired. The economic rewards were negligible, and the Cape Verdeans deeply resented the humiliations of plantation life: 'Many Cape Verdean labourers could read and write properly, and had a sense of their own dignity and worth which the white foremen did not understand or tolerate. They did not like restraint, and would not put up with some of the humiliating corporal punishments to which the European foremen tried to subject them' (p. 129).

284 **Portuguese slavery: Britain's dilemma.**
John H. Harris.   London: Methuen, 1913. 127p.

The Reverend John Harris was a leading light in the British Anti-Slavery Society, and active against Portuguese abuses of the Angolan contract workers. As Duffy notes in

A question of slavery, (q.v.), 'Harris gave a selective account of Portuguese conduct. His dismissal or disregard of Portuguese efforts since 1910 to improve the system was typical of Harris's kind of blind humanitarianism' (p.219). Harris first assembles an emotive collection of witnesses to the capture and trade of slaves in Angola for shipment to São Tomé and Príncipe. These include H. M. Stanley, C. A. Swan, H. W. Nevinson, M. Teixeira de Mattos, Colin Harding, F. Schindler, D. Crawford and Joseph Burtt. Official disclosures from Augusto de Vasconcellos at the Portuguese Foreign Ministry and Sir Edward Grey at the British Foreign Office also figure in the text and evidence used in the libel action between Cadburys and Standard Newspapers in Birmingham in 1908 is cited. The irregularities and deficiencies of the repatriation procedures are attacked and Harris insists that the Portuguese defence that conditions on the plantations are good 'does not transform slavery into freedom' (p. 92-93). The final section of the book concerns the international treaties on the slave trade and Britain's relationship with Portugal.

285 **A question of slavery.**
James Duffy.   Oxford: Oxford University Press, 1967. 240p.
2 maps.

A clearsighted and balanced view of slavery, the slave trade and labour policy in the Portuguese African colonies between 1850 and 1920 and the protest which it aroused in Britain. This is, of course, a subject of acute relevance to São Tomé and Príncipe. From the shipment of one hundred Angolan slaves by João Maria de Sousa e Almeida in 1853 to his plantation on Príncipe, to the final implementation of repatriation legislation after the First World War, the events and the controversies surrounding labour recruitment to the islands are charted in this volume. It is particularly valuable in its survey of the changing labour regulations, and of the campaigns waged by the English humanitarians. It also helps unravel the various laws and treaties concerning the ending of the slave trade and the abolition of slavery. Nevertheless, the demand for labour from the booming cocoa islands seemed insatiable and 'in Portuguese Africa the habits of centuries were not to be broken easily, and the slave-trade continued, on a much reduced scale, in devious ways and under different names. Slavery became free labour, contract labour, forced labour, and the slave became a worker, but a traditional relationship was unchanged' (p. 4). Sadly lacking in a bibliography, the primary sources used for this account were British Foreign Office records, Anti-Slavery Society and Aborigines Protection Society publications, Portuguese and British periodicals and newspapers, and the official gazettes of Portugal and her colonies.

286 **Relatorio da Sociedade de Emigração para S.Thomé e Principe.**
(Report of the Society for Emigration to São Tomé and Príncipe.)
Lisbon: Sociedade de Emigração para S.Thomé e Principe, 1912-68.
annual.

This is the annual report of the non-profit-making organization formed by the planters to recruit labour. It is also a source of statistics on plantation labour. During its early years this was a handsome publication with an eye to impressing English critics of the system.

287 **O trabalho indígena nas colónias de S.Tomé e Príncipe e Angola.**
Estado actual e evolução desejável. (Native labour in the colonies of
São Tomé and Príncipe and Angola. Current situation and desirable
development.)
Júlio Freire. In: *Congresso do Mundo Português. Publicações. XVI
volume.* Lisbon: Comissão Executiva dos Centenários, 1940,
p. 250-290, bibliog. (Memórias e Comunicações Apresentadas ao
Congresso Colonial [IX Congresso], vol. 3, section 3).
An unapologetic apologia for Portuguese colonial labour policy, it begins with a
history of the movement of labour from Angola to São Tomé and Príncipe. This spans
the period from the slavery of the first settlement of the islands to the labour
regulations of the late 19th and early 20th centuries. The second section is concerned
with the contemporary situation, the legislation in force and recruitment in drought-
stricken Cape Verde. The tone of the work can be deduced from Freire's description
of the great benefits for Angola in having its natives 'educated' and 'civilized'
through the medium of plantation labour in São Tomé and Príncipe. The final section
contains proposals for future policy. It praises the Angolan head tax and contract
labour: banning re-contracting would, he argues, be denying the workers their free
choice of employment. This is a fascinating revelation of colonial attitudes.

S.Tomé e Príncipe: do colonialismo à independência.
See item no. 138.

**Contribuição para o estudo do problema demográfico de S.Tomé e
Príncipe.**
See item no. 144.

Statistics

288 **Anúario estatístico.** (Statistical Yearbook.)
São Tomé: Direcção do Plano e Finanças, [1986?]- . annual.
A compendium of statistical information.

289 **Boletim Trimestral de Estatística.** (Quarterly Statistical Bulletin.)
São Tomé: Secção Central de Estatística, 1939-48 and 1971-[?].
quarterly.
These official statistics were previously published under the title *Boletim de Informação* (Information Bulletin) between 1949 and 1953. Between 1964 and 1971 the Serviços de Economia e Estatística Geral produced another quarterly publication, *Boletim Informativo dos Serviços de Economia e Estatística Geral* (Information Bulletin of the Economic and General Statistical Services). As well as publishing statistics it reprinted articles on the coffee and cocoa industries.

290 **Dados estatísticos de base.** (Basic Statistical Data.)
São Tomé: Ministério da Saúde e Desporto, Direcção de Plano, [1983?]- . biennial.
Statistical information, mainly concerned with health is reproduced here.

291 **Semana nacional de estatística: sistemas de informação estatística.**
(National statistics week: systems of statistical information.)
[São Tomé]: Embaixada de Portugal, Centro Cultural Portugues, 1989. 23p.
Produced in a collaboration between the Direcção de Economia e Estatística (Directorate of Economics and Statistics) from São Tomé and Príncipe and the Portuguese Instituto Nacional de Estatística (National Statistical Institute) and Instituto para a Cooperação Económica (Institute of Economic Co-operation), this is a collection of tables and graphs showing demographic and economic statistical data.

1º recenseamento geral da população e da habitação.
See item no. 145.

Education

292 **A educação na República Democrática de S.Tomé e Príncipe.**
(Education in the Democratic Republic of São Tomé and Príncipe.)
Roberto Carneiro, Fraústo da Silva, Marçal Grilo. Lisbon: Fundação
Calouste Gulbenkian, 1986. 2 vols. bibliog. maps. (Estudos
Africanos).

This consists of the report, impressions and main conclusions of a study mission sent
to the islands in December 1983. It includes statistical data. Beginning with a
discussion of the socio-cultural and economic context, the authors highlight the low
level of development, the external dependency and lack of enthusiasm for agricultural
or technical work and an absence of any community spirit. This is followed by a
comprehensive description of the education system from pre-school to adult
education and literacy programmes. Student numbers, expenditure, school facilities,
and levels of educational achievement are all covered. The administrative structure is
described and foreign aid for educational projects noted, with France and UNESCO
of some importance. In 1982-83 certain reforms in the education system took place
and these are also pointed out in the report. The authors then identify some of the
formidable problems facing the education sector. The relevance of the education
provided is limited, with no agricultural courses, only poor quality vocational
education, and teachers have little practical experience. There is also a lack of data on
the careers of school-leavers and a lack of manpower-needs forecasts. The system has
huge demands placed on it since the islands have a high birthrate (4.5 per cent) and
the population is young, with about one third being between six and eighteen years of
age. The quality of education is also a problem: there are high failure rates; the staff
are poorly qualified; school facilities are poor; the lack of facilities has led to a
curtailed primary curriculum; and some children have a poor nutritional status or
difficult family circumstances. Finance for education is constrained. Problems also
exist related to the administrative structure, as there is poor co-ordination between
agencies and managers are ill-qualified. The study mission team sets out some
objectives for improving the situation. Buildings and school facilities need to be
rehabilitated and their use better planned to enable them to move from triple to double
capacity use. More relevant courses, in agricultural and technical subjects, should be

developed and quality could be improved through better teacher training, a revision of textbooks and the implementation of a school meals programme. The role of the Gulbenkian Foundation in this work is explained in a preface by its administrator. There is a summary in English.

293 **Ensino secundário básico 1989/90. Educação em matéria de população e para a vida familiar. Livro de referência.** (Basic secondary instruction 1989/90. Education in population issues and for family life. Reference book.)
Edited by Elisa Andrade, Victor Bonfim. [São Tomé]: [Ministério da Educação e Cultura], [1989]. 329p. 5 maps.

The introduction to this collection of teaching materials describes some of the overwhelming social problems which are faced by São Tomé and Príncipe - instability in the relations between couples, de facto polygamy, an increasing incidence of sexually-transmitted diseases, sexual permissiveness amongst young people, multiple early pregnancies, back street abortions and sexual inequality. The demographic consequences of these trends affect economic development, the environment, health and family well-being. In 1981 the Ministry of Education and Culture decided to take educational action in these spheres, and this phase of the project aims to incorporate teaching on population and family life into the normal school programme. The project hopes to contribute towards the population policy of São Tomé and Príncipe's development programme, to resolving social problems, and to creating a more relevant education. The lessons themselves are designed to be integrated into various school years and into various academic disciplines - social studies, economics, natural sciences, Portuguese, geography and biology. The teaching materials use data about the islands and represent, in fact, an excellent collection of data describing contemporary society.

294 **Oralité et écriture en Afrique: processus d'alphabétisation et de post-alphabétisation a São Tomé et Príncipe.** (Orality and writing in Africa: the literacy and post-literacy process in São Tomé and Príncipe.)
Antonio Faundez, preface by Paulo Freire. Geneva: Conseil Oecumenique des Églises, 1986. 99p.

Treating the literacy programme in São Tomé and Príncipe and the philosophy behind it this collection of texts is heavily inspired by the teachings of Paulo Freire. The first chapter, 'Culture orale, culture écrite et processus d'alphabetisation' (Oral culture, written culture and the process of literacy) (p. 11-62), has also been published in Spanish (Quito: CEDECO, 1984) and in Portuguese (*Educação e Sociedade*, no. 19 [December 1984]). Paulo Freire became involved in the MLSTP's literacy programme in 1976 and the application of his methods to the São Tomense situation is described. Literacy is seen as adding a new dynamic to autochthonous culture, rather than destroying and devaluing oral culture. Problems associated with literacy are not ignored however: these include the changes in the social power structure when women learn to read and when children are teaching adults. Literacy is seen as part of adult education in a broader sense: the appended excerpts from the exercise books, which have been specially written for São Tomé and Príncipe, seem to illustrate this. The second chapter, 'Alphabétisation, post-alphabétisation et culture' (Literacy, post-literacy and culture) (p. 65-72) addresses the issue of language. Although for historic reasons and for the link which it provides with the outside world the Portuguese language should be taught, there is a danger of giving value to Portuguese culture at the expense of São Tomense oral culture. As a countermeasure local subject matter has been chosen for the exercise books. Ideally the indigenous languages should also be studied and bilingual versions of the exercise books produced. Subsequent chapters briefly discuss the history of the adult education movement inspired by Freire; make comparisons between São Tomé and Príncipe's literacy programme and that of Nicaragua; and describe Faundez's 1980 visit to the islands.

295 **A reforma integral de ensino. Seu fundamento e objectivo no sistema nacional de educação.** (The complete reform of teaching. Its foundations and objectives in the national education system.)
Ministério da Educação e Cultura, Gabinete de Estudos e Pesquisas Pedagógicas. S.Tomé: Empresa de Artes Gráficas, 1982. 155p.

Produced with the help of a Cuban advisor as a reference handbook for education professionals, this is very much a document reflecting the prevailing ideology of the time. Born from an awareness of education's role in overcoming the legacy of colonialism, the shadow of the one-party state is not entirely absent. It describes a rational, scientific, theoretical pyramid of learning with absolutely no reference to the actual conditions of life on São Tomé and Príncipe. The curriculum, organizational structure of schools and educational methodology are all prescribed with a level of detail which is not commensurate with any practical guidance related to the availability of resources. A flavour of the style can be gleaned from the following explanation of the objectives of methodological preparation for teachers, 'Elevar o nível político-ideológico, científico-teórico e pedagógico-metodológico do processo docente' (To raise the politico-ideological, scientific-theoretical and pedagogical-methodological level of the teaching process) (p. 76).

Literature

Criticism and history

296 **Alguns nomes da literatura são-tomense.** (Some names from the literature of São Tomé.)
Fernando Reis. *Espiral*, vol. 1, no.4-5 (Winter 1964-65), p. 110-13.

This text consists of brief notes on writers from São Tomé and Príncipe. In the case of novelists these have to be supplemented by the inclusion of foreign authors who have written about the islands, since Viana de Almeida is the only native novelist of whom Reis is aware. More attention is given to the poets Caetano da Costa Alegre, Francisco Stockler and Herculano Pimentel Levy. Both Alegre and Levy were of mixed race and Reis cites poems which illustrate their concern with issues of race.

297 **Almada Negreiros e Costa Alegre, o poeta de S.Tomé.** (Almada Negreiros e Costa Alegre, the poet from São Tomé.)
António Ambrósio. *Boletim Cultural da Guiné Portuguesa*, vol. 28, no. 110 (1973), p. 335-44.

Biographical notes on the poet Caetano da Costa Alegre are accompanied by examples of his poetry. Ambrósio points out that although his birthplace, the town of Trindade, was shared by the artist Almada Negreiros, the two had completely opposite reactions to their mixed racial origins. Costa Alegre was acutely aware of his race, whereas Almada Negreiros seems never to have referred to it. António Lobo de Almada Negreiros, the artist's father, knew of Costa Alegre, and his praise of the poet in *História ethnographica da ilha de S.Tomé* (q.v.) is cited.

298 **Cape Verde and São Tomé-Príncipe: a search for ethnic identity.**
Richard A. Preto-Rodas. In: *Critical perspectives on Lusophone
literature from Africa.* Edited by Donald Burness. Washington,
DC: Three Continents Press, 1981, p. 119-41.

Covers the work of Caetano da Costa Alegre, Viana de Almeida, Alda do Espírito
Santo, Maria Manuela Margarido and Tomás Medeiros, but devotes most attention to
Francisco José Tenreiro. Unlike Cape Verde, São Tomé and Príncipe was an ideal
environment in which the literature and ideology of negritude could develop. It was 'a
reaction of a small non-white elite determined to create a distinct ideology for a
society separated by color from the ruling establishment' (p. 130).

299 **As descobertas da descoberta ou a dimensão de uma mensagem
poética.** (The discoveries of the discovery or the measure of a poetic
message.)
Frederico Gustavo dos Anjos. São Tomé: Empresa de Artes Gráficas,
1985. 36p.

An essay on the poetry of São Tomé and Príncipe.

300 **Estudos sobre literaturas das nações africanas de língua
portuguesa.** (Essays on the literature of the Portuguese-speaking
African nations.)
Alfredo Margarido. Lisbon: A Regra do Jogo, 1980. 559p.

This is an anthology of Margarido's critical essays. Alongside those of general
relevance to the literature of Portuguese-speaking Africa, there are four essays which
concern São Tomé and Príncipe: 'As mutações da poesia africana de expressão
portuguesa: os exemplos de Francisco José Tenreiro e de Viriato Cruz' (Changes in
African poetry in the Portuguese language: the examples of Francisco José Tenreiro
and Viriato Cruz) (p. 121-28); 'Quintés roças e roças de Forro' (Cleared yards and
Forro plantations) (p. 513-18) which concerns the landholdings of the indigenous São
Tomense rather than literature; 'Poetas de São Tomé e Príncipe' (Poets of São Tomé
and Príncipe) (p. 519-52) which was previously published as the preface to *Poetas de
S.Tomé e Príncipe*, (q.v.); and 'As negras do brasileiro Gonçalves Crespo e do são-
tomense Costa Alegre' (The black women of the Brazilian Gonçalves Crespo and the
São Tomense Costa Alegre) (p. 553-59).

301 **Francisco José Tenreiro a preto e branco - II.** (Francisco José
Tenreiro in black and white - II.)
Pires Laranjeira. In: *Les littératures africaines de langue portugaise:
à la recherche de l'identité individuelle et nationale.* Edited by the
Fundação Calouste Gulbenkian. Paris: Fondation Calouste
Gulbenkian Centre Culturel Portugais, 1985, p. 423-27.

The use of racial terms in Tenreiro's poetry is enumerated and analysed. Laranjeira
concludes that he writes most frequently about the universal black, then the white,
and least frequently about the mixed race São Tomense. He notes that Tenreiro's
poetry - its negritude, its idealization of Africa and identification with Africans - is in
surprising contrast to his apparently successfully-assimilated life in Portugal.
Sentiment and experience are in conflict in his poetry.

302 **Insularidade e literatura, o mar e a originalidade da literatura santomense.** (Insularity and literature, the sea and originality in the literature of São Tomé.)
Inocência Mata. *Revista Internacional de Língua Portuguesa*, no. 4 (January 1991), p. 119-24.

Mata looks at the treatment of insularity in colonial and national literature, the style of which ranges from the exotic to the ironic. He makes interesting observations on the role of the sea in this literature, and the contrasting pairing of plantation and sea. For the São Tomense writer the sea is a means of survival rather than a cause of isolation. Some of the author's other works on the islands' literature include 'A poesia de Tomaz Medeiros: "Um canto de acusação"' (The poetry of Tomaz Medeiros: 'A song of accusation') (*Angolê*, no. 2 [July-September 1986], p. 5-6) and his 1986 dissertation from the University of Lisbon *A prosa de ficção no período colonial: S.Tomé e Príncipe* (The prose of fiction from the colonial period: São Tomé and Príncipe).

303 **Die jüngere lusographe Dichtung und Prosaliteratur der Inseln São Tomé und Príncipe im Überblick.** (An overview of recent Portuguese language poetry and prose from the islands of São Tomé and Príncipe.)
Luciano Caetano da Rosa. In: *Studien zur lusographen Literatur in Afrika*. Edited by Luciano Caetano da Rosa, Axel Schönberger. Frankfurt am Main: Teo Ferrer de Mesquita and Domus Editoria Europaea, 1991, p. 35-97.

Covers the work of Caetano da Costa Alegre, Francisco José Tenreiro, Alda Espírito Santo, Marcelo da Veiga, and Tomaz Medeiros in detail, and also mentions in brief several lesser-known poets. The prose writers covered are Landerset Simões, Mário Domingues, Viana de Almeida, Fernando Reis, Luís Cajão, Francisco Alves Preto, Horácio Nogueira, Sum Marky, Ruy Cinatti, Albertino Bragança, with brief notes on J. Rafael Branco, Sacramento Neto and Manu Barreto. The article contains useful bibliographical information on these writers, as well as illustrating the originality of their literature within the wider context of Portuguese-speaking Africa.

304 **Littératures du Cap Vert, de Guinée-Bissao, de São Tomé et Príncipe.** (Literature from Cape Verde, Guinea-Bissau, São Tomé and Príncipe.)
Paris: CLEF, 1993. 152p. bibliog. (Notre Librairie, no. 112).

This collection of short essays includes Inocência Mata 'Du journalisme contestataire à l'éclosion de la littérature' (From protest journalism to the dawning of literature) (p. 114-17) which looks at nationalism and negritude in 20th-century literature and its precursors in the late 19th century. In addition, Françoise Gründ 'Le tchiloli' (The *tchiloli*) (p. 118-23) describes a performance in the village of Boa Morte, São Tomé; Frederico Gustavo dos Anjos 'Les autres manifestations théâtrales' (Other theatrical forms) (p. 124-26) looks at the *Danço Congo* (Congo Dance), and at the popular theatre which performs scenes from daily life, puppet theatre and carnival; and Alda do Espírito Santo 'Sur les chemins battus de Francisco Tenreiro' (Along the paths trodden by Francisco Tenreiro) (p. 127-29) gathers together comments on Tenreiro's life and poetry.

305   **O livro de Costa Alegre.** (The book of Costa Alegre.)
Lopes Rodrigues.   Lisbon: Agência-Geral do Ultramar, 1969. 128p.
(Figuras e Feitos de Além-Mar, no. 7).

The first part of this literary biography covers the publishing history and poetic output of Caetano da Costa Alegre (1864-90), a poet often referred to as São Tomé and Príncipe's first. Rodrigues points out certain unsatisfactory aspects of the 1950 and 1951 editions of *Versos* (q.v.), originally published in 1916. He also discusses various themes which recur in Alegre's poetry, including love, race and resonances of his experiences as a medical student in Lisbon. Although contemporaries indicated that Alegre lamented being black, Rodrigues is keen to downplay any suggestion of racism in Portugal. He suggests that Alegre's feeling for São Tomé and Príncipe - which he left at the age of ten - was simple homesickness, not a reaction to the alien nature of Lisbon. The second part of the book provides a chronology of the poet's life, including facsimiles of some documents and dates for poems. Rodrigues also describes the place of the Lisbon medical school within Portuguese society at the turn of the 19th century. An appendix contains an anthology of nine of Alegre's poems.

306   **A new bibliography of the Lusophone literatures of Africa.**
Gerald Moser, Manuel Ferreira.   London: Hans Zell, 1993. 2nd ed.
432p. (Bibliographical Research in African Literature, no. 2).

This is a completely revised sequel to the *Bibliografia das literaturas africanas de expressão portuguesa* (Bibliography of literature from Portuguese-speaking Africa) (Lisbon: Imprensa Nacional-Casa da Moeda, 1983. 405p.) and has been updated to cover works of literature and literary criticism up until 1991. It is regrettable that the high production and visual standards of the first edition have been sacrificed in the later edition. Another departure from the first edition is the decision to concentrate on monographs rather than material from periodicals, and the section on literary periodicals has also been dropped. However, this should not detract from the welcome given to such an important bibliography. The section on São Tomé and Príncipe (p. 275-85) contains fifteen entries for oral literature, eighty-four entries for creative writing and twenty-seven entries for literary criticism. Of general interest is Moser's essay 'A brief social history of Africa's lusophone literatures' (p. 19-26) and the bibliography of general works (p. 31-58). Brief biographical notes are provided for most of the writers and the book is indexed by author and title.

307   **Parágrafos de literatura ultramarina.** (Paragraphs on overseas literature.)
Amândio César.   Braga, Portugal: Sociedade de Expansão Cultural, 1967. 340p.

Short pieces on Caetano de Costa Alegre and Francisco José Tenreiro are included in this collection of César's essays on literature from the Portuguese colonies.

308 **Le poids des valeurs portugaises dans la poésie de Francisco José Tenreiro.** (The weight of Portuguese values in the poetry of Francisco José Tenreiro.)
Manuela Margarido. In: *Les littératures africaines de langue portugaise: à la recherche de l'identité individuelle et nationale.*
Edited by the Fundação Calouste Gulbenkian. Paris: Fondation Calouste Gulbenkian Centre Culturel Portugais, 1985, p. 429-36.

Margarido discusses the importance of race, African identity and the experience of racism in Tenreiro's poetry. She also suggests that there were some irreconcilable dichotomies in his life, between being Portuguese and at the same time African, between being a scientist and being an artist, between the political caution of his professional life and the beliefs of his personal life. Margarido has also published 'De Costa Alegre a Francisco José Tenreiro' (From Costa Alegre to Francisco José Tenreiro) *(Estudos Ultramarinos,* no. 3 [1959], p. 93-107).

309 **S.Tomé e Príncipe.** (São Tomé and Príncipe.)
Manuel Ferreira. In: *Literaturas africanas de expressão portuguesa.*
[Lisbon]: Instituto de Cultura Portuguesa, 1977, p. 79-85.

Ferreira introduces the poetry of Francisco José Tenreiro, Alda do Espírito Santo, Maria Manuela Margarido, Tomaz Medeiros and Marcelo Veiga. He is slightly more reserved in his praise of the islands' prose writers, Viana de Almeida, Mário Domingues and Sum Marky and touches on the use of the creole languages in the written literature.

310 **Voices from an empire: a history of Afro-Portuguese literature.**
Russell G. Hamilton. Minneapolis, Minnesota: University of Minnesota Press, 1975. 450p. bibliog.

Probably the most illuminating English-language work on the colonial literary history of Portuguese-speaking Africa, it contains a valuable section on São Tomé and Príncipe (p. 365-88). Unlike in Cape Verde, there was no regional ethos uniting São Tomense writers and Hamilton ascribes this to the highly stratified plantation society, where those people fortunate enough to get an education would probably have found it in Portugal. Instead he looks for some recurring themes. He groups together the poets Alda do Espírito Santo, Tomás Medeiros and Maria Manuela Margarido under the heading of 'humanist solidarity and an incipient voice of militancy' (p. 370). He then looks at the work of three islanders who spent most of their lives in Lisbon, and their different perspectives on the experience of not being white in Europe. Mário Domingues' novel *O menino entre gigantes* (The boy amongst giants) (Lisbon: Prelo, 1960) is about a boy, the son of a Portuguese administrator and an African plantation worker, growing up in bourgeois Lisbon. Perhaps inadvertently, it gives an interesting description of alienation caused by race. The next subject of study is Caetano da Costa Alegre. Hamilton points out an often ignored 'parody of the traditional love lyricism of that era' (p. 380), more usually interpreted as the poet's misery at his lack of romantic success with white women. The final writer to be considered is Francisco José Tenreiro. The influence of Aimé Cesaire, Countee Cullen, Langston Hughes and negritude is acknowledged, and many of Tenreiro's poems are described in detail. In his partial paraphrase of 'Amor de África' (Love of Africa) Hamilton comes up with perhaps as good an encapsulation of Tenreiro's poetry as is possible in one sentence, 'But smiling through the woolen overcoat façade of his Europeanism, and with Africa in his heart and his heart in Africa, the poet counts the minutes until that time when humanity will be reborn' (p. 384). Hamilton extends his study to the post-independence era in *Literatura africana, literatura necessária II. Moçambique, Cabo Verde, Guiné-Bissau, São Tomé e Príncipe* (African literature, essential literature II. Mozambique, Cape Verde, Guinea-Bissau, São Tomé and Príncipe) (Lisbon: Edições 70, 1984. 300p. bibliog.)

311 **The West African area: Cape Verde, Guinea-Bissau, São Tomé and Príncipe.**
N. Araujo. In: *European-language writing in sub-Saharan Africa.*
Edited by A. S. Gerard. Budapest: Akademiaikiado, 1986, p. 267-89.
(A comparative history of literatures in European languages, vol. 6).

The work of Caetano da Costa Alegre, Francisco Stockler, João Maria de Fonseca, Viana de Almeida and Francisco José Tenreiro is discussed (p. 286-89) and the author identifies a theme of 'racial self-awareness'.

Auswahlbibliographie zu Sprache und Literatur São Tomés und Príncipes.
See item no. 409.

Poetry

312 **Anguéné: gesta africana do povo Angolar de S.Tomé e Príncipe.**
(Anguéné: African romance of the Angolar people of São Tomé and Príncipe.)
Fernando de Macedo, introduction by Natália Correia. Lisbon:
Livraria Sá da Costa Editora, 1989. 142p.

The Kingdom of Anguéné is part of the mythology of the Angolar people, and has inspired this volume of poetry by the son of an Angolar woman. It is an ambitious epic work, tracing the history of the Angolars. Poems cover the lost King Amador and the uprisings of the 16th century and there is a glossary for terms used in the Angolar language. Macedo has recently published another collection of poetry, entitled *Mar e Magóa* (Sea and sorrow) (São Tomé: Instituto para Cooperação e Desenvolvimento, 1994. 99p.).

313 **Antologia poética de S.Tomé e Príncipe.** (Anthology of poetry from São Tomé and Príncipe.)
Arquivo Histórico, preface by Alda Espírito Santo, introduction by
Carlos Agostinho das Neves. São Tomé: Imprensa Nacional, 1977. 136p.

Includes work by Francisco Stockler, Caetano Costa Alegre, Nhanha (João dos Santos Lima), Marcelo Francisco Veiga da Mata, Francisco Tenreiro, Alda Espírito Santo, António Medeiros (Tomás Medeiros), Maria Manuela Margarido, Carlos do Espírito Santo, Francisco Costa Alegre, Armindo Vaz, Carlos Neves and Ana Maria Deus

Lima. Both Stockler and Nhana write in creole. A brief biography is provided for each poet. The prefatory material puts the collection in the context of 'cultural liberation'.

314 **Antologia poética juvenil de S.Tomé e Príncipe.** (Anthology of young people's poetry from São Tomé and Príncipe.)
Edited by António Pinto Rodrigues. Lisbon: Tipografia Macarlo, 1977. 100p.

Most of the poems by these unnamed secondary school students are on the theme of the International Day of the Child. Two are written in creole. The volume also contains a short piece of literary criticism by José Palla e Carmo, the biographies of the poets Tomás de Medeiros, Francisco José Tenreiro and Caetano Costa Alegre, and a short history of the islands which concentrates on incidents of resistance to slavery and colonialism.

315 **Antologia temática de poesia africana.** (Thematic anthology of African poetry.)
Edited and with prefaces by Mário de Andrade. Lisbon: Sá da Costa, 1976, 1979. 2 vols.

Poems by Alda do Espírito Santo, Francisco José Tenreiro and Tomás Medeiros are included in this anthology of poetry from Portuguese-speaking Africa. One of the themes throughout the anthology is the experience of the contract worker (vol. 1, p. 205-40), and there are some interesting and moving poems about the plantations of São Tomé and Príncipe from the Angolans Agostinho Neto and Alexandre Dáskalos and the Cape Verdeans Osvaldo Alcântara, Gabriel Mariano, Ovídio Martins and Onésimo Silveira.

316 **O canto do ossôbo.** (The song of the *ossôbo*.)
Marcelo da Veiga, preface by Manuel Ferreira, introduction by Inocência Mata. Linda-a-Velha, Portugal: África: Literatura, Arte e Cultura, 1989. 275p. (Colecção para a História das Literaturas Africanas de Expressão Portuguesa).

Marcelo da Veiga (1892-1976) was born in Príncipe, educated in Lisbon, and then returned to Príncipe to run his own plantation. He was twice briefly imprisoned by PIDE, the Portuguese security police. Some of Veiga's poetry was published during his lifetime, but this is the best collection to date containing 374 poems. Ferreira received twenty notebooks from Veiga's family, dating from 1917 to 1975 and his preface provides bibliographical information and explains his arrangement of the poems in this volume. Mata's introduction is a useful piece of literary criticism which traces Veiga's development as a poet and some of the important themes in his work.

317 **50 poetas africanos: Angola, Moçambique, Guiné-Bissau, Cabo Verde, São Tomé e Príncipe.** (50 African poets: Angola, Mozambique, Cape Verde, Guinea-Bissau and São Tomé and Príncipe.)
Edited by Manuel Ferreira. Lisbon: Plátano Editora, 1989. 487p. (Obras de Manuel Ferreira).

This anthology of pre-independence poetry was selected on the grounds of quality. The poets chosen from São Tomé and Príncipe (p. 431-65) are Caetano Costa Alegre,

Marcelo da Veiga, Francisco José Tenreiro and Alda do Espírito Santo. There are biographical and bibliographical notes for each poet.

318 **Coração em África.** (Heart in Africa.)
Francisco José Tenreiro, prefaces by Manuel Ferreira and Fernando J. B. Martinho.   Linda-a-Velha, Portugal: África: Literatura, Arte e Cultura, 1982. 148p. bibliog. (Para a História das Literaturas Africanas de Expressão Portuguesa).

Tenreiro was born in São Tomé in 1921 and died in Lisbon in 1963. A distinguished geographer, he is also one of the greatest African poets to have written in the Portuguese language, and his work could easily stand comparison on a wider stage. This edition of his poetry brings together the poems from *Ilha de nome santo* (Island of the holy name) (Coimbra, Portugal: [s.n.], 1942, 55p. [Novo Cancioneiro, no. 9]) and an unpublished collection also entitled 'Coração em África'. There is a substantial commentary on the poems in Martinho's preface (p.17-45), who also provides a valuable bibliographical essay (p.145-48). This edition contains the same works that were published in *Obra poética de Francisco José Tenreiro* (The poetic works of Francisco José Tenreiro) (Lisbon: Livraria Editora Pax, 1967, 134p). Tenreiro was the first of the Portuguese African poets to discover negritude, and the appeals of a world-wide black and African culture are not hard to find. African-American writers and artists had particular influence: 'E se ainda fico triste / Langston Hughes e Countee Cullen / Vêm até mim / Cantando o poema do novo dia / ai! os negros não morrem / nem nunca morrerão.' (And if I am still sad / Langston Hughes and Countee Cullen / Come to me / Singing the poem of the new day / ah! the blacks haven't died / and will never die!), from 'Fragmento de blues' (Blues fragment), (p.106). Tenreiro's love for Africa did not preclude a body of poetry dedicated to the island of São Tomé. 'Ilha de nome santo', for example, gives a fine description: 'Terra! / das plantações de cacau de copra de café de coco a perderem-se de vista / que vão morrer numa quebra ritmada / num mar azul como o céu mais gostoso de tudo o mundo! (Land! / of plantations of cacao of copra of coffee of coconut losing themselves to view / that go dying in a cadenced crash / into a sea as blue as the most delicious sky in all the world) (p. 91). He is also acutely aware of local social issues. In 'Ciclo do álcool' (Alcohol cycle) and 'Romance de Seu Silva Costa' (Romance of Mr. Silva Costa) he comments on the success of the white merchants at the expense of the São Tomense; in 'Romance de Sinhá Carlota' (Romance of Mrs. Carlota) his subject is the fate of the female African contract worker and her black and *mestiço* children. The son of a Portuguese administrator and a São Tomense woman, Tenreiro's attitude to his own racial background might be found in these lines from 'Canção do mestiço' (Song of the *mestiço*): 'Quando amo a branca sou branco... / Quando amo a negra sou negro' (When I love a white woman I'm white... / When I love a black woman I'm black) (p.62).

319 **O coro dos poetas e prosadores de São Tomé e Príncipe (antologia).** (The chorus of poets and writers of prose from São Tomé and Príncipe [anthology].)
Prefaces by José Luís Fontenla, A. Viegas da Graça.   *Cadernos do Povo: Revista Internacional da Lusofonia*, nos. 23-26 (1992), 62p.

This special issue is a result of co-operation between the Irmandades da Fala de Galiza e Portugal (Fellowship of the Language of Galicia and Portugal) and the União

Nacional dos Escritores e Artistas de São Tomé e Príncipe (National Union of Writers and Artists from São Tomé and Príncipe). The thirteen well-chosen poems are by Francisco Tenreiro, Marcelo da Veiga, Caetano Costa Alegre, Francisco Costa Alegre, Alda Espírito Santo, Conceição Lima, Tomás Medeiros, Olinda Beja, Armindo Vaz de Almeida, Caustrino Alcântara, Manuela Margarido, Francisco Stockler and Lima Ermelinda. Prose extracts are from works by Rufino Espírito Santo, Albertino Bragança, Lúcio Pinto, Rafael Branco and Frederico Gustavo dos Anjos. This anthology also includes a homage to the late Manuel Ferreira by Inocência Mata and a review by Fernanda Pontífice of *Anguéné* (q.v.).

320 **A descoberta das descobertas ou as descobertas da descoberta.**
(The discovery of the discoveries or the discoveries of the discovery.)
Direcção de Cultura. São Tomé: Empresa de Artes Gráficas, 1984.
40p.

Here is a collection of poems which contains the work of São (Conceição Lima), Alda Espírito Santo, Camucuço (Carlos Vaz de Almeida), Armindo Aguiar, Armindo Vaz and Frederico Gustavo dos Anjos.

321 **É nosso o solo sagrado da terra: poesia de protesto e luta.** (The
earth's sacred soil is ours: poetry of protest and struggle.)
Alda Espírito Santo. Lisbon: Ulmeiro, 1978. 184p. (Colecção Vozes
das Ilhas, no. 1).

Alda Espírito Santo (1926-) is one of São Tomé and Príncipe's leading cultural figures. Imprisoned at one time by the Portuguese for her political activities, she was for a long time an active member of the MLSTP, becoming a government minister after independence. Her preface (p. 5-25) to this collection places her poetry in the context of the struggle for independence. The arrangement in which the poems appear in this handsome volume is an illustration of the course of political events: 'Poemas da juventude' (Poems of youth); 'Poema mensagem' (Message poem); 'Por entre os muros da repressão' (Between the walls of repression); 'Aos combatentes da liberdade' (To the freedom fighters); 'A legítima defesa' (The legitimate defence) which refers to the Batepá massacre; 'Cela non vugu' (We must go on). The poems are in Portuguese with the use of some creole terms, for which there is a glossary.

322 **A horse of white clouds: poems from Lusophone Africa.**
Selected and translated by Donald Burness, foreword by Chinua
Achebe. Athens, Ohio: Ohio University, 1989. 193p. (Ohio
University Center for International Studies, Monographs in
International Studies. Africa Series, no. 55).

This anthology includes four works by poets from São Tomé and Príncipe: 'Maria' by Caetano da Costa Alegre; 'Romance de Seu Silva Costa' (The ballad of Mista Silva Costa) and 'Fragmento de blues' (Blues fragment) by Francisco José Tenreiro; and 'Costa Alegre' by Marcelo Veiga. The poems are given in their original as well as in English translation. Burness confesses that he has 'not been a timid translator', which is indeed revealed in his interesting translations of Tenreiro's poems into Black American English. Biographical notes are appended.

323 **Lembranças para S. Tomé e Príncipe.** (Souvenirs of São Tomé and Príncipe.)
Ruy Cinatti. Évora, Portugal: Edição de Instituto Universitário de Évora, 1979. 71p.

This is a collection of forty-eight poems giving Cinatti's impressions of the islands and their people.

324 **Madala.** (Madala.)
Francisco Costa Alegre. São Tomé: EMAG, 1990. 64p. (Gibela).

A collection of poetry with many resonances of São Tomense life, and an awareness of the relationship between regional and universal themes. Another collection of poetry by the same author is *Cinzas do Madala* (Ashes from Madala) ([São Tomé]: s.n., [1991] 80p. [Gibela]).

325 **Natal. Poemas e versos, anedotas e adivinhas, 'uma salada de frutas'.** (Christmas. Poems and verses, jokes and riddles, 'a fruit salad'.)
Teófilo Braga de Macedo. São Tomé: Empresa de Artes Gráficas, 1986. 95p. (Folhetim no. 10).

Most of this miscellaneous collection of writings consists of poetry in São Tomense creole. Included however are a handful of recipes, notes on the islands' musical groups, and the author's opinions on a variety of other topics.

326 **No reino de Caliban II.** (In Caliban's kingdom II.)
Manuel Ferreira. Lisbon: Plátano Editora, 1988. 2nd ed. 506p.

The second volume of Ferreira's essential anthology of the pre-1975 poetry of Portuguese-speaking Africa covers Angola and São Tomé and Príncipe and was first published in 1976. The section on the islands (p. 421-88) also contains an essay, 'Berço de negritude' (Cradle of negritude) by Ferreira. He traces the development of poetic expression in the islands, with particular reference to the importance of race and the presence of Africa. The poets represented in the anthology are Caetano da Costa Alegre, Francisco José Tenreiro, Alda Espírito Santo, Marcelo da Veiga, Maria Manuela Margarido, Tomás Medeiros and Francisco Stockler. A bio-bibliography is provided for each poet.

327 **Paga ngunu.** (Put out the torch.)
Amadeu Quintas da Graça, preface by Frederico Gustavo dos Anjos.
São Tomé: Empresa de Artes Gráficas, 1989. 53p.

Two short prose passages containing dialogue in São Tomense creole are followed by an interesting collection of poems in both Portuguese and creole (with Portuguese translations). Evidence of the oral tradition can be found in the creole poetry. The poem 'Amadeu nón' (Our Amadeu), for example, which was written in 1964 when Graça was a reluctant soldier in the Companhia de Caçadores de S.Tomé (Riflemen's Company of São Tomé), addresses his companions in a satirical fashion: 'Bô ni bancu réu tassondu / Ka guada zustiça / Quê qua bô fé / Nozolino nón sá padê / Migu Lúgi sá s'tudantxi / Cu sá atali s'ca orá / S'ca pigi pedon da bô' (You sitting in the dock /

Waiting for justice / What have you done? / Our Nozolino is priest / Friend Lúgi is sacristan / They are at the altar praying / Begging forgiveness for you) (p.52).

328 **Poesia do colonialismo.** (Poetry of colonialism.)
Carlos Espírito Santo. Lisbon: África Editora, 1978. 100p. (Colecção Cântico Geral).

Carlos Espírito Santo (1952-) was an active member of the MLSTP. The editor's foreword acknowledges that his poetry is political, inspired by anti-colonialism and that a considerable part of its value is as a record of that time in the history of São Tomé and Príncipe. The collection also contains three short love poems in São Tomense creole with Portuguese translations.

329 **Poesia negra de expressão portuguesa.** (Black poetry in the Portuguese language.)
Francisco José Tenreiro, Mário Pinto de Andrade, preface by Manuel Ferreira. Linda-a-Velha, Portugal: África: Literatura, Arte e Cultura, 2nd ed. 1982. 87p. (Colecção Para a História das Literaturas Africanas de Expressão Portuguesa).

With the addition of Ferreira's preface and some photographs, this is a facsimile of the first edition (Lisbon: Editora Gráfica Portuguesa, 1953). Tenreiro and Andrade selected these poems for their representation of negritude. The poems chosen from São Tomé and Príncipe are Tenreiro's 'Coração em África' (Heart in Africa) and Alda Espírito Santo's 'Lá no Água Grande' (There in the Água Grande river). Also included are the Angolan poets Agostinho Neto, António Jacinto and Viriato da Cruz and the Mozambican Noémia de Sousa. A poem by Nicolás Guillén, from Cuba, prefaces the collection. Andrade's introduction (p.47-52) gives a brief outline of negritude's history and aims and Tenreiro's afterword (p.81-82) is his defence of negritude. Ferreira's preface, entitled 'Metamorfose e premonição' (Metamorphosis and forewarning) (p.13-39), puts the book into its context . He covers the political and literary development of the generation of Africans who studied in Lisbon and Coimbra in the 1940s and 1950s. The political background of repression and the clandestine activities of the Portuguese Communist Party, are also treated.

330 **Poetas de S.Tomé e Príncipe.** (Poets from São Tomé and Príncipe.)
Preface by Alfredo Margarido. Lisbon: Casa dos Estudantes do Império, 1963. 98p.

This is an important early anthology of some of the best poetry from the islands. It contains work by Caetano da Costa Alegre, Francisco José Tenreiro, Alda do Espírito Santo, Tomás Medeiros, Manuela Margarido, Marcelo da Veiga and Francisco Stockler. Alfredo Margarido provides a substantial preface (p. 1-35).

331 **Solilóquio.** (Soliloquy.)
Frederico Gustavo dos Anjos. São Tomé: The Author, 1986. 25p.

Solilóquio is a discursive, wide-ranging poem. Anjos (1954-) studied in East Germany, which perhaps accounts for his citations from Crista Wolf.

332 **Versos.** (Verses.)
Caetano de Costa Alegre, edited by Artur da Cruz Magalhães.
Lisbon: Livraria Ferin, 1916. 163p.

Caetano de Costa Alegre (1864-90) is one of the islands' earliest poets. He left São Tomé for Lisbon at the age of ten, and it was there that he studied medicine until his early death from tuberculosis. Of mixed parentage, his handling of racial themes in his poetry is of particular interest. Perhaps Alegre's most cited poem is a sarcastic work describing the reaction of women of various nationalities to the colour of his skin: 'Passa uma ingleza, / E logo acode, / Toda supreza, / All afluster / What black my God!' (If an Englishwoman passes by, / She suddenly rushes, / What black my God!). Ninety-three of Alegre's poems are contained in this posthumous edition, together with a preface by Magalhães. A second edition (Lisbon: Papelaria Fernandes, 1950) reproduces the first, but with some errors in the texts of poems. A third edition (Lisbon: Livraria Ferin, 1951) edited by the poet's nephew, Norberto Cordeiro Nogueira Costa Alegre omits some of Magalhães' notes.

Antologia da terra portuguesa. Volume 16: Cabo Verde, Guiné, S.Tomé e Príncipe, Macau e Timor.
See item no. 333.

A palavra perdida e outras histórias. / Poemas.
See item no. 341.

Prose

333 **Antologia da terra portuguesa. Volume 16: Cabo Verde, Guiné, S.Tomé e Príncipe, Macau e Timor.** (Anthology from the Portuguese lands. Volume 16: Cape Verde, Guinea, São Tomé and Príncipe, Macau and Timor.)
Introduction by Luís Forjaz Trigueiros.   Lisbon: Livraria Bertrand, [1963?]. 241p. 5 maps.

This is an anthology of poetry, prose and non-fiction in which the São Tomé and Príncipe section (p. 137-68) contains material by Maria Archer, Luís de Camões, Augusto Casimiro, Rui Cinatti, Caetano da Costa Alegre, Manuel Henriques Gonçalves, Fernando de Araújo Lima, José Brandão Pereira de Melo, Vitorino Nemésio, Joaquim Paço d'Arcos, Fernando Reis and finally, Francisco José Tenreiro.

334 **Bandeira para um cadáver.** (A flag for a corpse.)
Frederico Gustavo dos Anjos, preface by Armindo Aguiar.   São Tomé: Empresa e Artes Gráficas, 1984. 16p. (Caderno Gravana Nova, no. 1).

This is a short story set around a funeral.

335 **A estufa.** (The hot house.)
Luís Cajão.   Lisbon: Sociedade de Expansão Cultural, 1964. 299p.
This novel is set in Príncipe, where Cajão (1920-) lived between 1958 and 1960.

336 **Fortunas d'África.** (African fortunes.)
Manuel Récio, Domingos S. de Freitas.   Lisbon: Casa Ventura
Abrantes, 1933. 250p.
This novel follows the experiences of a Portuguese emigrant to the islands, who
uncovers a traffic in workers to the Spanish colony of Fernando Pó. São Tomé
crushes, overwhelms and vanquishes the ordinary man. The authors' foreword
explains that the novel has been inspired by the suffering of all those who labour in
São Tomé and is intended to brand the 'shamelessness and manifest indifference of
those who create fortunes in Africa without ever having been there'.

337 **A lezíria e o equador.** (The water meadow and the equator.)
Fernando Reis, preface by José Galeno.   Lisbon: Editorial Adastra,
1954. 203p.
Most of the eleven short stories in this collection are set in São Tomé's plantations.
Some of the African characters are given a rather exotic treatment. In 'Amy-só', for
example, the principal characters are a feverish white planter, his female servant
Naguinga and Chicenda, an old sorceress with triangular teeth who is rumoured to
have been a cannibal in Africa. Chicenda gives Naguinga a magical herb - *amy-só* - to
make her master fall in love but after drinking the love potion the planter dies, and the
two women are found dead in the forest. Naguinga has her hands around Chicenda's
throat and nearby is the corpse of a poisonous black snake. Reis (1917-92) lived in
São Tomé between 1949 and 1970. His other works of fiction with a São Tomense
setting include the novel *Roça* (Plantation) (Lisbon: Adastra, 1960. 259p.) and the
five short stories in *Histórias da roça* (Plantation stories) (Lisbon: Sociedade de
Expansão Cultural, 1970. 271p.).

338 **Maiá Pòçon.** (Maria from the city.)
Viana de Almeida.   Lisbon: Edições Momento, 1937. 173p.
Published in this collection are seven short stories by one of the first São Tomense
writers of fiction. Plantation life and the place of the *mestiço* feature in these stories.
Almeida (1903-) moved to Lisbon as a child but writes about 'the characters whose
paths crossed mine during my life in Africa, land of my birth, and which since then
have not ceased to populate my imagination' (p. 168).

339 **A nau de Quixibá.** (The Quixibá ship.)
Alexandre Pinheiro Torres.   Lisbon: Moraes Editores, 1977. 220p.
(Círculo de Prosa).
Torres' introductory note explains the history of this autobiographical novel which
was written in 1957 but not published at this time because of censorship in Portugal.
The story is set in São Tomé where a young Portuguese boy goes to join his father
after an absence of seven years. As well as dealing with the relationship between
father and son, the novel calls into question Portuguese imperialism and fascism.
Quixibá is an islet off the coast of São Tomé. Torres (1923-) has also written poetry

inspired by his experiences of São Tomé. See, for example, *A terra de meu pai* (My father's land) (Lisbon: Plátano Editora, 1972. 134p.).

340 **Ossobó - história dum pássaro de S.Tomé.** (*Ossobó* - story of a São Tomense bird.)
Ruy Cinatti. Lisbon: Sociedade Industrial de Tipografia, 1936. 7p.

This is a short story, set in the dense mysterious forest, in which the *ossobó* bird is killed by a venomous black snake.

341 **A palavra perdida e outras histórias. / Poemas.** (The lost word and other stories. / Poems.)
Rufino do Espírito Santo, Ayto Bonfim. [São Tomé]: Edição CDTC, [1990]. 58p.

Short stories by Espírito Santo and poems by Bonfim are gathered together in this book. Bonfim (1955-) has also published a novel, entitled *O Suicídio cultural* (Cultural Suicide) (São Tomé: Empresa de Artes Gráficas, 1992. 208p.). It is the story of a released prisoner who discovers that the society he grew up in no longer exists.

342 **Peneta.** (Destiny.)
Sacramento Neto. [Lisbon?]: Sociedade Astória, 1989. 126p. (Ficção Africana, no. 3).

The title of this novella comes from a São Tomense saying, 'Peneta sa nancê' (Destiny is fixed at birth) and the destiny of the protagonist Sun Telvino is, indeed, relentless. He is dispossessed from his plantation by a Portuguese colonist, prevented from carrying out his trade as a palm-wine maker by colonial laws favouring wine imported from Portugal, and arrested and condemned to forced labour at the time of the Batepá massacre. Telvino's personal life is equally troubled, by childlessness, polygamy and infidelity. This is not perhaps the best-crafted of literary works, but it is full of local issues.

343 **Rosa do Riboque e outros contos.** (Rosa of Riboque and other stories.)
Albertino Bragança, preface by Amadeu da Graça do Espírito Santo.
São Tomé: Empresa de Artes Gráficas, 1985. 95p. (Cadernos Gravana Nova, no. 2).

Set amidst the day to day life of rural São Tomé, this collection of four stories includes such aspects of traditional culture as the *piadô zaua* (healers who take diagnosis from urine samples), *nozado* (a ritual held in memory of the dead) and *soía* (stories told at *nozados*). The first story, 'Rosa do Riboque' (Rosa of Riboque) (p.13-48), tells the story of the eponymous heroine's participation in the struggle against colonialism which ends in her death in prison. 'Reencontro' (Reunion) (p. 51-73) is a family tragedy set on a plantation. 'Solidariedade' (Solidarity) (p. 77-80) reunites two enemies with the donation of blood to an injured child whom the *piadô zaua* cannot save. Mento Muala, the protagonist of the final story, 'Solidão' (Solitude) (p. 83-89), is an inveterate womanizer who comes to a pathetic end. Although the stories are written in Portuguese a useful glossary of creole terms is included.

344 **Sam Gentí!** (Mrs Tina!)
   Manu Barreto.   São Tomé: Publicações Povo, 1985. 70p.

This is a rather touching short story set in the village of Caixão Grande, São Tomé, at the coming of independence. It concerns the mysterious illness of Argentina, also known as Sam Gentí, a washerwoman and the single mother of three children. Blaming her lover's wife, she seeks the help of various traditional healers and spiritualists. Nothing works, not even some explicitly-described medical practices, and she eventually dies. The tale is a simple evocation of rural life, interspersed with some poetry.

345 **Toda a gente fala: sim senhor.** (Everyone says 'yes sir'.)
   Onésimo Silveira.   Sá da Bandeira, Angola: Imbondeiro, 1960. 35p.

Silveira (1935-), a Cape Verdean, spent the years from 1956-59 in São Tomé and Príncipe. This short story and three poems reflect the experiences of Cape Verdeans working on the cocoa plantations.

346 **Vila Flogá.** (House of fun.)
   Sum Marky.   Fundão, Portugal: Jornal do Fundão, 1963. 294p.

Set in São Tomé, this novel describes the lives of Europeans and São Tomense as they are caught up in scenes of violence based on the Batepá massacre. The atmosphere of rumour and the intimidating presence of jeep-loads of armed men is strikingly evoked, and there are some unpleasant prison sequences. Sum Marky is the pseudonym of José Ferreira Marques (1921-).

O coro dos poetas e prosadores de São Tomé e Príncipe (antologia).
See item no. 319.

Culture and the Arts

General

347 **Aguêdê zó véssu.** (Riddles and proverbs.)
Carlos Espírito Santo. Lisbon: Grafitécnica, 1979. 75p.
Riddles and aphorisms, maxims and proverbs are like linguistic building blocks for
the language of the oral culture of São Tomé and Príncipe, as well as forming a genre
in their own right. This is a selection from the many variants available, reproduced in
their original creole, together with translations and explanations in Portuguese. Many
of the riddles are based on the human body or on the islands' flora, for example:
'Galafa mélé ni baçu son' (A bottle of honey under the ground = sweet potato). The
brief introduction suggests that the proverbs can reveal the islanders' character,
beliefs and way of life, for example: 'A na ca ximiá baná / Ni lóça lendadu fá' (Don't
plant bananas / In a rented plantation).

348 **Almada Negreiros - africano.** (Almada Negreiros - African).
António Ambrósio. Lisbon: Editorial Estampa, 1979. 191p. bibliog.
(Colecção Polémica, no. 22).
This is a rather curious biography of the great Portuguese modernist artist and poet,
Almada Negreiros (1893-1970). It attempts to supply every piece of information
concerning the São Tomense heritage which the subject's own complete indifference
has omitted from all his artistic works and autobiographical writing. There have even
been reports that Negreiros was born in Lisbon, so to prove his São Tomense origins
the birth certificate is included amongst the facsimiles of documents. Negreiros'
father was António Lôbo de Almada Negreiros (1868-1939), an active colonial
administrator and writer who was based in São Tomé between 1891 and 1899. His
mother, who died when her son was three, was born in São Tomé to an Angolan
woman and a Portuguese plantation owner, José António Freire Sobral. Sobral,
although childless by his wife, had children by three different women in São Tomé.
He and his family in Lisbon were responsible for Negreiros' upbringing when he

moved there at the age of two, never to return to his country of birth. Given Negreiros' brief stay on São Tomé it is hardly surprising that this biography becomes more a study of his relatives and their milieu. Negreiros senior took a keen scientific and intellectual interest in the islands: this is described, accompanied by a twenty-two item annotated bibliography of his publications and the reproduction of some of his poems.

349 **L'apport africain à São Tomé.** (The African contribution to São Tomé.)
François Gaulme.   In: *Les littératures africaines de langue portugaise: à la recherche de l'identité individuelle et nationale.*
Edited by the Fundação Calouste Gulbenkian.   Paris: Fondation Calouste Gulbenkian Centre Culturel Portugais, 1985, p. 419-22.

Gaulme has put together a rather sketchy overview of some of the areas of São Tomense language, society and culture which may show an African influence. The creole of São Tomé, for example, contains vocabulary of Nigerian and Congolese origin. Similarities with Gabonese culture are found in the *de facto* practice of polygamy and in the religious belief in ancestral spirits. Riddles and narratives from the oral tradition have Bantu equivalents. The creole poetry of Francisco Stockler is also thought to have (unspecified) African influences and this is contrasted with the 20th-century poets of negritude who turned to Africa in a very conscious way.

350 **Aspectos fundamentais da magia entre os Forros.** (Basic features of magic amongst the Forros.)
Carlos Espírito Santo.   *África: Literature, Arte e Cultura*, vol. 7, no. 12 (January-March. 1986), p. 85-88.

The indigenous São Tomense have a strong belief in magical forces, elements of which are dealt with in this article. The *fitxicêlu* (sorcerer) has hereditary supernatural powers, usually passed down from mother to daughter, and is greatly feared. These sorcerers are known for their healing powers, but are often consulted to discover the causes of deaths and misfortunes. São Tomense also believe in *contla* (amulets), made from animal teeth, herbs and roots, which protect against the forces of evil. Finally, in less serious circumstances, there are a wide variety of curses to call upon to confound one's enemies.

351 **Um breve esboço dos costumes de S.Thomé e Principe.** (A brief outline of the customs of São Tomé and Príncipe.)
António Maria de Jesus Castro e Moraes.   Lisbon: Typographia Adolpho de Mendonça, 1901. 96p.

Arranged in three parts, this is a miscellaneous collection of material on the people and customs of the islands. The first section looks at the lifestyle of the indigenous São Tomense, and includes comments on the different categories of women - married, single and 'washerwomen' (who often form relationships with Europeans). Religious practices, festivals, traditional medicine and 'superstitions' are described and the *Danço Congo* (Congo Dance) (including the text of some of the songs) and the *Auto da Floripes* (Drama of Floripes) from Príncipe are also covered. The second section contains a poem by João Maria de Sousa e Almeida which was written on the tombstone of Manuel da Vera-Cruz Almeida, and a collection of six documents from

1807-08 written by Governor Luiz Joaquim Lisboa. One of the more interesting of these documents outlines measures to be taken against fugitive slaves and bans dancing and music in the evenings. Castro e Moraes rescued these documents from being burnt. The final section, 'A traição porque foi colhido o capitão de fragata Joaquim Bento d'Almeida no reinado de D. Miguel I' (The treason for which the frigate captain Joaquim Bento d'Almeida was seized in the reign of D. Miguel I) contains a poem by José de Beldrode Ferreira Vaz. This poem concerns the events of 1834 when Governor Bento was imprisoned for supporting the wrong side in the dispute over the Portuguese succession. Bento is heavily criticized in this poem.

352 **Cancioneiro do Grande Festival da Canção Popular.** (Song book from the Grand Festival of Popular Song.)
Introduction by Albertino Bragança. São Tomé: Empresa de Artes Gráficas, 1984. 42p.

A summit of the five Portuguese-speaking African countries was held in São Tomé and Príncipe in February 1985. In honour of this occasion a song contest was staged, with musical accompaniment provided by the group Sangazuza. Twenty-seven songs from the contest are published here. The vast majority take the conference as their theme, welcoming the leaders to the islands and most of the songs are written in creole.

353 **A carta São Tomé e Príncipe.** (The São Tomé and Príncipe letter.)
São Tomé: Direcção Nacional de Cultura, 1992. 4p.

This is a photocopied publication, produced under the auspices of the Centro de Documentação Técnica e Científica (Centre for Technical and Scientific Documentation). It contains two articles on the islands' history, one of which is by Armindo Aguiar, and an article surveying the work of contemporary São Tomense artists by A. Leylavergne 'Les arts à São Tomé: entre Afrique et Europe' (The arts in São Tomé: between Africa and Europe) (p. 4).

354 **Cultura em Movimento: Revista Cultural.** (Culture in Motion: Cultural Review.)
Edited by Armindo Aguiar. São Tomé: Direcção Nacional de Cultura, 1989- . quarterly.

Poems, stories from the oral tradition and reports of cultural events are published in this review. It also contains material on the Direcção Nacional de Cultura (National Directorate of Culture), the União Nacional dos Escritores e Artistas (National Union of Writers and Artists), the Arquivo Histórico de S.Tomé e Príncipe (Historical Archive of São Tomé and Príncipe), the Centro de Documentação Técnica e Científica (Centre for Technical and Scientific Documentation) and other library services.

355 **Danço Congo.** (The Congo Dance.)
Manuel Ferreira. *África: Literatura, Arte e Cultura*, vol. 1, no. 2 (October-December 1978), p. 196-97.

Ferreira provides a brief description of this traditional dance, identifying the characters of the plantation owner, the previous plantation owner's children, the witch doctor, the devil, angels, and assorted dancers, musicians and men on stilts. It includes a colour reproduction of one of Pascoal Viegas's naïve paintings of the dance.

356 **O Danço Congo de São Tomé e as suas origens.** (The Congo Dance of São Tomé and its origins.)
António Ambrósio. *Leba*, no. 7 (1992), p. 341-72. bibliog.

The *Danço Congo* has been subjected to many different interpretations, most of which are soundly criticized in this interesting article. Ambrósio, a clergyman, applies a Christian interpretation to the dance, based on the popular Marian worship of Our Lady of Penha de França. This is the tale of how Mary rescued a believer from a giant lizard. Ambrósio tracks the story's diffusion from the Iberian peninsula to the Gulf of Guinea, São Tomé and Príncipe and Brazil. He suggests that the 'Congo' of the title refers to the location of its first performance in this form. The lizard is nowadays replaced by the Devil, although early descriptions seem to mention a dragon-like figure named Ukué which swallows a boy. His mother begs for heavenly assistance and the captain, angels and soldiers of the piece force the creature to release the boy. The dragon flees at first, then tries to return, but is stopped by the angels. Several verses from songs associated with the dance are cited in the article. Ambrósio's enthusiasm for accumulating evidence to support his thesis takes some imaginative forms: *Pôvô flogá - o povo brinca* (q.v.) notes that the *Danço Congo* troupes are often named after insects, such as the Sinkuá (flea) and Bissuitchi (a tree-destroying larva) and suggests that these are chosen to represent the troupes' perenniality. Ambrósio, however, thinks that the insects are small-scale vestiges of the legendary dragon. A by-product of this article is its historical information concerning the clergy of São Tomé and the history of the Catholic Church on the islands. It contains a number of colour illustrations, including two of Pascoal Viegas's paintings of the dance, from 1936 and 1969.

357 **Folclore musical da ilha de São Tomé.** (The musical folklore of the island of São Tomé.)
M. Barros. In: *Conferência Internacional dos Africanistas Ocidentais 6ᵃ Sessão. Volume V.* [Lisbon]: Commission for Technical Co-operation in Africa South of the Sahara; Scientific Council for Africa South of the Sahara, 1956, p.101-13.

Contains music and lyrics, in Portuguese translation as well as the original creole, for the São Tomense dances known as the *lundum, irmandade, ússua* and *sôcopé*. There are also notes on the types of musical instruments used.

358 **Indumentária dos nativos da ilha de São Tomé.** (Dress of the natives of the island of São Tomé.)
Maria do Céu Marques de Figueiredo do Espírito Santo. In: *Conferência Internacional dos Africanistas Ocidentais 6ᵃ Sessão. Volume V.* [Lisbon]: Commission for Technical Co-operation in Africa South of the Sahara; Scientific Council for Africa South of the Sahara, 1956, p. 159-65.

The author describes the clothing of the indigenous population of São Tomé, which is very similar to Portuguese dress, except that the women rarely wear shoes. There is a summary in English.

359 **Para a história do folclore são-tomense.** (Towards the history of São
     Tomense folklore.)
     António Ambrósio. *História*, no. 81 (July 1985), p. 60-89.

A variety of topics are covered, many supported by 19th-century documents. A
fascinating contribution to the history of the *tchiloli* and theatre in São Tomé is the
biography of Estanislau Augusto Pinto, whom Ambrósio credits with the authorship
of the prose text of the *tchiloli*. Pinto was the founding president of a musical and
dramatic society, the Sociedade Africana 23 de Setembro (African Society of the 23rd
September). He was also a clerk in the São Tomé court, which would have given him
first-hand experience of Portuguese bureaucracy and the legal system. Ambrósio also
provides a biography of Pascoal Viegas (Pascoal Viana de Sousa e Almeida Viegas
Lopes Vilhete), the naïve painter and creator of painted wooden sculptures, and the
article concludes with a survey of the literature about the islands' popular culture.

360 **Pôvô flogá - o povo brinca.** (The people make merry.)
     Fernando Reis, introduction by Fernando de Castro Pires de Lima.
     São Tomé: Edição da Câmara Municipal de São Tomé, 1969. 241p.
     bibliog.

This is an exceptionally beautiful book, from its typeface to its line drawings and
stunning photographs. Reis writes about various manifestations of the popular culture
of the islands, slightly compromised by his search for evidence of Portuguese
influences. He describes the dances, music and musical instruments associated with
the *socopé* run by organized societies, the *ússua*, the *tuna*, the *fundões*, the *deixa* from
Príncipe and the *semba* which is held the night before a funeral mass. The *Plo Mon
Desu* (By the hand of God) is held on Ash Wednesday and begins with Catholic
prayers in a chapel, but continues with flamboyantly-dressed dancers and improvised
songs. Reis interprets the *Dânço Congo* (Congo Dance) or *Dança do Capitão do
Congo* (Dance of the Congo Captain) as the story of four clowns who inherit their
father's plantation. They invite the captain to guard it but a sorcerer kills an angel.
The clowns don't see this as any reason to stop the party, so the music, singing and
dance continue. This does not, perhaps, shed a great deal of light on a performance of
six hours' duration, but the descriptions of costumes and dance are fascinating. The
text of the *tchiloli* as performed by the Formiguinha troupe from Boa Morte, São
Tomé is reproduced next, in full, both the 16th-century verse play by Baltasar Dias
and the 20th-century prose passages. A French translation by José Maria Queiros of
part of this text can be found in 'La tragédie du Marquis de Mantoue et de l'Empereur
Charlemagne' (The tragedy of the Marquis of Mantua and the Emperor Charlemagne)
(*Internationale de l'Imaginaire*, no. 14 [Spring 1990], p.75-112). Reis describes the
staging of the *tchiloli*, the costumes and masks, sets, dance and music: in sum, it is a
'mixture of dance and pantomime' (p.57). Reis also includes the text and stage
directions for the *Auto da Floripes* (Drama of Floripes), again from the Charlemagne
cycle, which is held on the feast day of St. Laurence in Príncipe. This is a huge
spectacle which, with its battles between the Christians and the Moors, completely
takes over the town of Santo António. A similar play is performed in the village of
Neves in northern Portugal, and Reis is convinced that Príncipe had settlers from this
region. As in the *tchiloli*, roles tend to be hereditary. This is not the case, however,
for the girl who plays Floripes and who must be a virgin. See also Reis 'Folclore de
São Tomé e Príncipe' (The folklore of São Tomé and Príncipe) (*Boletim Cultural da
Guiné Portuguesa*, no. 109 [1973], p. 23-33).

361 **Presença cultural.** (Cultural presence.)
Alda Espírito Santo. *África: Literatura, Arte e Cultura*, vol. 1, no. 2
(October-December 1978), p. 189-95.

Notes on some aspects of the islands' popular culture are prefaced by a brief history
of the exploitation of colonialism. The rituals which are associated with newborn
babies and sick children are described and illnesses are attributed to a spirit double
attempting to reclaim the child: this spirit has to be appeased with gifts. Funerals, too,
incorporate rituals to ensure that the spirits of the deceased do not disturb the living.
The article goes on to explore the music and dance of the *(ússua*, the islands' oldest
dance form, which used to be associated with the religious ceremonies of mutual aid
associations. Finally, the *Danço Congo* is covered: it is suggested that the dance
expresses the indigenous population's dispossession from the land, caused by the
creation of the plantations.

362 **Presença do arquipélago de S.Tomé e Príncipe na moderna cultura
portuguesa.** (Presence of the archipelago of São Tomé and Príncipe in
modern Portuguese culture.)
Edited by Amândio César.   São Tomé: Edição da Câmara Municipal
de S.Tomé, 1968. 266p.

In this anthology of writing about the islands, items about popular culture are of
interest, and poems and extracts from fictional works are included. The volume
contains a number of illustrations, unfortunately not in colour, several of which are by
Pascoal Viegas.

363 **Some cultural aspects.**
Armindo Aguiar.   *The Courier*, no. 85 (May-June 1984), p. 46-47.

This is a brief survey of popular culture and religion. Aguiar's interpretation of the
Danço Congo is that it might be an expression of the male slaves' virility.

364 **Stern's guide to contemporary African music.**
Ronnie Graham.   London: Zwan; Off the Record Press, 1988. 315p.
26 maps. bibliog.

The entry on São Tomé and Príncipe (p. 225) gives a brief description of the contemporary music scene and has a discography of albums made by África Negra,
Conjunto os Leononses and Sum Alvarinho. See also Caroline Shaw 'Land of
lundum: music of São Tomé and Príncipe' in *The rough guide to world music* (edited
by Richard Trillo, et al. London: Rough Guides, 1994, p. 335-36).

Das portugiesische Kreolisch der Ilha do Príncipe.
See item no. 161.

A religiosidade entre os Forros.
See item no. 173.

Oral narratives

365 **Cinco fábulas da ilha do Príncipe.** (Five stories from the island of Príncipe.)
António de Almeida. Lisbon: Instituto Superior de Estudos Ultramarinos, 1957. 13p. bibliog.

These oral narratives were told by two women from Príncipe and have been transcribed in Portuguese. In 'A tartaruga-macho e o txíntxi' (The turtle and the fish) the familiar figure of the *tartaruga* (turtle) comes to a bad end from laziness. He is more successful in 'A tartaruga-macho e o rei' (The turtle and the king), in which he tricks the king into enjoying an unprestigious type of fruit. In 'A tartaruga-macho glutona' (The greedy turtle) he tricks a party of diners into fleeing from their feast, only to die of indigestion. 'Txíntxim tangulà, txíntxim tangulà, San Bilanza Sousà, tangulà, txim guini, ou o macaco e a menina' (The monkey and the maiden) tells the story of the monkey who cures a girl's disfiguring skin disease only to make it return when she breaks her promise to marry him. Finally, in 'O macaco e o caracol' (The monkey and the snail) the monkey is beaten by the snail in a race to the top of Pico do Príncipe mountain because he stops to eat bananas. Almeida comments on how aspects of these stories relate to life on Príncipe.

366 **Contos infantis.** (Stories for children.)
São Tomé: Direcção Nacional da Cultura, 1984. 2nd ed. 77p.

This illustrated collection of ten stories for children, some told by the children themselves, was produced with the support of UNICEF. They clearly fall within the tradition of São Tomense oral narratives.

367 **Contos tradicionais santomenses.** (Traditional stories from São Tomé.)
Introduction by Carlos Agostinho das Neves. [São Tomé]: Direcção Nacional da Cultura de S.Tomé e Príncipe, 1984. 79p.

An enjoyable collection of nine stories has been compiled from the oral literature of São Tomé, prepared and illustrated with a young readership in mind. The stories are presented in Portuguese, with any creole terms accompanied by explanatory footnotes. In 'História do rei e do gigante' (Story of the king and the giant) a giant cures the king's blindness and is given his daughter in return. 'História da tartaruga' (Story of the turtle's wife) tells how *tartaruga* tricks his wife out of the food she has been saving for a feast day. In 'Todos os males têm o seu castigo' (Every wrong has its punishment) one friend murders another whilst out hunting. História do munquém e da rola' (Story of the pigeon and the dove) explains the songs of the two birds. 'A lenda de Canta Galo' (The legend of Canta Galo) gives the origin of this toponym, which means 'cock crows'. In 'Um grão de milho é o preço de um escravo' (A grain of corn is the price of a slave) *tartaruga* proves this price to the king. 'Quando os cães deixaram de falar' (When the dogs stopped talking) explains the silence of dogs and in 'A grande escolha' (The big choice) a girl turns down lots of good suitors, but ends up marrying a monkey. Finally 'A velha e a galinha' (The old woman and the hen) is the story of a bereaved mother (see 'A velha e a galina [fábula nativa da ilha de S.Tomé]' [q.v.]).

368 **Egoísmo castigado: fábula angolar.** (Selfishness punished: an Angolar fable.)
António de Almeida, Maria Cecília de Castro. *Garcia de Orta*, vol. 5, no. 2 (1957), p. 319-25. bibliog.

This traditional story of the trickster *tartaruga* (turtle) is prefaced by a short history of the Angolar people, some comments on the genre of turtle stories, and background notes on such things as the São Tomense foods and traditional medicine which feature in the narrative. In this story *tartaruga* wants to eat the pig which his wife is raising. He feigns illness and, imitating a traditional healer, tricks his wife into making a feast to cure him. However, his punishment for greed is to be stuck to a rock and then eaten by a soldier. A similar version of this story appears under the title 'História da tartaruga' (Story of the turtle) in *Contos tradicionais santomenses* (q.v.).

369 **Fablier de São Tomé.** (Tales from São Tomé.)
Françoise Massa, Jean-Michel Massa, translations by Emilio Giusti. Paris: Edicef, 1984. 145p. 2 maps. bibliog. (Fleuve et Flamme).

Within this volume is contained the text of fourteen oral narratives in parallel Portuguese and French versions, with illustrations and explanatory footnotes. 'Vem aí chuva' (Here comes the rain) is about the feckless *ossôbo* bird and 'Origem das braçadeiras' (Origin of the forest soldiers' armbands) explains why the soldiers need to identify themselves. In 'Tartaruga manhosa' (The cunning turtle) *tartaruga* wins himself the king's daughter. 'Lenda do Rio Água Grande' (The legend of the River Água Grande) tells the tale of a river goddess and 'O espírito do Rio Contador' (The spirit of the River Contador) is about a river god. The nine stories which appear in *Contos tradicionais santomenses* (q.v.) are also included. The Massas' introduction provides a background to São Tomé's history and culture, and some notes on the stories selected for this anthology.

370 **O galo, a galinha e o falcão: fábula angolar.** (The cock, the hen and the hawk: an Angolar fable.)
António de Almeida, Maria Emília de Castro e Almeida. *Garcia de Orta*, vol. 7, no. 1 (1959), p. 187-92. bibliog.

A Portuguese transcription of a story told by an Angolar man, it concerns a cock who arranges to give his chicks to the hawk in exchange for a cure for his eye disease. Naturally the hen refuses to co-operate. The commentary on this story covers the use of animals in oral narratives, sun-worship and astrolatry amongst the Angolars, hens and hawks in São Tomé and the Angolar perception of male and female psychology.

371 **Soiá: literatura oral de São Tomé.** (Story: oral literature from São Tomé.)
Fernando Reis. Braga, Portugal: Editora Pax, 1965. 129p. (Colecção Metrópole e Ultramar, no. 9).

This collection of oral literature from São Tomé contains the lyrics of a number of popular songs, in São Tomense creole and Portuguese translation, and proverbs and sayings in both languages. Its principal attraction, however, is the inclusion of five oral narratives told by Arriaga Quaresma and transcribed in Portuguese. They are 'A tartaruga e o seu compadre gigante' (The turtle and his friend the giant); 'Branca Flor e cidade de Bigi-Bigi' (Branca Flor and the city of no return); 'A tartaruga e Pedro

Andrade' (The turtle and Pedro Andrade); 'As sete feiticeiras' (The seven witches); and 'Me Mama' (Little woman). In *Soiá II* (Story II) (Lisbon: Sonotexto, 1978, 74p.) Reis transcibes a further six stories as told by Manuel do Sacramento Pontífice: 'Estória do João Alfaiate e do seu filho' (The story of João Alfaiate and his son) which is about Aladin; 'A tartaruga adivinhadora' (The soothsaying turtle); 'Festa da Mãe do Céu' (The feast of the mother of heaven); 'A lenda da tartaruga' (The legend of the turtle); 'Estória da rainha ciumenta' (The story of the jealous queen); and 'A tartaruga e os filhos' (The turtle and his sons).

372 **Tluqui de Deçu.** (Tluqui of God.)
Carlos Espirito Santo. *África: Literatura, Arte e Cultura*, vol. 1, no. 3 (January-March 1979), p. 307-09.

Remembered from childhood and transcribed in São Tomense creole and Portuguese, this is the story of a bird called Tluqui who every morning sings a blessing to a certain man. One day, however, the man is away and his wife becomes so irritated by the singing that she kills, cooks and eats the bird. At no point however, does Tluqui stop singing. In desperation the wife cuts open her stomach, lets out the bird, and dies. The majority of the text is in verse.

373 **A velha e a galina (fábula nativa da ilha de S.Tomé).** (The old woman and the chicken [native story from the island of São Tomé].)
Maria Cecília de Castro. *Garcia de Orta*, vol. 8, no. 2 (1960), p. 391-97. bibliog.

Originally narrated by an Angolar woman, this story has been transcribed in Portuguese although with some creole words retained. The tale concerns an old woman who becomes ill following the death of her only daughter. It dwells on the medical details of her symptoms and the cures attempted by the *doutor encartado* (certified healers), the *stilijon* (surgeons), the *piá dôz áua* (specialists in diagnoses from urine) and the medicinal plant specialist. The woman is finally cured when she hears of the hen's stoicism despite losing all of her fifteen children. A substantial commentary is appended to this transcription. Hens and how they are perceived in Africa are discussed and there is some very interesting background material on the training and work of the traditional healers alluded to in the story.

Das portugiesische Kreolisch der Ilha do Príncipe.
See item no. 161.

Tchiloli

374   **A contribuição portuguesa ao tchiloli de São Tomé.** (The
Portuguese contribution to the *tchiloli* of São Tomé.)
Juliet Perkins.   *Revista do Patrimônio Histórico e Artístico Nacional,*
special issue (1990), p. 131-41.

Perkins provides a useful study of the textual element of the *tchiloli*. She looks at the
career of the 16th-century Madeiran playwright, Baltasar Dias, who wrote the verse
text *Marquez de Mantua: tragedia do Marquez de Mantua, e do Imperador Carloto
Magno* (q.v.) which is at the core of the *tchiloli*. The origins of the literature about
Charlemagne in general, and the literary history of Dias' play, are outlined. Although
Tomaz Ribas' view that the play arrived in São Tomé and Príncipe with Madeiran
sugar-planters in the 16th century is endorsed, many unanswerable questions about
the survival of the play between that date and the 19th century are raised. Perkins
goes on to discuss the actual performance of the *tchiloli*, and finds connections with
Portuguese and Brazilian popular culture, and with English mummers' plays and
Morris dancers. The psychological and symbolic significance of various aspects of the
performance are touched upon, and she sees a clear political resonance between the
plays' discussion of authority and the experience of colonialism in São Tomé and
Príncipe. Another study which places the *tchiloli* in a wider cultural perspective is
Lucien Clare 'Le passé dans le présent: du tchiloli de São Tomé aux courses de bague
brésiliennes' (The past in the present: from the *tchiloli* of São Tomé to the Brazilian
ring races) (*Internationale de l'Imaginaire*, no. 14 [Spring 1990], p. 175-202). Clare
uses the tchiloli as a starting point for a survey of the Iberian tradition of spectacular
performance.

375   **'Les jours de tchiloli, je mettais mon costume de Ministre de la
Justice et je parlais a Charlemagne sévèrement'.** ('On *tchiloli* days
I put on my costume as the Minister of Justice and spoke sternly to
Charlemagne'.)
Françoise Gründ.   *Internationale de l'Imaginaire*, no. 14 (Spring
1990), p. 61-74.

Gründ conducts an invaluable and illuminating interview with the septuagenarian
Artur Pinho, who has performed the role of Minister of Justice in the *tchiloli* since
1937. Topics covered include the role of patron saints, ancestor worship and the
history of the famous *Formiguinha* troupe. The description of the role of a *tchiloli*
actor is fascinating: he retains the same role for his entire career; owns and elaborates
his own costume; and the dialogue and dance steps which he memorizes are unlikely
ever to be changed. The organization of the troupe is also of interest. The
Formiguinha troupe is so successful because it is largely a family affair, with plenty
of young men eager to participate. The group also exercises a certain amount of
discipline over its members' behaviour. Pinho is also informative on the evolution of
the text. Modifications to the prose text were made in the 1930s and again in the
1950s, when the lawyers' parts were introduced. He can envisage the *tchiloli* evolving
over time, but insists that the verse text would remain the same. Pinho is a canny
interviewee, not averse to giving a matter-of-fact answer to a loaded question. This
lively article is illustrated with some cartoons of scenes from the *tchiloli*.

376 **Marquez de Mantua: tragedia do Marquez de Mantua, e do Imperador Carloto Magno.** (The Marquis of Mantua: tragedy of the Marquis of Mantua, and the Emperor Charlemagne.)
Baltasar Dias. Lisbon: Typographia de Mathias José Marques da Silva, 1860, 19p.

This is one of many editions of the 16th-century verse play which is at the core of the *tchiloli*. The poor print quality, flimsy paper and crude illustrations suggest that this was one of the cheap editions of the text which were so popular in the 19th century. The play may have arrived in São Tomé at this time, rather than three centuries earlier as some commentators suggest. The text as used by performers of the *tchiloli* can be found in *Pôvô flogá - o povo brinca* (q.v.).

377 **Originalités du tchiloli.** (Originalities of the *tchiloli*.)
Jean-Michel Massa. *Internationale de l'Imaginaire*, no. 14 (Spring 1990), p. 203-18.

Massa looks at the textual history of the *tchiloli*. He concludes that the verse play is, indeed, the marginally modified work of Baltasar Dias and makes a strong case for its introduction to São Tomé in the late 19th century. The *tchiloli*'s originality is both theatrical and national: theatrical in the semi-improvised prose passages; national in its satire of the Portuguese colonizers.

378 **Pourquoi 'tchiloli'.** (Why '*tchiloli*'.)
Jean-Louis Rougé. *Internationale de l'Imaginaire*, no. 14 (Spring 1990), p. 57-60.

The etymology of the word *tchiloli* is traced using the rules of phonological change between the Portuguese language and São Tomense creole. Rougé arrives at the Portuguese word *teoria*, which has an erudite meaning of 'procession' as well as the more usual 'theory'. Educated clerics, he suggests, might have introduced this usage.

379 **Le tchiloli de São Tomé: un exemple de subversion culturelle.** (The *tchiloli* de São Tomé: an example of cultural subversion.)
Christian Valbert. *Internationale de l'Imaginaire*, no. 14 (Spring 1990), p. 32-56.

Valbert has an interesting approach to the *tchiloli*, and his article is particularly valuable for its comprehensive description of both plot and performance. He thinks of the *tchiloli* as an act of cultural resistance, and in interpreting it as a drama of colonialism he places Charlemagne as representative of the president of Portugal, Carloto as the governor of the islands, and the court of the Marquis of Mantua as the people of São Tomé. Appropriating the European form of the play, the African São Tomense used it both to criticize their colonial government, and as a vehicle for rituals of African origin. Valbert describes the significance and symbolism of the dances, masks, costumes and continuing use of Dias' archaic Portuguese language. He draws parallels with Brazil and other African cultures, in particular those from Gabon, and is especially interested in finding vestiges of ancestor worship in the *tchiloli*. Also described is the social organization of the troupes who perform it. There is an appendix on the pre-independence dance societies of Luanda, which are in some ways comparable to the *tchiloli*. Another version of this article is published in *Les littératures africaines de langue portugaise: à la recherche de l'identité individuelle et nationale* (African literatures in the Portuguese language: in search of individual and national identity), edited by the Fundação Calouste Gulbenkian (Paris: Fondation Calouste Gulbenkian Centre Culturel Portugais, 1985, p. 437-44). Valbert has also published a general description of the history and culture of the islands, 'Présentation de São Tomé et de sa culture' (Introduction to São Tomé and its culture) (*Internationale de l'Imaginaire*, no. 14 [Spring 1990], p. 10-31).

380 **O 'tchilôli' ou as tragédias de São Tomé e Príncipe: um exemplo teatral da aculturacção afro-portuguesa.** (The *tchiloli* or the tragedies of São Tomé and Príncipe: a theatrical example of Afro-Portuguese acculturation.)
Tomaz Ribas. *Espiral*, vol. 2, nos. 6-7 (Summer 1965), p. 70-77.

These are straightforward accounts of the *tchiloli*, the *Auto da Floripes* (Drama of Floripes) from Príncipe and the *Danço Congo*. 'Simultaneously ritual and spectacle', Ribas wonders if they might be unique examples of African and European acculturation in theatrical genres and speculates about the *tchiloli* having its origins with Madeiran sugar-masters working on São Tomé and Príncipe in the 16th century. Baltasar Dias, the author of *Marquez de Mantua: tragedia do Marquez de Mantua, e do Imperador Carloto Magno* (q.v.), the play at the core of the *tchiloli*, did, in fact, come from Madeira. Also, the *Auto da Floripes* is a piece of popular theatre performed in Neves, northern Portugal, a region from which many Madeirans had emigrated. Ribas' interpretation of the *Danço Congo*, which uses mime, dance and song rather than oral expression, is that it tells the story of an African king brought to the islands as a slave. It uses figures from Portuguese theatre, such as Lucifer, clowns and Algoz the executioner, as well as ritual African dances. He also mentions the *chola*, a procession of fishermens' canoes which possibly represents the arrival of the first colonizers, and various dances and other musical events.

381 **Tchiloli: viagens entre mundos, entre tempos.** (*Tchiloli*: journeys between worlds, between times.)
Carlos Porto. *Adágio: Revista de Arte e Cultura*, vol. 2, no. 8 (January-February 1992), p. 27-35.

As well as providing a general description of the *tchiloli*, with the usual emphasis on the Baltasar Dias text and speculation about its route to the islands, Porto comments on two performances which were held in Lisbon. These were sponsored by the Calouste Gulbenkian Foundation and took place in 1973 and 1990. He is aware that the performances lack the audience participation, in the form of comments and jokes, that could be expected in São Tomé. They are also, at only ninety minutes, considerably shorter than their usual length of six hours. The only substantial difference between the 1973 and 1990 productions is the reduction in number of actors, down from thirty-six to seventeen. Black-and-white photographs from the performances are included.

149

Libraries, Archives and Research

382 **African studies information resources directory.**
Edited by Jean E. Meeh Gosebrink. Oxford: Hans Zell, 1986. 572p.

This is a guide to sources of information and documentation on sub-Saharan Africa located in the United States of America. The only institution specifically cited for material on São Tomé and Príncipe is the Hispanic Division of the Library of Congress.

383 **Boletim.** (Bulletin.)
São Tomé: Arquivo Histórico de S.Tomé e Príncipe, 1969-80. irreg.

The Arquivo Histórico de S.Tomé e Príncipe was set up in 1969, and produced eight issues of the *Boletim* in which its holdings up to 1920 were listed. It provides a guide to material from the Secretaria Geral do Governo (General Secretary of the Government), 1802-1920; the Câmara Municipal do Príncipe (Town Council of Príncipe), 1665-1920; the administrative council of Príncipe, 1844-1920; and the *curadoria* (curate) of workers on Príncipe, 1891-1916. A more detailed listing and indexing was begun for documents from the Secretaria Geral do Governo. Sadly, only 42 of the 581 boxes in the archive were completed in this way before staff shortages brought the work to a halt. A. da Silva Rego wrote an introduction to the first issue which gives some background information on the archives and the islands' historical documentation.

384 **Cent'Doc Info. Gazeta.** (Centre for Technical and Scientific Documentation Information Gazette.)
São Tomé: Centro de Documentação Técnica e Científica, [1992?]- . bi-monthly.

This is a brochure which lists programmes of lectures, exhibitions and other activities of the Centro de Documentação Técnica e Científica (Centre for Technical and Scientific Documentation). The influence of French co-operation aid is very visible.

385   Fontes para a história do antigo ultramar português. Volume II
      São Tomé e Príncipe. (Sources for the history of the former
      Portuguese overseas territories. Volume II São Tomé and Príncipe.)
      Academia Portuguesa da História.   Lisbon: The Author, 1982. 264p.

Various archive sources for historical documentation concerning the islands are listed in
this guide. See also Fernando Castelo-Branco 'Documentação histórica remetida de
S.Tomé para a metrópole no século XIX' (Historical documentation sent from São Tomé
to Lisbon in the 19th century) (*Stvdia*, no. 37 [December 1973], p. 287-96). In 1891 all
of the colonies' pre-1834 documents no longer in use were ordered to be sent to the
Arquivo da Torre do Tombo (Torre do Tombo Archive) in Lisbon. However, the process
was not carried out very efficiently in the case of São Tomé and Príncipe. Castelo-
Branco found some of the islands' documentation mixed up with material from
Mozambique in the Biblioteca Nacional de Lisboa (Lisbon National Library) and he
takes this opportunity to list and describe these documents. António Brásio 'As fontes
arquivistas da história de S.Tomé' (The archival sources for the history of São Tomé)
(*Portugal em África*, vol 21 [May-August 1964], p. 148-53) is a brief guide to the
archives of Portugal and São Tomé and Príncipe. He also points out areas in which
useful work might be carried out in the archives of Spain, France, Germany and the
Vatican. Information and locations for thirty-three manuscripts relating to São Tomé and
Príncipe and dating from 1506-1812 can be found in Luiz Fernando de Carvalho Dias
'Notícia dos documentos da Secção dos Reservados, Fundo Geral, da Biblioteca
Nacional de Lisboa, respeitantes às províncias ultramarinas de Angola, Cabo Verde,
Guiné, Macau, Moçambique, S.Tomé e Príncipe e Timor' (News of the documents in the
Reserved Section, General Fund, of the Lisbon National Library, relating to the overseas
provinces of Angola, Cape Verde, Guinea, Macau, Mozambique and São Tomé
and Príncipe) (*Garcia de Orta*, vol. 5, no. 2 [1957], p. 347-67; vol. 5, no. 3 [1957],
p. 569-89).

386   **Guia de fontes portugueses para a história de África.** (Guide to
      Portuguese sources for the history of Africa.)
      Instituto Português de Arquivos.   Lisbon: Imprensa Nacional-Casa da
      Moeda, 1991. 154p. (Guide to the Sources of the History of Africa).

Holdings are arranged by depository and indexed. This valuable series is prepared by
the International Council on Archives under the auspices of UNESCO. Other volumes
cover France, Germany, Italy, the Netherlands, Scandinavia (Denmark, Norway and
Sweden) and the Vatican.

387   **The SCOLMA directory of libraries and special collections on
      Africa in the United Kingdom and in Europe.**
      Edited by Tom French.   London: Hans Zell, 1993. 5th ed. 355p.

Produced under the auspices of the Standing Conference on Library Materials in
Africa, this is a guide to European institutions with collections in the field of African
studies. It contains addresses, phone numbers and contact names as well as brief
descriptions of the collections. This edition includes Russia and Eastern Europe, but
the eight Portuguese institutions are of most obvious use.

388   **The social sciences in Angola, Cape Verde, Guinea-Bissau, Mozambique and Sao Tome and Principe.**
José Gonçalves.   Dakar: CODESRIA, 1992. 46p. (CODESRIA Monograph Series, 1/92).

This is an interesting overview of the state of social science research in Portuguese-speaking Africa, from the colonial era of the Junta de Investigações do Ultramar (Council for Overseas Research), through the hegemony of Marxism, to the present day. A short section is devoted to São Tomé and Príncipe (p. 15-16), 'the country with the scantiest record of work accomplished' (p. 15). Although a government agreement has been made with the Centre for the Study of Bantu Civilizations and a development studies agency has been set up, any research on the country has so far been carried out by individuals rather than institutions. Researchers mentioned, most of whom are based in Portugal, are Agapito Mendes Dias, Leonel d'Alva, Arlindo Carvalho, Armindo Vaz, Guilherme Otaviano, Maria Alves Trovoada, Nazare Ceita and Carlos Neves.

Periodicals

General

389 **África Hoje.** (Africa Today.)
Lisbon: Africa Hoje, 1985- . monthly.
Current affairs and business developments in Portuguese-speaking Africa are covered
in this glossy magazine.

390 **Catálogo das publicações em série africanas de língua portuguesa.**
(Catalogue of African serial publications in the Portuguese language.)
Introduction by Maria Fernanda Casaca Ferreira. Lisbon: Biblioteca
Nacional, 1988. 69p.
The Biblioteca Nacional de Lisboa (Lisbon National Library) has listed its holdings
of periodicals from the former Portuguese African colonies, covering 1854 to 1975.
Twenty-nine periodicals from São Tomé and Príncipe have been identified, dating
from 1881 to 1974. These are mostly newspapers and other non-official publications.

391 **A informação na Guiné, em Cabo Verde e em São Tomé e Príncipe
(achegas para o seu estudo).** (Information in Guinea, in Cape Verde
and in São Tomé and Príncipe [contributions towards its study].)
José Júlio Gonçalves. In: *Cabo Verde, Guiné, São Tomé e Príncipe:
curso de extensão universitária, ano lectivo de 1965-1966.* Lisbon:
Universidade Técnica de Lisboa, Instituto Superior de Ciências
Sociais e Política Ultramarina, 1966, p. 165-376.
This is a good source of interesting and useful information on official, non-official,
religious and cultural periodicals and includes clandestine pamphlets in creole.
Facsimile pages from some of the publications are reproduced. Cinema, the *tchiloli*,
radio, postal services, telecommunications and tourism are briefly noted.

392 **Informafrica.**
Lisbon: Informafrica, 1987-91. monthly.
Sometimes published fortnightly, this is a record of events of political and economic significance in Portuguese-speaking Africa, or of interest to Portuguese-speaking Africa. With items ranging from a paragraph to a page in length, this English-language edition of *África Confidencial* (Africa Confidential) (1985-89) constitutes the raw material of contemporary research. It is continued by *Informafrica Confidencial*.

393 **Periodicals from Africa: a bibliography and union list of periodicals published in Africa.**
Carole Travis, Miriam Alman.   Boston, Massachusetts: G. K. Hall, 1977. 619p.
Produced under the auspices of the Standing Conference on Library Materials on Africa, this bibliography of periodical publications contains nineteen entries for São Tomé and Príncipe. The first supplement, published in 1984, contains twenty-five entries on the islands.

Relatorio da Sociedade de Emigração para S.Thomé e Principe.
See item no. 286.

Catálogo de publicações.
See item no. 412.

From São Tomé and Príncipe

394 **Boletim Oficial.** (Official Gazette.)
São Tomé: Imprensa Nacional, 1857-1975. weekly.
New legislation and information on the business of the government and bureaucracy were disseminated through the medium of this official publication.

395 **Crónica.** (Chronicle.)
São Tomé: [Crónica], 1991- . monthly.
Covers political and economic affairs with some international news and is edited by Ambrósio Quaresma.

396 **Labor.** (Labour.)
São Tomé: Sociedade de Notícias, 1989- . bi-weekly.
This is a single sheet independent newspaper, run by Manuel Barreto.

397 **Notícias.** (News.)
São Tomé: Direcção de Impresso e Publicação, 1992- . weekly.

At around twenty pages per issue this government-owned newspaper carries features as well as news and sports reports. Until his dismissal in 1993 the editor was Martinho Tavares. Tavares had previously edited the newspaper *Revolução* (Revolution) under the MLSTP regime.

398 **Nova República.** (New Republic.)
São Tomé: Nova República, 1992- . weekly.

Rafael Branco is the director of this independent newspaper which manages to fill four to six pages weekly with news, political intrigue and sport.

399 **A província de S.Tomé e Príncipe: jornal comemorativo do 5 de Outobro de 1927.** (The province of São Tomé and Príncipe: commemorative paper for the 5th of October, 1927.)
Edited by Antonio Pequeno Rebelo. São Tomé: João de Carvalho Alfeirão, 1927.

Seventeen years of the Portuguese republic are celebrated in this unique issue of the paper. Alberto Veloso contributes an article listing the illustrious men of São Tomé and Príncipe's history in 'Galeria d'honra' (Gallery of honour) (p. 7-8). Otherwise, this publication is of more interest for the insight which the advertisements give into island life.

400 **S.Tomé e Príncipe. Boletim de Informação, Propaganda e Estatística.** (São Tomé and Príncipe. Information, Propaganda and Statistical Bulletin.)
São Tomé: Imprensa Nacional de S.Tomé e Príncipe, 1951-[19??]. monthly.

This is a digest of government news, official statistics, short features and legislation.

401 **S.Tomé Informa.** (São Tomé Informs.)
São Tomé: Sociedade de Notícias, [1993-]. [weekly?].

Osvaldo Aguiar heads this newspaper.

402 **A Voz de São Tomé.** (The Voice of São Tomé.)
São Tomé: Delegação em S.Tomé da União Nacional, 1947-74. fortnightly.

A government-controlled newspaper which published local and international news and cultural pieces, including poems and prose. Martinho Pinto da Rocha was director until 1950 when Raul Simões Dias took over.

Anúario Estatístico.
See item no. 288.

Boletim Trimestral de Estatística.
See item no. 289.

Periodicals. From São Tomé and Príncipe

Dados Estatísticos de Base.
See item no. 290.

Cultura em Movimento: Revista Cultural.
See item no. 354.

Boletim.
See item no. 383.

General Reference Works

403 **Africa: a guide to reference material.**
John McIlwaine. London: Hans Zell, 1993. 507p. (Regional Reference Guides, no. 1).
Useful as a guide to more general sources, the section on São Tomé and Príncipe (p. 313-14) contains material up to 1968.

404 **Africa Contemporary Record.**
Edited by Colin Legum. New York; London: Africana Publishing. 1968-69- . annual.
This authoritative review of events in Africa appears in three sections: the first contains essays on significant topics; the second has reports on the economic, political and social situation of individual countries; and the third has documents and statistics on economic, social, regional, constitutional and international relations issues.

405 **Africa South of the Sahara.**
London: Europa Publications, 1971- . annual.
A directory in three parts: the first contains background essays, often on historical themes; the second covers regional organizations; the third is a country-by-country survey with brief notes on geography, recent history, the economy, statistics, bibliography and information on government ministries and businesses. Since 1973 contributions to the section on São Tomé and Príncipe have been made by William Gervase Clarence-Smith, Basil Davidson, René Pélissier and Thomas Young.

406 **Congo, Sao Tome & Principe, Guinea-Bissau, Cape Verde: Country Report.**
London: Economist Intelligence Unit, 1993- . quarterly.
This quarterly report represents an extremely valuable summary of political and economic events. In the absence of any other reliable or accessible source the

economic statistics which this publication produces are of particular value. For the years 1986-92 the islands were covered in the volume *Angola, São Tomé & Príncipe.*

Bibliographies

407 Africa bibliography.
Edinburgh: Edinburgh University Press, 1984- . annual.
Both periodical and monographic material in the social sciences, arts and humanities is represented in this bibliography. Items are arranged thematically within regional and country sections, and are indexed by author and subject. As well as a section on São Tomé and Príncipe, there is a special section on Portuguese-speaking Africa.

408 Africana: bibliographies sur l'Afrique luso-hispanophone (1800-1980). (Africana: bibliographies on Portuguese- and Spanish-speaking Africa [1800-1980].)
René Pélissier.   Orgeval, France: Éditions Pélissier, 1980. 205p.
Only five entries refer specifically to São Tomé and Príncipe, but the general section is more substantial. Annotations are provided.

409 Auswahlbibliographie zu Sprache und Literatur São Tomés und Príncipes. (A selective bibliography of the language and literature of São Tomé and Príncipe.)
Luciano Caetano da Rosa.   In: *Studien zur lusographen Literatur in Afrika.*   Edited by Luciano Caetano da Rosa, Axel Schönberger. Frankfurt am Main, Germany: Teo Ferrer de Mesquita and Domus Editoria Europaea, 1991, p. 99-132.
This is a selective bibliography, in five sections, which takes a surprisingly broad view of its subject. It lists ten anthologies, twenty-five entries under literature, and a useful fifty-seven secondary works on literature and culture. Seventy-eight items are listed as secondary works on the islands' languages: a footnote acknowledges that material covering the whole of the Portuguese-speaking world is included. The final section, general secondary works, contains an eclectic ninety-one entries, from historical works on the islands, to William Shakespeare.

410 **Bibliografia da Junta de Investigações Científicas do Ultramar sobre ciências humanas e sociais.** (Bibliography of the Council for Overseas Scientific Research on the human and social sciences.) In: *Colóquio sobre educação e ciências humanas na África de língua portuguesa, 20-22 de Janeiro de 1975.* Lisbon: Fundação Calouste Gulbenkian, 1979, p. 329-76.

Publications of the Junta de Investigações Científicas do Ultramar are listed in sections covering history, the social sciences in general, physical anthropology, ethnology and cultural anthropology, human geography, demography, linguistics, literature and religion. Bibliographies produced by the Centro de Documentação Científica Ultramarina (Centre for Overseas Scientific Documentation) include *Contribuição para uma bibliografia sobre a demografia, etnografia, etnologia de Cabo Verde e S.Tomé e Príncipe* (Contribution towards a bibliography on the demography, ethnography and ethnology of Cape Verde and São Tomé and Príncipe) and *Contribuição para uma bibliografia sobre a economia e sociologia de S.Tomé. Trabalhos publicados desde 1952* (Contribution towards a bibliography on the economy and sociology of São Tomé. Works published since 1952).

411 **Bibliografia das publicações sobre a África de língua oficial portuguesa.** (Bibliography of publications on Portuguese-speaking Africa.) Jill R. Dias. *Revista Internacional de Estudos Africanos*, no. 2 (June-December 1984), p. 201-27; no. 3 (1985), p. 241-61; nos. 4-5 (1986), p. 355-74; nos. 6-7 (1987), p. 307-31; nos. 8-9 (1988), p. 339-49; nos. 12-13 (1990), p. 501-24.

A useful and fairly regular feature of this journal, the bibliographies are arranged by country with a section for general works. Journal articles are listed as well as monographs. The series began with 'Bibliografia das publicações sobre a África de língua oficial portuguesa entre Janeiro de 1975 e Janeiro de 1983' (Bibliography of publications on Portuguese-speaking Africa between January 1975 and January 1983) (no. 1 [January-June 1984], p. 243-303). The *Revista Internacional de Estudos Africanos* occasionally publishes more specialized bibliographies. To date these include three compiled by Franz-Wilhelm Heimer: 'Obras em língua alemã sobre a África de expressão oficial portuguesa: a "colheita" dos primeiros anos oitenta' (German-language works on Portuguese-speaking Africa: the 'harvest' of the early 1980s) (no. 2 [1984], p. 177-99); 'O Estado pós-colonial em África: uma bibliografia' (The post-colonial state in Africa: a bibliography) (nos. 12-13 [1990], p. 475-500); and 'Bibliografia sobre a crise, ajustamento estrutural e democratização em África, com atenção especial à África de língua oficial portuguesa' (Bibliography of the crisis, structural adjustment and democratization in Africa, with special reference to Portuguese-speaking Africa) (nos. 14-15 [1991], p. 315-34).

412 **Catálogo de publicações.** (Catalogue of publications.) Lisbon: Instituto de Investigações Científica Tropical, 1992. 353p.

Lists the publications in series, publications not in series and the contents of journals which fall under the umbrella of the Instituto de Investigações Científica Tropical (Institute of Tropical Scientific Research). Series which are good sources of material on São Tomé and Príncipe are *Anais* (Annals) (1946-60), *Estudos de Ciências*

Políticas e Sociais (Political Science and Social Studies) (1956-72), *Estudos, Ensaios e Documentos* (Studies, Essays and Documents) (1950-), *Garcia de Orta* (1953- , various disciplines), *Leba* (1978-), *Memórias* (Memoirs) (1943- , various disciplines), *Revista Internacional de Estudos Africanos* (International Review of African Studies) (1984-) and *Stvdia* (1958-).

413 **Catálogo sumário da exposição bibliográfica e cartográfica de S.Tomé e Príncipe.** (Brief catalogue of the bibliographical and cartographical exhibition on São Tomé and Príncipe.)
In: *Conferência Internacional dos Africanistas Ocidentais 6ª Sessão. Volume I.* [Lisbon]: Commission for Technical Co-operation in Africa South of the Sahara; Scientific Council for Africa South of the Sahara, 1956, p. 255-60.

The catalogue is arranged by the contributors to the exhibition.

414 **Listagem alfabética por títulos de algumas obras sobre São Tomé e Príncipe.** (Alphabetical listing by title of some works on São Tomé and Príncipe.)
Lisbon: Centro de Informação e Documentação Amílcar Cabral, 1993. 17p. (Informação Bibliográfica).

The Centro de Informação e Documentação Amílcar Cabral (Amílcar Cabral Centre for Information and Documentation) periodically publishes bulletins listing its collections of material from the former Portuguese colonies. It is a particularly valuable source of grey literature.

415 **Portuguese-speaking Africa 1900-1979. A select bibliography. Volume 3: Portuguese Guinea/Guinea Bissau, Cape Verde, São Tomé e Príncipe, Portuguese-speaking Africa as a whole.**
Susan Jean Gowan. Braamfontein, South Africa: South African Institute of International Affairs, 1983. 350p. 9 maps. (South African Institute of International Affairs Bibliographical Affairs Bibliographical Series, no. 11).

Material, in general divisions by country and by pre- and post-independence date of publication, is listed by author within four sections: a general section (including bibliographies); politics and government (including liberation movements); foreign relations; and economics and development. The 2,399 entries are indexed by author and subject. Elna Schoeman's *Portuguese-speaking Africa 1900-1979. A select bibliography. Volume 4: United Nations documentation on Portuguese-speaking Africa* (44p.), also published by the South African Institute of International Affairs, is bound together with *Volume 3*. It is intended as a guide to United Nations documentation on the process of decolonization and attainment of independence.

416 **S.Tomé e Príncipe.** (São Tomé and Príncipe.)
[Lisbon]: [s.n.], 1980. 42p.

In February 1980 the Biblioteca Nacional de Lisboa (Lisbon National Library) hosted a bibliographical exhibition of works relating to São Tomé and Príncipe. The exhibition was organized by the embassy of São Tomé and Príncipe. It aimed not only to disseminate information about the islands, but also to contribute to the task of making inventories of material. The principal source of exhibits was the Biblioteca Nacional de Lisboa. Material was also contributed by the Arquivo Histórico de S.Tomé e Príncipe (Historical Archive of São Tomé and Príncipe), the Biblioteca Nacional de S.Tomé e Príncipe (National Library of São Tomé and Príncipe), the Centro de Informação e Documentação Amílcar Cabral (Amílcar Cabral Centre for Information and Documentation) and the Sociedade de Geografia de Lisboa (Lisbon Geographical Society). The 186 items listed in this catalogue form an excellent core bibliography for the last 400 years. Material is arranged by author within chronological subsections of the following divisions: manuscripts; monographs; periodicals; manuscript maps; printed maps; and engravings; drawings and postcards.

417 **Síntese bibliográfica das ilhas de S.Tomé e Príncipe.** (Bibliographic synthesis for the the the islands of São Tomé and Príncipe.)
Isaú Santos. São Tomé: Imprensa Nacional, 1973. 561p.

Clearly aiming to be as comprehensive as possible, this substantial bibliography contains 3,094 entries. These are split into five sections: authored works; unauthored works; documents from the 15th to the 18th centuries; periodical publications and maps. Although most legislation has been omitted, the preface indicates the Portuguese official publications in which it can be found. A vast quantity of valuable material is listed, but without any indexes or arrangement by subject this is rather an overwhelming reference tool.

Bibliografia geológica do ultramar português.
See item no. 31.

A new bibliography of the Lusophone literatures of Africa.
See item no. 306.

Catálogo das publicações em série africanas de língua portuguesa.
See item no. 390.

Periodicals from Africa: a bibliography and union list of periodicals published in Africa.
See item no. 393.

Africa: a guide to reference material.
See item no. 403.

Index

The index is a single alphabetical sequence of authors (personal and corporate), titles of publications and subjects. Index entries refer both to the main items and to other works mentioned in the notes to each item. Title entries are in italics. Numeration refers to the items as numbered.

Alegre, N. da Costa 231
Alexander, J. 71
Allen, W. 102
*Alma negra! Depoimento
sobre a questão dos
serviçais de S.Tomé*
267
*Almada Negreiros –
africano* 348
Alman, M. 393
Almeida, A. de 3, 143,
147-48, 163, 365, 368,
370
Almeida, C. Rebello
Marques de 3, 246,
259
Almeida, C. Vaz de 320
Almeida, E. X. de *see*
History
Almeida, M. da Vera-Cruz
351
Almeida, Viana de 296,
298, 303, 309, 311,
338
Alva, L. M. de 206, 209,
388
Alvares, M. G. de Araujo
189
Alves, A. Correia 42,
51-52, 54, 56
Alves, M. L. Gomes 73,
77
Amadon, D. 66
Amador *see* History
Ambrósio, A. 128, 137,
176, 297, 348, 356,
359
Amphibians and reptiles
11, 58, 63
Anais 412
Ancestor worship 173
see also Tchiloli
Andrade, E. 293
Andrade, Mário de 108,
315, 329
Angola 1, 138, 229, 326,
329, 406
cultural similarities 379
historical links 125, 129
linguistic influence 161
literature about São
Tomé and Príncipe
315

relations with São Tomé
and Príncipe 200,
203-04, 215-16
trade with São Tomé
and Príncipe 233
see also Armed forces;
History (labour
procurement in
Angola)
*Angola, Moçambique,
S.Tomé* 1
*Angola, São Tomé &
Príncipe* 406
Angolans
legal status in São Tomé
and Príncipe 124
comparison in physical
anthropology 142-43
plantation workers 4,
109, 161, 244, 247,
267, 269, 278, 280
Angolar language 148,
150-51, 155-57,
159-61, 164-65, 312
Angolars 4, 146-50
architecture 148
diet 148, 187
education 146, 180
health 187
in literature 312
names 147
oral narratives 368, 370,
373
physical anthropology
142-43, 148
religion 146, 148, 150,
370
women 194
see also History; São
João dos Angolares
*Anguéné: gesta africana
do povo Angolar de
S.Tomé e Príncipe*
312, 319
Animals 57-91, 189
see also
Amphibians and
reptiles; Bats;
Birds; Insects; Marine
life; Snails; Snakes;
Spiders
Anjos, F. G. dos 299, 327,
331, 334

L'année africaine 1991
209
Annobon 100, 140
geological similarities
33
linguistic similarities
157, 160, 165
similarities in flora 38,
41
Anthropology 150
bibliographies 410
see also Physical
anthropology
Anti-Slavery Society 281,
284-85
*Antologia da terra
portuguesa. Volume
16: Cabo Verde,
Guiné, S.Tomé e
Príncipe, Macau e
Timor* 333
*Antologia poética de
S.Tomé e Príncipe*
313
*Antologia poética juvenil
de S.Tomé e Príncipe*
314
*Antologia temática de
poesia africana* 315
Anúario Estatístico 288
Araújo, C. A. de 53
Araújo, M. F. C. de 52
Araujo, N. 311
Archaeology 149
Archer, M. 333
*Archipelagic straight
baselines: São Tomé
and Príncipe* 22
Architecture 8, 13, 174
see also Angolars
Archives *see* Libraries and
archives
Armed forces 8, 103, 200,
204, 247
Angolan garrison 203,
215-16
see also History
(mutinies)
Arquivo da Torre do
Tombo 385
Arquivo Diocesano 176
Arquivo Histórico de São
Tomé e Príncipe 176,

164

C

Map of São Tomé and Príncipe

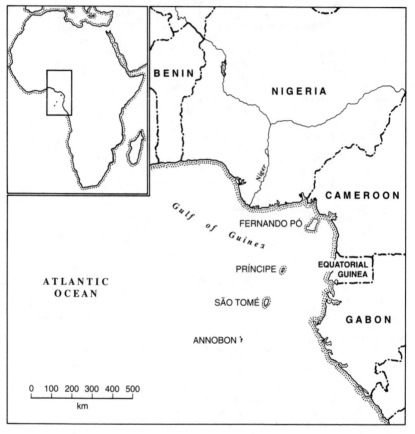

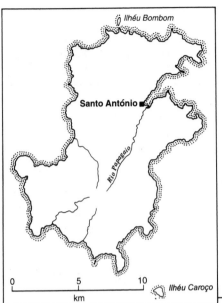

Príncipe

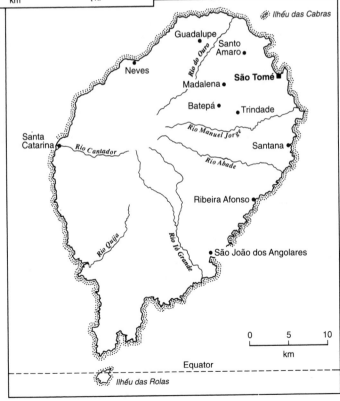

São Tomé

ALSO FROM CLIO PRESS

INTERNATIONAL ORGANIZATIONS SERIES

Each volume in the International Organizations Series is either devoted to one specific organization, or to a number of different organizations operating in a particular region, or engaged in a specific field of activity. The scope of the series is wide-ranging and includes intergovernmental organizations, international non-governmental organizations, and national bodies dealing with international issues. The series is aimed mainly at the English-speaker and each volume provides a selective, annotated, critical bibliography of the organization, or organizations, concerned. The bibliographies cover books, articles, pamphlets, directories, databases and theses and, wherever possible, attention is focused on material *about* the organizations rather than on the organizations' own publications. Notwithstanding this, the most important official publications, and guides to those publications, will be included. The views expressed in individual volumes, however, are not necessarily those of the publishers.

VOLUMES IN THE SERIES

TITLES IN PREPARATION